# Understanding Industrial Society

# Understanding Industrial Society

A. P. Sanday
M.A. (Oxon)
Senior Educational Adviser,
Coventry Local Education Authority

P. A. Birch
B.A. (London)
Inspector of Schools
Warwickshire Local Education Authority

HODDER AND STOUGHTON
LONDON SYDNEY AUCKLAND TORONTO

ISBN 0 340 16187 6

First Published 1976



Printed in Great Britain for
Hodder and Stoughton Educational,
a division of Hodder and Stoughton Ltd,
St Paul's House, Warwick Lane, London EC4P 4AH
by Hazell Watson & Viney Ltd, Aylesbury, Bucks

# Contents

## Part 2 Expanding the firm

**Part 3 Allocating our resources – the choice before us**
'O' level version

The authors and publishers would like to thank the following for permission to reproduce the photographs and other illustration material in this book (page numbers in brackets):

British Steel Corporation (6), *Farmers Weekly* (6), Joseph Lucas Ltd (6), Esso Petroleum Co. Ltd (6), *Punch* – Handelsman (17), Companies Registration Office (19), WCB – Clares Ltd (21, 25), Montague Burton Ltd (28), Spar (29), Comet (30, 37), The Boots Co. Ltd (33), John Lewis (35), The Littlewoods Orgn Ltd (35), Fine Fare (36), Birkenhead and District Co-operative Society (38), Vending Centres (Holdings) Ltd (39), *Financial Times* – Christies (51), The Stock Exchange (52), Ford Motor Co. Ltd (61, 79, 169), *The Guardian* (70), National Union of Railwaymen (70), Volvo Concessionaires Ltd (80), *Private Eye* – M. Heath (83, 109), Griffin and George Ltd (85), Sony (UK) Ltd (86), Autocar (86), Philips Electrical Ltd (87), Wallis and Co. (Costumers) Ltd (88), Kosset Carpets Ltd (91), Institute of Trading Standards Administration (104), British Standards Institution (105), British Electrotechnical Approvals Board for Household Equipment (105), *Punch* – M. Heath (106), Scientific and Technical (109), Ransom Hoffmann Polard Ltd (114), Hoover Ltd (116), Lever Bros Ltd (116), *Private Eye* – H. Breeze (129), F. W. Woolworth and Co. Ltd (141), National Coal Board (141), Mecca (143), Forestry Commission (145), BBC (147), Thames Water Authority (147), *Financial Times* (163), BBC – Pan's People (168), British Farmer and Stockbreeder (169), UNESCO – F. Bibal (172), Friends of the Earth (174), Greater London Council (174), Keystone Press Agency (177).

The authors and publishers are grateful to the following for permission to reprint copyright material:
*The Sunday Times*, Documents 13B, 16A, 19A; AA magazine *Drive*, Document 13A; The Controller of Her Majesty's Stationery Office, Documents 10A, B, C, Tables 16A, B, 18A, B, C, 19A.

# About this course

Whether you are at present at school or at college, sooner or later you will go into employment. You will then need to understand what happens to people in industry and commerce, and why they behave in the way they do.

*Why are people always striking for higher wages?*
*Why are some people better off than others?*
*Why can't some people get jobs?*
*Why are prices in the shops always rising?*

It is these and similar questions that this course tries to answer.

In order to help you understand our industrial society, we shall imagine first of all that we are setting up our own small firm. We shall decide to manufacture something – it might be something you have already made in craft lessons or it might be an entirely new idea. We shall then have to do some market research to see if people will buy it, how much they will pay for it and whether we can sell it at a profit.

We shall have to find out how to get the money to set up our factory and then study a real factory so that we shall know how to organise our own. We shall meet people doing all kinds of different jobs and no doubt we shall want to ask them about their jobs and what they think about them. We shall also have to find out the best ways of selling our product so we shall make a study of various shops and other ways in which goods are sold these days.

When we have made a success of our small firm we shall almost certainly want to expand. This will create a number of problems. Where should be build our new large factory? Should we get the extra money we need through the Stock Exchange? Will we require more expensive machinery? How shall we increase our orders? Again, we need to study a real factory, but this time a large one, to find the answers to these questions.

For most of the time so far we have been thinking of ourselves as owners or managers, but now we ought to imagine ourselves as the workers in our firm. How can we organise ourselves so that we get a share of the increased profits? What kind of problems might come up in the firm, and how shall we deal with them? How can we get more pleasure out of our work? Now that we have thought of ourselves as managers and as workers, it is time to put ourselves into the shoes of the consumers or customers. Do firms or shops try to deceive or even cheat us? What kind of protection do we need?

We have felt something of what it is like to be managers or workers or consumers. In real life we may be each of these at various times. Is there any conflict of interest between the different parts we as citizens shall play in our industrial society? For example, as a consumer I want firms to produce the kind of goods I need as cheaply as possible. But as a worker I want high wages and not to lose my job simply because people no longer require the goods my factory has always made. Can conflicts such as these be resolved?

Some goods and services are provided by private firms, others through local and national government. Have we got the balance right? How do local and national governments decide how much to spend and what to spend it on? Where do they get the money from? How do national governments try to stop such things as unemployment and rising prices? Should some people and some countries be far wealthier than others? Should the rich help to keep the poor? Could this be achieved fairly?

From these questions you can get some idea of the decisions which have to be made in this and every country. We shall try to understand how these decisions are made, and how we could influence them if we wished to do so.

We think you will find the work very interesting. Much of it will involve you in doing things, not just making notes and learning them. When your parents were at school, they were not able to do a course like this. Perhaps you might like to let them read this introduction. They may even wish to help you with some of the work. They will most likely enjoy it, too!

# Part 1 Starting a small firm

# Would you like to be your own boss? 1

When you have been looking at television you have probably watched scenes such as the following:

an argument between workers and their bosses about higher wages,

workers complaining about being made redundant,

a woman shopper complaining about rising prices and saying that manufacturers were getting too much profit,

someone complaining about industrial firms causing pollution by putting their waste products into a river.

During this course we are going to try to understand why people in business behave in the way they do.

When you leave school or college to go to work, you will almost certainly be employed by someone. You will be an employee – a worker – not an owner or a manager. You will soon find out how a worker feels and thinks, because you will be one yourself, but it will be very useful if you have some idea also why the boss behaves in the way he does. So this is where we will start.

About one and a half million people in Britain are their own bosses. They own or manage small firms – by 'small' we mean about one to fifty workers. Many of these owners started the firm themselves. Documents 1A and 1B give the case histories of two of these firms. Read them now.

As you see from these case histories, people usually start up in business in a trade they already know something about. They do so for the satisfaction of running things themselves, and often at first they work much harder for less money. Sometimes they never do as well as if they were working for someone else, but sometimes they do very well and expand and become big businesses. We shall be looking at expansion in the second part of our course.

There are three types of industries:

1. Primary industries which produce raw materials, e.g. mining iron ore, coal mining. Agriculture also is a major primary industry.
2. Secondary industries which manufacture products from raw materials. These products are sold as components to other manufacturers or direct to the consumer.
3. Tertiary industries or service industries. These do not manufacture a product but provide a service to industry or the consumer. Examples are shops, garages, hairdressers and banks.

Primary industries

Mining metal ores

Farming

Secondary industry

Making cloth

Tertiary industry

Garage

In an underdeveloped country most people are employed in primary industries. Often these countries depend mainly on one crop or mineral, e.g. in Africa, Ghana depends mainly on cocoa and Zaire mainly on copper. As countries develop, more and more people are employed in manufacturing, and in an industrially developed country, such as Britain, most people are employed in manufacturing and service industries. The proportion of people employed in service industries is gradually increasing.

To start up a business in a primary industry in a developed country such as Britain requires a lot of capital, and people who start up in business on their own usually start a small manufacturing firm or provide a service.

We are going to imagine ourselves setting up a small manufacturing enterprise. Discuss with your friends the kind of article you might manufacture. It must be fairly easy to make, and something which is sold direct to the customer (not, for example, an electric meter which is sold as a component to another manufacturer). Perhaps the work you have done in science or craft will give you some ideas. Like the people in Document 1A, you must have some reason why you think your product will sell.

If you were to invent some very novel device, you would want to prevent other people copying it. You can do this by registering it as a 'patent'. Make a list of all the articles you come across which have a patent number ('Pat. No.') stamped on them, or for which their inventors have applied for a patent ('Patent Pending' or 'Pat. Pend.').

## Document 1A *'Bangles and Dangles' Ltd*

John, Jane, and Paul went to a college of art and did a course in jewellery and silversmithing. John and Jane married in their last year at college. When they left college, John and Paul went to work for silversmiths, and Jane worked in a jeweller's shop.

None of them really liked working for other people, because they felt that their abilities were not fully used – they were bored. They would like to have had the freedom to organise their own lives.

From their knowledge of the trade they felt that there was a need for a business to do small, quick repairs, to make up jewellery to customers' specifications, and to produce good but relatively cheap hand-made jewellery for young people.

To get going they borrowed money from relations, arranged a £600 overdraft from the bank, and set up a small workshop in John and Jane's house. They sold their products on a stall in the market hall in the city where they lived.

They found they had to work very hard indeed, much harder than they had worked for someone else, and at first they made less money.

However, they had been right in thinking that there was a big demand for good, cheap hand-made jewellery, and they decided to expand.

In order to get more capital they formed a limited company. They took a shop with a big workshop attached in the area of the city where many jewellers worked, but they also kept their stall in the market. They opened up similar stalls in neighbouring towns and they employed a representative to visit gift shops and persuade them to stock their wares.

They are now very prosperous and still expanding.

## Document 1B *Green and Son, Carpenters*

Mr Green had worked all his life for a medium-sized firm of furniture makers. A lot of their work was school furniture, such as desks. When his son left school he went into the same firm.

At sixty Mr Green was very active, but he knew that at sixty-five he would have to retire. In his spare time he had done a lot of work for neighbours, putting up storm-porches and fitted cupboards, so he now decided to retire early from his old firm to form a full-time business with his son, partly so that he would be able to carry on working after sixty-five and partly so that his son would eventually have a business of his own.

However, soon after he started there was a bit of a slump and he was not able to get enough business. They were almost out of money altogether before trade picked up again, and Mrs Green nearly had a nervous breakdown with worry.

In order to get more business they now erect wooden home-extensions also, but to do this they have to employ a brick-layer to build the foundations.

Business is still not good, and sometimes the brick-layer employee takes home more than Mr Green the boss.

# Will our product sell? 2

The first and probably the most difficult thing to decide is whether our product will sell, and if so at what rate it will sell (i.e. how many per week?) because this determines the size of factory we must set up.

In general, we wish to produce as much as possible to make as much profit as possible, but if we make a mistake and produce more than we can sell, we shall go bankrupt.

One way of finding the answer to our question might be to make a prototype and ask people whether they would buy it and, if so, how much they would pay for it. What would be the difficulties in doing this?

We cannot ask all possible customers. We can afford the time to ask only a small sample, and the difficulty is to make sure that our small sample represents our customers as a whole. In 1936 an American magazine called *Literary Digest* took the largest sample ever known in order to discover who would win the presidential election in that year. The answer calculated from the replies proved in the event to be wrong. The reason was that the magazine sent questionnaires to a random selection of people chosen from telephone numbers and car registration numbers, and the people who own telephones and cars are not representative of the population as a whole. Furthermore, those who reply to questionnaires of this nature might not be a representative sample of those who were sent questionnaires.

We must therefore decide what factors will determine who would buy our product, and ensure that these are represented in our sample in the same proportions in which they exist in the population who will be asked to buy our product. Possible factors are sex, age, and income.

A statistician can calculate what size sample we must take in order to get the desired degree of certainty in our result. You may have done some work in sampling in mathematics; if not, try the following experiment.

There are four black jars labelled 1, 2, 3, and 4. Each contains red and yellow beads, and they are marked on the bottom (so that you cannot see the letter) as follows:

| | *Red* | *Yellow* |
|---|---|---|
| A | 10 | 40 |
| B | 20 | 30 |
| C | 30 | 20 |
| D | 40 | 10 |

Gently shake jar 1, extract a bead, and note its colour. Return the bead to the jar, shake gently, extract a second bead, note its colour. In this way extract five beads. Your record may be something like YRRYR. Do this sampling for each jar marked 1 to 4. From your experiment, can you tell with certainty which jar is A, which is B, etc.?

Repeat the experiment, this time taking a sample of ten (in ones) from each jar. Then try a sample of fifteen. How large must the sample be before you are certain which jar is which? What general conclusion can you draw from this experiment?

In general, market-research organisations cannot afford to take the size of the sample to give them the degree of certainty they would like.

Two methods of sampling which are widely used by market-research firms are as follows:

### 1 Three-stage random sampling

Within the area required, Parliamentary constituencies are chosen at random, and within each of the selected constituencies starting addresses are chosen at random from the electoral register. The interviewer calls at the starting address: if no-one is in, he calls at the next ascending house number, and so on until he makes an effective interview. After each effective call he misses out four dwellings before starting again. (Why do you think he does this?) If the interviewer comes to a turning, he turns into it and carries on as before (even if this is not now in ascending house numbers). (If this type of interviewing were done during the day-time, what kind of bias would there be in the result?)

### 2 Stratified random sample, or quota sample

The population can be divided into the occupational groupings shown in Table 2A.

TABLE 2A Occupational Groupings

| *Group* | *Occupational type* | *Percentage of population* |
|---|---|---|
| A | Higher managerial, administrative, or professional – e.g. company director, doctor, senior civil servant, headmaster | 13% (A and B) |
| B | Intermediate managerial, administrative, or professional – e.g. owner of medium-sized shop, industrial scientist, engineer, university lecturer | |
| C1 | Junior managerial, administrative, or professional, plus supervisory and clerical – e.g. bank clerk, foreman, bus inspector | 19% |
| C2 | Skilled manual worker | 32% |
| D | Semi-skilled and unskilled manual workers | 36% (D and E) |
| E | Those existing on state pensions without other income | |

The interviewer is given a quota in which the numbers from each group are in the proportions shown in the table. He has to find the right number of people of each kind.

The advantage of this type of survey is that it may reveal that our product is particularly attractive to a particular section of the community. We can therefore slant our advertising at this group.

The second difficulty about market-survey work is framing questions. For example, a firm had invented a light-dimmer: this is a knob fitted instead of the light-switch so that you can control the brightness of the light. They wished to find out whether it would sell.

You might think they could send interviewers round the houses asking, 'Would you like to buy one of these?' 'How much would you pay for it?' People would be likely to say 'Yes' and to indicate that they would be prepared to pay quite a high price for it, but without really meaning it.

The firm did a stratified random sample of *men* using the questionnaire, Document 2A. What information would they have found out, and how would it be useful to them?

You are now to plan a market-research survey for your product. Write out a) instructions to the interviewer (based on three-stage random sampling or stratified random sampling), b) a questionnaire.

Market-research-type surveys are used not only to find out whether products would sell, but also by newspapers, for example, to sound out public opinion on various matters, such as which political party would win an election. From the work you have done you can see that the reliability of these must depend very much on how carefully the sampling is done and the way in which the questions are framed.

Sometimes institutions such as trade unions carry out referenda among their members, and again great care must be taken in framing the questions. For example, if a union received a pay offer which the national executive of the union were inclined to reject and go on strike for a better offer, they might ask:

1 'Do you wish to accept the present offer?'

2 'If not, are you willing to strike for a better offer?
or 'Will you support your national executive in striking for a better offer?'

Why might the way in which the questions are framed get different answers?

## Document 2A *Market-research survey on a 'dimmer' switch*

My firm has invented this light-dimmer and we are trying to discover whether people would find it useful.

(Show the prototype and explain what it does.)

1 If a light-switch in your house gets broken, do you replace it yourself or get an electrician to do it?

2 If the answer to question 1 is 'self', ask, 'Are you yourself an electrician?'

3 If the answer to question 1 is 'get an electrician', ask, 'Have you had an electrician to work in your house recently?'

4 If the answer to question 3 is 'no', ask, 'If you needed an electrician, how would you find the name and address?'

5 Have you ever installed or had installed any special electrical fittings such as wall lighting or a fluorescent tube?

6 Which do you think is the most important reason why people might buy a 'dimmer'?:

because they would like to have dim lights for relaxing and bright lights for working?

because it would save electricity?

7 Can you think of any other reason why people might buy one?

8 In which rooms of the house do you think people might fit 'dimmers'?

9 If you saw these advertised in a newspaper or on TV and decided to buy one, would you fit it yourself or get an electrician to fit it?

10 How much would you expect to pay for one of these in a shop?

11 Comparing these with all the other things you would like to have, would you be likely to buy one of these

a) in the near future?

b) sometime?

c) probably not at all?

# Can we make a profit? 3

## 3.1 Deciding a price

From the results of our market research we shall be able to get some idea of the number of articles we might sell and the kind of price we might get. We must now calculate whether we can produce the articles so as to sell them at a profit.

In order to manufacture our product we shall:

a) buy or rent a factory and office,
b) buy or hire machinery,
c) pay wages to workers,
d) buy raw material or components.

Are there any other costs?

Some of these costs are the same whether the factory is producing only a few articles or working at full capacity. These are sometimes called *fixed costs*. Which are the fixed costs?

Some of the costs vary according to the number of articles produced. These are sometimes called the *variable costs*. Which are the variable costs?

Suppose the fixed costs are £5000 per year and the variable costs are £10 per article. What would be the cost of each article if we produced 1000 articles per year?

What would be the cost of each article if we produced 2000 articles per year?

Why is the cost per article less if more are produced?

We must now decide what a reasonable profit would be. Suppose we must invest £10 000 to set up our business. If instead we invested this money in a building society, what interest would we get (before tax)? Why should we expect to get more if we invested the £10 000 in a business? What do you think would be a reasonable return on the £10 000?

One way of determining our price is to decide what number of articles we expect to produce each year, calculate the cost, add the total profit we expect, and divide by the number of articles. If the fixed costs are £5000, the variable costs are £10 per article, we produce 1000 articles per year, and we hope for a total profit of £1500, what price should we charge?

If we make 1500 articles per year and still charge the same price, what would the total profit be?

If we make only 500 articles per year, what would be the result?

Working on similar lines, carry out the following calculation: the fixed costs are £10 000 and the variable costs are £15 per article.

a) If we manufacture 2000 articles per year, at what price must we sell each article to produce a profit of £2000 per year?

b) What would be the total profit if we made 3000 articles and sold them at the same price per article as in (a)?
c) What would be the result if we sold only 1000 articles at the same price per article as in (a)?

What we have been discussing is sometimes called 'cost-plus-profit' pricing. Research shows that a lot of goods are priced in this way. Of course the 'price' we have been discussing is the price at which the manufacturer sells to the retailer (usually a shopkeeper). The shopkeeper adds his own profit margin, and we shall discuss this in a later section.

If our product is similar to one which is already on the market, we can price it by comparison with our competitors. If they are charging considerably higher than the 'cost-plus-profit' price, we might fix our price just below theirs. Alternatively we might put our price the same or even a bit higher and hope that the customers assume from our advertising that our product has an important difference which makes it worth buying rather than our competitor's. We shall be thinking more about these kind of tactics later in the course.

Suppose the price we determine on a cost-plus-profit basis is considerably less than the price which market research shows that our customers would be willing to pay? Is it right to charge the higher price and make a very high profit?

### 3.2 'Break-even' point

Suppose that the fixed costs are £5000 per annum and the variable costs are £5 per article. Draw a graph, to an appropriate scale, of fixed costs against number of articles produced up to 1000 articles. On the same diagram draw the graph of total costs against number of articles produced.

Let us suppose we designed the factory to produce a maximum of 1000 articles per year. Let us assume that we might normally produce and sell 800. What is the total cost of the 800 articles?

We decide that a reasonable total profit is £1200. What would be the total selling price of 800 articles? Plot this as a point on your graph and draw a straight line from the origin through this point. What does this line tell you?

If sales fall below a certain number, you will make a loss not a profit. From your graph calculate the number of articles you must sell to break even, i.e. when the income from sales just equals the total costs.

# Where does the money come from, and who gets the profits? 4

## 4.1 Getting money from a bank

We shall need to raise money for two main purposes:

a) To buy buildings and machinery. Money used in this way is usually called *fixed capital.*

b) To buy raw materials which we turn into finished products and sell to the consumer, thus earning money which is used to buy more raw materials. Money used in this way is called *circulating capital.*

The first thing which would probably occur to most of us is to go to a bank.

Document 4A describes an interview between someone who wishes to start a business and his bank manager. Study the document and then answer the following questions.

1 Why do you think that banks are often reluctant to make loans to new firms?

2 What is meant by collateral (e.g. for a bank loan)?

3 Why do banks need to charge interest on loans and overdrafts?

4 Mr B can have an overdraft of up to £1000 at 10% per annum. On 1 January he draws £500 and on 1 June another £500. On 31 August he repays £250, and on 31 December the other £750. Complete this schedule for his account:

| *Month* | *Amount outstanding* | *Monthly interest (10% per year)* |
|---|---|---|
| January | £500 | £4·17 |
| February | £500 | £4·17 |
| March | | |
| April | | |
| May | | |
| June | £1000 | |
| July | | |
| August | | |
| September | £750 | |
| October | | |
| November | | |
| December | | |

What is the total interest for the year? If he had had a bank loan of £1000 for a year at 10%, how much would he have paid in interest? Why can he not use only the cheaper of the two – loan and overdraft – to meet all his financial needs?

5 What other services can the bank provide to a small business?

### 4.2 Forming a limited company

When we set up in business there are several types of business organisation we might choose, each of which has its advantages and disadvantages. The characteristics of the different types of business unit are described in Document 4B. Use this information to answer the following questions:

1 Why might it be easier for a sole trader rather than a limited company to obtain credit from suppliers?

2 Why do you think it was necessary for a government at some time in the past to pass a Companies Act which allowed the formation of 'limited' companies?

3 Outline the procedure for the formation of a private limited company.

4 What protection does the founder of a private limited company have against being 'taken over'?

5 Suppose that, as a shareholder in a company, I object to the way in which the company is being directed. What can I do about it?

6 A company has issued 1000 £1 ordinary shares, of which I own 100. In one year the profit to be distributed is £500. What dividend shall I receive?

7 A small private limited company has the following capital structure:

| | |
|---|---|
| 1000 8% preference shares of £1 | £1000 |
| 1000 ordinary shares of £1 | £1000 |

Complete the table below:

| *Year* | *Trading profit* | *Preference shares profit* | | *Ordinary shares profit* | |
|---|---|---|---|---|---|
| | £ | £ | % | £ | % |
| 1970 | 500 | 80 | 8 | 420 | 42 |
| 1971 | 160 | | | | |
| 1972 | 100 | | | | |
| 1973 | 60 | | | | |

What conclusions can you draw about the relative advantages and disadvantages of owning preference or ordinary shares?

8 Why, if the business is successful, would holders of ordinary shares expect to get a greater return on their money than if they had invested it in a bank or a building society?

**9** What else might the directors decide to do with part of the profits rather than distribute them to the shareholders?

**10** Directors are expected to run a business to make as much money as possible for the shareholders (otherwise the shareholders might elect new directors at the next annual general meeting). In what ways might the interests of the shareholders clash with the interests of the workers?

**11** What changes could be made in company law to ensure that directors run businesses in the interests of both shareholders and workers?

## Document 4A *An interview with the bank manager*

A man who wishes to start a small business, Mr B, has arranged an interview with his bank manager, Mr M.

Mr B: In my letter I told you about my background and about the small business I would like to start. Can you lend me

***"I sometimes wish that I, too, were working for myself, and not just for humanity."***

(Reprinted with acknowledgement to Punch)

the money to get going?

Mr M: Well, first of all Mr B, what money are you putting into the firm yourself?

Mr B: All our savings, about £2000, and about £3000 I have borrowed from friends.

Mr M: Well, if instead of buying premises and machinery, you rent the buildings and hire machinery, you will not need a lot more money. We can lend it to you in two ways. One way is a bank loan. For example, we might lend you £1000 to be paid off over two years. The interest we would charge would be £200, so you would have to pay back £600 each year.

However, we should need some collateral – something which we could sell to get our money back if you went broke. For example, if you have already paid up over the £1000 we are lending on a life-assurance policy, we could use that.

Another way is by a bank overdraft – in other words, we let you overdraw on your current account. This will work out cheaper than a loan, but you can use the money only for circulating capital, not for fixed capital. We review overdrafts each year and, if national economic circumstances are tight, we sometimes have to press customers to reduce their overdrafts.

Bearing in mind that you have had a current account here for some time which you have never overdrawn, I am willing to offer you a loan of £500 if you can produce the collateral, and an overdraft of up to £500. Perhaps you would like time to consider it and let me know what you wish to do.

## Document 4B *Chief types of business unit*

### 1 Sole proprietor

In this type of business, all the equity capital is provided by one person. He or she gets all the profits, but they have unlimited liability, i.e. if the business loses money they may be made bankrupt and compelled to sell all their private property to pay their business debts. The British bankruptcy law is extremely exacting, and a bankrupt may be left with only the clothes he wears, his bedding, and the tools of his trade!

### 2 Partnership

In this type of business, the capital is provided by up to twenty people. Usually, although not necessarily, they draw up a legal agreement. Sometimes one or more of the partners provides capital but is not actively engaged in running the business, and such partners are often referred to as 'sleeping partners'. As with the sole proprietor, each of the partners has unlimited liability. Any partner may dissolve the partnership at any time he wishes.

### 3 The private limited company

The limited-liability or joint-stock company (which usually has the abbreviation 'Ltd' after the name) has the following characteristics.

a) The minimum number of shareholders is two and the maximum is fifty (with the exception of employees and former employees).

b) The shareholder's liability is limited to the nominal amount of his shareholding, which is usually the price paid for the shares when they were first issued. For example, if a person buys £1 shares when they are first issued, and pays the full £1 on each share, then he cannot be called upon to pay any more money if the firm becomes bankrupt. Some time later a second person might buy these shares from the first person for £0·50 each (paying less because the company has not been doing very well), but he is still not liable to pay out any more money at any future date because the full nominal value of the '£1 shares' was paid in the first place.

c) A private company cannot invite the public at large to buy its shares, and a shareholder cannot transfer shares to another person without the agreement of other shareholders.

d) In Britain, companies are formed in accordance with an Act of Parliament called the Companies Act, 1948 (there have been a series of Companies Acts between 1844 and 1967, the most important for most purposes being those of 1862 and 1948). This lays down that a company is to be run by a board of directors and a company secretary, the minimum number of directors being one in the case of a private company. Directors are voted into office and are removable from office only by the shareholders at a general meeting; a general meeting must be held annually. The shareholders are not permitted to interfere with the directors' day-to-day management of the business.

When a company is formed, a solicitor draws up two documents: the 'memorandum of association' and the 'articles of association'. The memorandum of association is a statement of the rules by which the company will regulate its dealings with the outside world. The articles of association are concerned with the internal affairs of the company within the general framework of the memorandum of association. It sets out the company's regulations concerning such matters as the rights and voting powers of shareholders, the powers and duties of directors, and so on. All these arrangements must comply with the Companies Act.

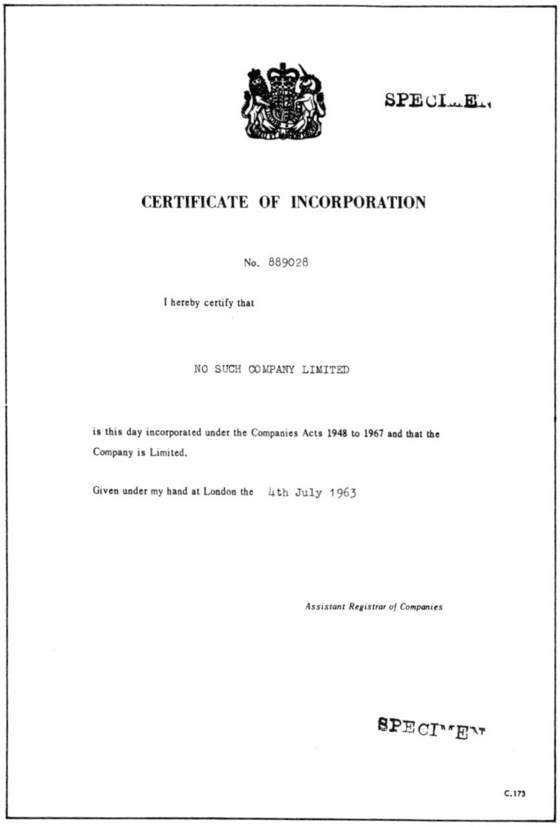

SPECIMEN

CERTIFICATE OF INCORPORATION

No. 889028

I hereby certify that

NO SUCH COMPANY LIMITED

is this day incorporated under the Companies Acts 1948 to 1967 and that the Company is Limited.

Given under my hand at London the 4th July 1963

*Assistant Registrar of Companies*

SPECIMEN

C.173

When the memorandum and articles are sent to Companies House (at present at 55–71 City Road, London EC1Y 1BB), the Registrar of Companies issues a Certificate of Incorporation, and upon receipt of this a private company may commence trading.

e) All companies are required by the Companies Acts to supply certain information annually to the Department of Trade. They must give details of the shareholders, the directors, and the company's assets and mortgages etc., and they must file a copy of the accounts.

f) There are two main types of shares: preference shares and ordinary shares.

Preference shares have a fixed rate of interest which must be paid in full before any dividend is paid on the ordinary shares. Ordinary shares do not have a fixed rate of interest, but the holders divide between them the remainder of the profits after all other claims have been met.

Debentures are not really shares but loans. They have a fixed rate of interest, and this must be paid before there is any distribution of profits to either preference or ordinary shareholders. Debenture holders are not members of the company.

### 4 The public limited company

This is in many ways similar to a private company, but with the following important differences.

a) It must have a minimum of seven shareholders and there is no maximum. There is a minimum of two directors.

b) It can invite the general public to buy its shares. This is usually done through the Stock Exchange, and since an issuing house (a firm which issues shares to the public through the Stock Exchange) will handle the shares only of a company of proven financial reliability, this form of finance is not in practice available to a small company starting from scratch. What usually happens is that a business starts as a private company and 'goes public' at a later date to raise additional finance (see Section 9).

# How shall we organise our factory? 5

An interior view of a wire factory

## 5.1 A study of the Wyre Company Ltd

We now have the problem of how to organise our works. Document 5A is a study of a small firm of the size we might set up. Read it through carefully, and then answer the following questions.

1 How many staff were employed at the time of the study? Make up a diagram showing their relationship to each other within the works.

2 What advantages does this small firm have over larger firms within the same type of trade?

3 Why has this firm been able to expand?

4 What are the advantages and disadvantages to this firm of being located in an area which has other firms producing metal goods?

5 What are the advantages and disadvantages to the workers in a neighbourhood of having several firms employing similar kinds of workers?

6 Why do the employees apparently think it is not necessary under their particular circumstances to belong to a trade union?

7 As far as we can tell from this study, what appear to be the most important factors in making employees decide to stay with the firm?

### 5.2 A study of a local firm

You will have the opportunity to study a local firm but, before you go, use the following suggestions to make out a questionnaire.

1 List the products of the firm. How many of each article were produced last year?

2 How are the orders obtained?

3 Where does the raw material come from? Who orders it?

4 Who plans the production, and how do they do it?

5 What outside services does the firm use?

6 What office work is done? If you can, obtain samples of any forms used, and trace an order through from the time it is made to the time it is paid.

7 How is the factory located relative to other similar factories?

8 What is the trade-union membership? How is wage bargaining carried out?

9 What are the safety regulations for various jobs? How well are they observed?

10 What is the history of the firm?

11 What is the present capital structure and turnover?

12 Draw a diagram of the workshop, show how the work flows through it, and find out what job each person does.

13 Make out a questionnaire such as the following for each worker.

TYPE OF JOB.............................. MALE/FEMALE
MARRIED/SINGLE

ASK: 'How important do you consider each of the following?'
Put a tick in one column against each.

| | Very important | Fairly important | Not very important | Not at all important |
|---|---|---|---|---|
| a) High wages | | | | |
| b) Working conditions | | | | |
| c) Being able to talk while working | | | | |
| d) Working with friends | | | | |
| e) Interesting work | | | | |
| f) Varied work | | | | |
| g) Responsible work | | | | |
| h) Canteen | | | | |
| i) Social club | | | | |

ASK: 'Do you live near any of the people you work with?'
YES/NO

ASK: 'Do you see any of the people you work with outside work?'
OFTEN/NOT OFTEN

ASK: 'Is there any other job you would sooner do?'
YES/NO
If yes, ask 'Why?' and 'Why don't you change to it?'

ASK: 'Do you expect any promotion?'

ASK: 'How did you receive your training for your present job?'

OBSERVE FOR YOURSELF:
Are they able to talk while working? OFTEN/NOT OFTEN
Is the work interesting? YES/NO
Is the work varied? YES/NO
Is there any opportunity to plan their own work? YES/NO
Is the work responsible? YES/NO

When you have gathered all this information and written it up, try to answer the same questions that we asked in Section 5.1.

### 5.3 Planning our own factory

Having regard to what we have learnt from our studies, you are now to plan in detail a factory organisation to manufacture your own product.

You will obviously bear in mind efficiency of production, but you will probably have formed some ideas about the way in which workers like to have the job organised, and you may be able to incorporate some of these ideas into the planning of your factory.

## Document 5A *The Wyre Company Limited*

(This document is based on a study of a Midlands firm, but certain details have been altered to prevent identification, and other details have been added to present a more general picture.)

### History

In 1926 a Mr Wyre (now deceased) was employed by a Midlands firm. He made wire components for their main products. But as the trade depression developed there was no longer sufficient work to keep one man fully employed on this job, and he was made redundant. However, each of the firms in the area still required *some* wire work, so Mr Wyre set up a room in his house to produce the wire components for two or three firms.

Soon after, he took over a bicycle shop, and he and his son ran the shop and did the wirework in a back room of the shop.

When trade began to improve, Mr Wyre found that there were quite a lot of firms in the area who occasionally required a quantity of wire components for special jobs, and there were shops in the area who would sell articles such as wire wastepaper baskets, incinerators, and decorative wirework. Since Mr Wyre had a specialist knowledge of where to get different kinds of wire, the best wire for different jobs, and the techniques for handling it, he was in a good position to supply this trade.

He and six others (mostly family) put up money to form a private limited company, and he rented a small factory, employing about twelve people. The work gradually increased.

In 1955 the seven shareholders plus one other increased the share capital to £12 000, so that they could move to a modern factory on a trading estate. They now employ about fifty people, and the turnover is about £120 000 per annum. The output is spread over a wide variety of products, but machinery guards and incinerators figure fairly prominently.

### Organisation

The managing director and majority shareholder is Mr Wyre senior (son of the founder of the firm). His elder son is the sales director, who works with one representative. Their method is to look up in a trade directory such as Kelly's (most public libraries have a copy) the names of all the firms who might use wire products as components and the large shops who might require a run of their goods. They then visit these firms to see whether they have any requirements which Wyre Co. Ltd could produce more easily than their present supplier, or, in the case of a shop, they might persuade them to sell a line of goods which they had not hitherto carried. Most of their business now comes from previous customers or firms recommended to them by previous customers.

The sales director obtains a working drawing from the customer, or in some cases this is drawn up by the assistant works manager. The managing director works out a price and, if this is accepted, the works manager orders the wire and any other components which may be required, and organises the production run. Types of wire which are used frequently are kept in stock and replaced as used.

There are two types of production run (refer to figure 5A – plan of Wyre works).

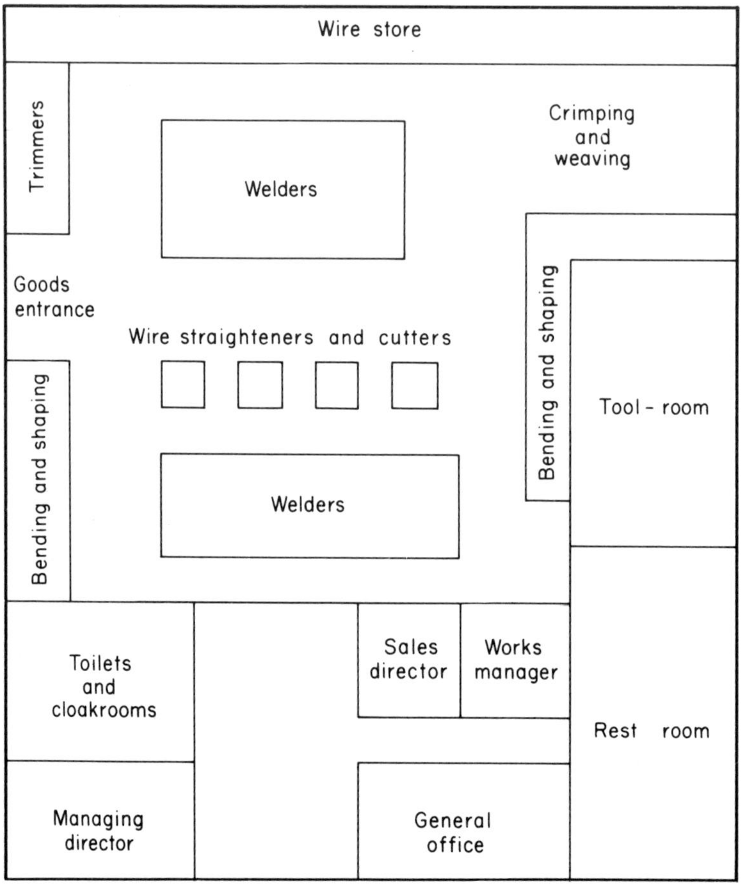


Figure 5A. Plan of Wyre Works

Straightening and cutting the wire

Trimming the components

Bending the wire

Attaching the wire to the sub-frames

Electric spot-welding

Plating the finished components

Most production runs start by the wire being straightened and cut into lengths. There are four electrically operated machines for doing this, attended by two men.

The wire then goes to the hand-operated bench presses for bending into shape. There are four men and six women working in this section.

The components are then put together by electric spot welding. The jigs for doing this have been produced in the tool-room at the time the works manager planned the production run. About fifteen people (two men and thirteen women) work in the welding section, each working at their own individual machine.

The article then goes to the side benches again, for trimming. There are two men and three women working in this section.

The other type of production run is where the wire is crimped, then woven and attached to a metal frame. This is done by seven people operating hand presses and tools.

Occasionally some of the articles are hand painted, but mostly they are sent to other firms for electroplating or plastics coating. One man is employed as van driver.

The finished goods are sent by British Rail or British Road Services.

The making of the jigs and the care of the tools is done by one man in the tool-room.

The managing director's wife is company secretary, and there are two girls employed in the office on general clerical work.

## The employees

None of the employees belong to a trade union, but the rates paid are the same as those in the larger union factories in the area.

There is no canteen, but there are facilities for heating up food. When the firm first moved to the new factory they had an hour for lunch, but the employees decided to reduce this to half an hour and leave earlier in the evening.

Most of the employees have been with the firm some time. The man in the tool-room has been with the firm the longest. Boys from school are encouraged to take apprenticeships and if they do they are given day-release, but they seldom decide to take them. It is difficult to get people to stay in the crimping-and-weaving section, and there is some turnover among the welders. Some of the welders move from one firm to another on the estate according to where the rates offered at a particular time are highest. The welders consider themselves more highly skilled than the side-bench workers. The side-bench workers have the most opportunity to talk to each other during working hours, and they have the most contact with each other outside working hours.

# Selling our product 6

## 6.1 The retailer

Our problem is, what is the best way of distributing our product to the customer? But before we can answer this, we need to have some knowledge of the retail trade.

We can begin by looking at the way we buy goods in our own household. Take home the following questionnaire, and fill it in with the help of your parents. Fill in the answers to the best of your ability – if you don't know exactly how far away a particular shop is, estimate the distance as nearly as you can – but make sure you complete the questionnaire.

| | How commodities are bought | | | | | | | | | |
|---|---|---|---|---|---|---|---|---|---|---|
| | | Shop | | | | | | | | |
| | | | | | Type of shop | | | | | |
| Individual questionnaire | Door to door | How far away? | How frequently used? | Av. cost of item | Independent | Voluntary chain | Multiple | Variety chain | Department | Mail order |
| Groceries | | | | | | | | | | |
| Greengroceries | | | | | | | | | | |
| Meat | | | | | | | | | | |
| Milk | | | | | | | | | | |
| Bread | | | | | | | | | | |
| Pharmaceuticals and cosmetics | | | | | | | | | | |
| Sweets and tobacco | | | | | | | | | | |
| Small household goods | | | | | | | | | | |
| Clothes | | | | | | | | | | |
| Shoes | | | | | | | | | | |
| Furniture | | | | | | | | | | |
| Electrical goods | | | | | | | | | | |
| Others: | | | | | | | | | | |

To help you, here is an explanation of each type of shop mentioned in the questionnaire.

### Independent shops

The small shop owned by an independent shopkeeper. The shopkeeper acts as his own accountant, display man, buyer, etc. In other words, he

A multiple shop – the Burton shop in Southampton

does much of the work himself – but is generally helped by his family. He may, however, own more than one shop but, as long as he owns less than ten shops, he is described as being independent.

### Multiple shops

Those shops that have many branches around the country but which specialise in a particular type of goods. An example would be Burtons for men's clothes.

### Variety chain stores

Again, these shops have many branches around the country, and in each branch they sell a range of goods. Examples are Littlewoods and Boots.

### Voluntary chain shops

These are groups of retailers who join together for the purpose of buying their goods. By buying a large amount they are able to obtain a discount, thus reducing their costs. These groups may be local – say in a small town – or they may cover a large part of the country such as Mace and Spar.

### Department stores

These are very large stores selling a very wide variety of goods. The store is divided into separate departments, e.g. hardware, furniture, clothing, toys, etc. They are often thought of as being several shops under one roof. Examples are Harrods, John Lewis and Selfridges.

A voluntary chain shop

### Mail order

Here the shopper buys the goods using a catalogue, or an advertisement in a newspaper or magazine, and the postal service. Examples of the firms are Janet Frazer and Kays.

When you return the questionnaire, your teacher will help you summarise the results for all your class.

1. Can you pick out any pattern from the information in the summary table?
2. Can you explain any pattern you pick out?
3. How might the pattern change if most families were to buy deep-freezers?

## 6.2 The wholesaler

Suppose you are the manager of a small hardware store. You sell a wide variety of goods – tools, paints, wallpaper, etc. If in each case you traded direct with the manufacturer, your time would be taken up by many visits from the various manufacturers' representatives, and, since there are very many small hardware shops, each manufacturer would need to employ a large number of representatives.

It is in a situation such as this that a wholesaler can provide a valuable service. He buys in bulk from each manufacturer and sells in smaller quantities to the retailer. The situation can be represented diagrammatically, as shown on the next page.

Manufacturers dealing with retailers without a wholesaler

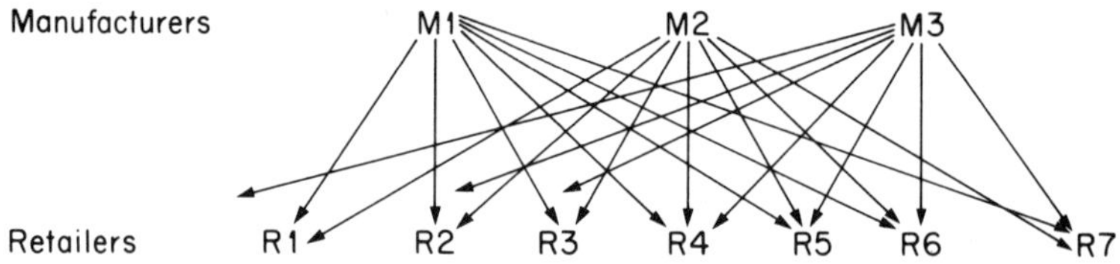


How many visits are required for each manufacturer to deal with each retailer?

Manufacturers dealing with retailers through a wholesaler

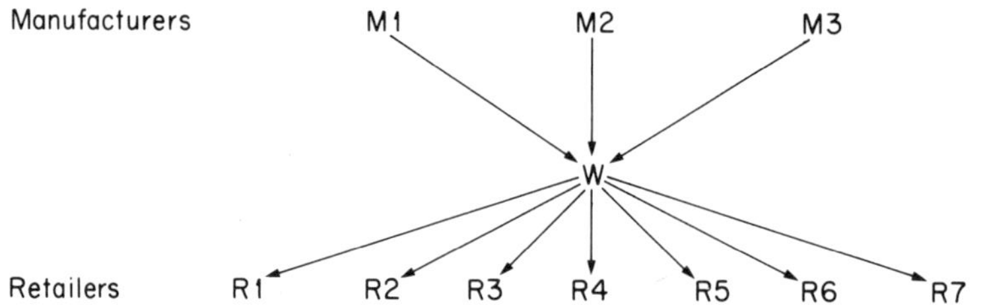


How many visits are required for each wholesaler to deal with each retailer?

Inside a wholesaler's warehouse

## Services which the wholesaler gives to the manufacturer and to the retailer

Services to the manufacturer:

1 He is able to inform manufacturers about the types of goods retailers are buying (and do not forget that retailers will want these goods as they are selling well in their shops). This can help the manufacturers to decide whether or not to increase the production of certain goods.

2 The manufacturer is able to devote his time and energy to *making* goods, as the wholesaler will buy them in large quantities and *store* them in his own warehouse.

3 The wholesaler will pay the manufacturer for the goods bought, promptly and in cash. The manufacturer is, therefore, able to use this to buy more raw materials, pay his labour, and produce more goods.

4 He transports goods to the retailers, thus freeing the manufacturer from this job.

5 He may pack the goods.

6 He is able to save the manufacturer a great deal of time, trouble, and money. Imagine a situation where a manufacturer had to deal directly with a large number of retail shops without the help of a wholesaler. The manufacturer would have to send bills, delivery notes, and all sorts of other communications to all the shops, and would have to hire extra staff to do all this. Postage costs would also increase, as would transport costs, for goods would have to be delivered in small quantities to many of these retailers.

The two diagrams should help to show the difference a wholesaler makes to the costs of a business.

Services to the retailer:

1 Retailers would find it very difficult and time-consuming if they had to deal with each manufacturer individually. The wholesaler offers goods from many manufacturers.

2 He sells to the retailer in small quantities.

3 He is generally situated near to the retailers and can supply the retailer quickly from his warehouse.

4 He is able to give the retailer advice on products, and can keep the retailer up to date with new products.

5 He is able to give credit to the retailer. This is very important to the small retail shops, as it is then possible to sell the goods to the public and then pay the wholesaler.

As can be seen, the wholesaler can be helpful to both the retailer and the manufacturer. Thus the normal chain of distribution looks like this:

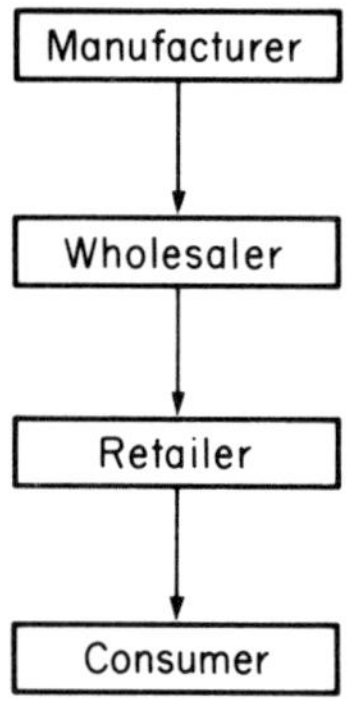


1 To what extent would each of the following types of retail establishment use a wholesaler, if at all?
   a) Independent shop selling a variety of low-cost goods – e.g. a grocer or a general hardware shop.
   b) Independent shop selling high-cost goods – e.g. furniture.
   c) Voluntary chain.
   d) Multiple and variety chain shops.
   e) Department store.
   f) Mail order.

2 It is sometimes said that, if the wholesaler were omitted, the price of goods would fall as there would be no wholesaler's profit. Is this necessarily so?

3 Thinking of the product which you originally decided to manufacture, how would you decide to sell it?

## 6.3 Advantages and disadvantages of different methods of distribution

Now let us look in more detail at some of the types of selling units which comprise the retail trade.

### 1 Independent shops

There are a very large number of independent shops in this country. However, their total share of the retail trade is declining steadily, due to strong competition from other types of retail units, e.g. multiple shops and mail order.

The independent shop is generally situated conveniently for local customers – they are able to shop without going into town. The owner may also be more flexible with regard to his opening and closing times; for example, he may stay open until late in the evening and part of the day on Sunday. Regular customers might well be able to obtain credit and a free delivery service. The shopkeeper may be prepared to exchange or alter goods with a minimum of fuss, and to cater for any special requirements of his customers. The atmosphere in the shop may be friendly and personal, with the shopkeeper often being willing and able to advise customers on the best articles for their requirements.

Prices, however, may be higher than in other larger stores, due to the fact that the small shopkeeper does not have the turnover or the storage space to buy his goods in large quantities and thus obtain discounts on bulk purchase from wholesalers or manufacturers. Due to his slow turnover, he may also find it difficult to keep up to date with new fashions and products, while being able to stock only a limited number of goods of any one variety. Due to lack of space, he might have to limit his display and advertising areas.

While the 'personal touch' in a small shop may appear inviting to the consumer, there is also the distinct possibility of queues and delays which can be frustrating to the shopper who has little time to spare.

The small shopkeeper is often found in greater numbers in relatively low-rent areas, and this may help to keep prices down to a competitive level if the volume of trade is high. However, small shopkeepers must usually buy through several wholesalers, each of whom must meet his costs and make a profit.

## 2 Multiple and variety chain stores

These stores have been increasing their share of the retail trade. They are usually joint-stock companies who are able to raise greater amounts of money than the small shopkeeper. They buy in large quantities and pay promptly, and can, therefore, obtain substantial discounts from suppliers. They have very fast sales and can charge lower prices. In other words, they

A variety chain shop – in the centre of a modern shopping centre

can afford to make a smaller profit on each item sold because they sell so many. This means that total profits are still high.

These types of shops can also employ very skilled people who specialise in managing, buying, market research, etc. More use can also be made of such aids to selling as trading stamps, special offers, sales, etc. The buying of goods is done at the head office of the company, and the goods are then distributed to the shops. Although each shop has a manager, many of the important decisions are made by head office, for example, the buying of goods and advertising on a national scale. The manager, however, must be able to organise his stock, staff, and accounts. It may not be easy, however, to control a large number of branches without complicated and therefore costly administration.

These stores are generally found in the shopping centres and certain suburbs of towns and cities, where rents and rates are high. Their siting may not be as convenient to customers as the siting of independent shops. The goods that are sold tend to be highly standardised and do not necessarily cater for local or individual variations in taste and demand. Many of these shops rely on consumer self-service to a greater or lesser extent. Often a multiple shop may sell goods due to its reputation, and consumers will be attracted by its familiar name and shop front.

### 3 Department stores

These offer convenience to the customer in that many articles can be bought without moving from place to place. On the other hand, they are situated in the centre of cities and so they may be inconvenient for the consumer who has to travel to them. The premises are large, with a number of floors. They are built on very expensive sites in the main shopping areas, where there are crowds. Sales floors are spacious, with plenty of room for the display of goods. Window displays are important, since an eye-catching display will bring goods to the notice of passers-by. Department stores provide a whole range of services to the customer, such as lounges, restaurants, hairdressing shops, escalators, lifts, pleasing decor, etc. They also provide experienced sales staff to advise customers on purchases.

Each selling department is controlled by a buyer, who must buy the goods for his department and also see how successfully they sell. In many of the chain department stores, however, e.g. Beatties of Wolverhampton, a central buyer works at head office, buying for all the department stores in order to get a discount for bulk buying.

Payment for goods in a department store is generally made in cash, but hire-purchase is often allowed on more expensive goods. Stores also operate monthly and/or budget accounts.

Many department stores now run mail-order departments to encourage customers who do not wish to travel. Because the shop is so large, other attractions can also be offered, e.g. exhibitions, demonstrations, Father Christmas, etc.

An important feature of department stores is the seasonal sales, when

John Lewis – a department store in Oxford Street

the prices of many goods are cut to encourage customers to buy them. The store is able to clear much of its old stock by this method. Special cheap lines of goods may also be purchased by the store for resale during this period.

Other firms may be allowed to hire part of the store in order to sell their goods or services, e.g. Aquascutum and Susan Small.

Department stores have very high costs, e.g. rent, rates, wages, heating, lighting. These costs are often passed on to the consumer in the form of higher prices. Multiple and variety chain stores, among others, can very often sell the goods more cheaply with a minimum of services offered.

## 4 Mail order

This type of selling method uses the postal service. There are mail-order firms who will send catalogues to prospective customers, and they may also employ agents to win custom for the firm. The agent is normally paid a 10% commission on any sales made. Credit is usually given on the goods bought. The catalogues contain a large variety of goods and are very expensive to produce. More than one is needed each year, the contents varying with the season.

The cover of a mail order catalogue

Another type of mail-order firm advertises goods in newspapers and in magazines. Credit may still be offered. Postage and packing may be extra charges.

For the consumer, there is the convenience of being able to choose goods at home, and the credit facilities. However, the goods cannot be seen or touched before being ordered, and therefore quality cannot necessarily be assessed properly. There may also be delays in the post and further delays if the goods are faulty, broken, or of the wrong type. Exchanges or refunds of money may not always be granted readily, if at all.

Mail-order firms may be situated in low-rent areas and do not have to be close to large centres of population. There are no display or sales assistants' costs. The major cost may be the printing of the catalogue. However, there are costs – such as bad debts, postage, administration of the weekly credit payments, and the 'breaking down' of bulk – which all have to be met. These costs may mean that mail order is not necessarily a cheaper method of selling than a conventional shop, and therefore prices cannot automatically be expected to be any less.

### 5 Supermarkets and self-service shopping

This has been one of the most important trends in retailing since the Second World War. Self-service as a method of selling is used now by many different types of shop, but one tends to associate this method with the multiple supermarket groups dealing with food. A self-service shop can only properly be called a supermarket if its area is at least 250 square metres.

Supermarkets deal mainly with goods that can be sold very rapidly; goods such as groceries and toilet requisites. They therefore buy in very large quantities and obtain handsome discounts. The goods are then sold to the consumer at the lowest price possible, thus increasing demand. Goods that have already been packed, wrapped, weighed, and priced are put on display for customers to see themselves. Once customers have made their selection, they pay for their purchases at the 'check-out points'.

This method of selling reduces labour costs, since fewer sales staff are needed. In fact, staff are really necessary only to stock the shelves and collect the money for purchases, as service is cut to a minimum since there is generally neither credit nor delivery.

A supermarket – large display shelves and trolleys for self-service

A great deal of time and effort is put into devising means by which the consumer is persuaded to buy the goods in the shop. Counters and shelves are carefully placed; the displays are eye-catching, with special offers, 'loss leaders', and trading stamps; and specially selected music may be played.

Many housewives regard supermarkets as a great help, as shopping can be done with the minimum of bother, although some prefer the independent shop because of the personal service and advice which is given. If the housewife wishes to buy only a few items, the independent shops may be more conveniently sited.

Make a table like this:

| | Manufacturer | | Retailer | | Consumer | |
|---|---|---|---|---|---|---|
| | Advantages | Disadvantages | Advantages | Disadvantages | Advantages | Disadvantages |
| 1. Independent shop | | | | | | |
| 2 Multiple and variety chain store | | | | | | |
| 3 Department store | | | | | | |
| 4 Mail order | | | | | | |

Then list the advantages and disadvantages to each person (manufacturer, retailer, consumer) of each type of shop (independent, chain, department). Remember that what is an advantage to one might be a disadvantage to another.

## Modern trends in retailing

1 Discount stores

Discount stores, such as Argos and Comet, may be termed supermarkets for consumer durables. (Consumer durables are items which last a long

A Comet discount store

time and which are not bought regularly – examples would be washing machines, television sets, and radios.)

The premises are usually a large warehouse, which need not be sited in a high-rent area of a city centre since customers are prepared to travel a little distance (especially with the rise in car ownership) to buy these goods at a lower price – and this is precisely the reason for the rapid rise in popularity of these stores.

Service is cut to a minimum. The goods are stacked up with no pretence of display, and the customer buys what he wants and drives it away himself (discount stores generally charge if they have to deliver the goods).

## 2 Hypermarkets

The Co-op 'superstore' – a hypermarket

These are huge stores, covering perhaps several hectares of ground, with parking space for hundreds of cars, situated outside towns or cities. The stores sell both consumer durables and consumables on the supermarket principle. All the advantages of a supermarket are multiplied for the retailer, because of the huge turnover of goods, and all the usual supermarket sales techniques are applied.

This type of shopping is again only possible due to the wide ownership of motor cars. The hypermarket started, as did the supermarket, in America and has since spread to Europe, but the European country in which they have developed most is France, the biggest firm being Carrefour.

In Britain, Woolworths have entered the field with their Woolco hypermarkets, such as the one situated on the outskirts of Bournemouth. Tesco also have a hypermarket near Leicester.

## 3 Automatic vending machines

The principle is not new – cigarettes and chocolate have been sold by this method for many years. However, the range of these machines has grown recently, and such goods as petrol, beverages, and tights are now sold by this method. In some parts of the country, there are shops where various types of prepacked food are sold through automatic vending machines. America is again a leader in this field, and shops exist where the housewife can order her goods by using a punched card. The goods are then selected and packed automatically. These shops can, of course, be used by customers at any time, and the shoppers' time is saved. On the other hand, prices tend to be higher than usual, due to the cost of the complicated electronic equipment needed for this type of operation.

Vending machines selling fresh drinks

## 6.4 A study of a department store

1 Read through Document 6A. What would be the important differences in your way of life if you worked in a shop rather than in a factory or an office? Which of the jobs described would you most like to do? Are there any aspects of the job you would not like?

2 Imagine you are a sales assistant. Which of the following do you think is the most important? Number them from 1 to 6 in order of importance:
   being clean and tidily dressed,
   keeping your part of the shop clean and tidy,
   leaving other jobs in order to wait on a customer immediately she requires your attention,
   giving the customer accurate information about the goods on sale,
   making the customer feel that she has enjoyed being in your shop,
   doing exactly what the departmental sales manager tells you to do.

3 From your own experience as a customer, which of the above do you feel that sales assistants consider to be the *least* important?

4 For each of the following statements, say whether you think it is true of all customers, true of some, partly true of all, partly true of some, or not true at all:

The customer knows exactly what she wants and she comes into the shop just to buy it.

The customer knows vaguely what she wants, but she needs some help in making a choice.

Most customers go shopping to give themselves a treat by buying something.

Many customers go shopping because they are lonely or bored and want something to do.

5 All the goods on sale in this store could be plastic-wrapped and sold in a supermarket-style store: the goods could be sold cheaper because fewer assistants need be employed. Why do many customers prefer to trade in a department store of this type?

6 'The customer is always right.' Say why you agree or disagree.

7 Plan the layout of a shop with the departments listed in Document 6A. Bear in mind that you want the customer to buy as many things as possible. Which articles are they most likely to come into the shop on purpose to buy? Which articles are they most likely to buy on impulse? You may decide to design the shop so that the customer must pass through 'impulse' departments on the way to and from the departments she intends to get to. Remember that children are accompanied by mothers.

Write a short account explaining your design.

8 Are there any goods you would add to the range sold in this shop?

9 At what times during the year might you expect trade to be slackest? What device do shops use to improve trade at these times?

10 The management decided to pay a commission on sales to the assistants. Do you think this is a good idea? Which would be the fairest: to pay according to the sales by individual assistants, according to the sales by departments, or according to the sales by the store as a whole?

## Document 6A *A study of a department store*

This store is situated in the main shopping centre of a town of 40 000 people. It is part of a chain of similar shops.

There are twelve selling departments, each under a departmental sales manager (who used to be called a buyer). The departments are as follows (number of assistants in brackets):

coats and suits (3),
gowns (3),
millinery (2),
blouses and knitwear (3),
teenage fashions (2),
childrens (2),
underwear (4),
dress fabrics (3),
haberdashery and knitting wools (5),
handbags, luggage, and fancy goods (3),
gloves, hosiery, and perfumery (10).

In this latter department, three of the assistants are employed by hosiery firms (Wolsey, Pretty Polly, and Charnos) to sell their own particular brand, and five of the assistants are paid partly by the firm and partly by a particular cosmetic manufacturer (Elizabeth Arden, Charles of the Ritz, etc.).

Most of the goods are bought by 'head office' and distributed to the shop. The departmental sales managers are responsible for recording deliveries and sales, ordering replacement stock, and requesting items from the firm's catalogue which they think will sell well. They also have control over a certain amount of money with which to order special lines from manufacturers: they must use their own judgment to order what they think will sell well in their department. (In some department stores all goods are bought centrally, whereas in others the departmental sales managers or buyers are responsible for all their own ordering. This firm operates a mixed system.)

In addition to the selling departments there are the display department (a manager and two assistants responsible for window dressing), dispatch (responsible for accepting deliveries and distributing to departments, and dispatching goods to customers), maintenance, and office (four staff responsible for accounts and wages).

All the departmental managers are responsible to the general manager of the store.

Most of the staff are women. School-leavers or married women without previous experience are given a short induction course (about eight hours) in which they are taught how to deal with the various ways of making a purchase (cash, cheque, credit), how to operate the till, and how to parcel up purchases. Their departmental sales manager teaches them how to behave towards customers.

All those who are interested are encouraged to train as departmental sales managers. This training can be started any time after the age of eighteen, and it lasts for two years. It involves working in various departments, and part-time study in the business-studies department at the local college of further education.

Senior management (general managers of stores and head-office buying staff) are recruited from specially selected departmental sales managers or university graduates. They are given a two-year training in the larger stores of the company, with some time at a business college and at head office. After that they become assistant general manager of one of the large stores or general manager of one of the smaller stores.

## Document 6B *Combines in the retail trade*

### Co-operative Movement

Turnover about £1500m. Over 150000 employees.
19250 shops, supermarkets and stores for about 240 local retail societies.
Food, clothing, shoes, furnishing, coal, hotel and catering, motor and petrol, farming etc.

The retail societies are supplied by the national Co-operative Wholesale Society (turnover £700m. 28 000 employees)

Allied Suppliers

Turnover in 1973/74 £295m.
2100 shops including Lipton, Home and Colonial, Pearks, Maypole.
Also has 62 restaurants, 44 launderettes, 38 hairdressing salons.
Owns factories which produce canned foods, pickles, jams etc.

Tesco

Turnover in 1973/74 £433·7m. 24000 employees.
800 supermarkets and stores.

Sainsbury

Turnover in 1973/74 £362m. 29 433 employees.
198 supermarkets and stores.

Fine Fare

Turnover in 1973/74 £225m. 23 000 employees.
810 supermarkets and shops.
Division of Associated British Foods.

Great Universal Stores

Turnover in 1973/74 £692m. 47 615 employees.
2750 shops, stores and warehouses, including:

*Men's clothing:* Hector Powe, Neville Reed, John Temple, Hope Bros., Willerby.
*Ladies' Fashions:* Jax and Paige.
*Furniture:* Cavendish Warehouse, Times Furnishing, Aston.

Largest mail-order business in Europe. Owns factories which produce clothing, shoes, furniture and bedding.

Marks and Spencers

Turnover in 1973/74 £605m. 40 827 employees.

United Drapery Stores

Turnover in 1973/74 £234m. 27 613 employees.
1000 department stores and shops, including John Collier, Alexandre and Richard Shops.

House of Fraser

Turnover in 1973/74 £259m. 27 800 employees.
131 department stores and shops including Harrods, Rackhams, Dickens and Jones, D. H. Evans, John Barker, Kendal Milne and Binns.

Debenhams

Turnover in 1973/74 £227m. 35 511 employees.
269 department stores and shops including Debenham and Freebody, Swan and Edgar, Harvey Nichols, Cresta, Lotus, Caters.

John Lewis Partnership

Turnover in 1973/74 £209m. 23 000 employees.
69 department stores, supermarkets (Waitrose) and shops.

British Shoe Corporation

Turnover in 1973/74 £233m. 45 000 employees.
2000 shoe shops including Lilley and Skinner, Dolcis, Saxone, True-Form, Freeman, Hardy and Willis, Manfield. Also Selfridges and Lewis's department stores.

Woolworth

Turnover in 1973/74 £452·6m. 82 443 employees. 1134 shops.

The Boots Co. Ltd.

Turnover in 1973/74 £441·5m. 66611 employees.
1900 shops, including Timothy White's.

# Managing a small firm 7

In this first part of our course we have imagined that we have set up a small firm. You may have got the idea that all you have to do is to set up a firm and then stand back while the money rolls in! In practice, however, the manager of a small firm has many problems, and it is all too easy to go bankrupt – sometimes just when you think business is doing well.

We are going to play a game which will help you to appreciate some of the manager's problems.

Suppose that you have set up a private limited company, with a fully paid-up ordinary-share capital of £4000. You have hired a plant capable of producing up to 100 articles per quarter. The fixed costs are £1000 per quarter and the variable costs are £20 per article. Your market research tells you that initially you can expect to sell about 60 articles per quarter, but the number may be higher if you fix a low price and lower if you fix a high price. The number of sales may change both up and down as time goes on.

You will be given copies of the 'Quarterly Decision Form' (see example over the page).

1 Decide on your output and fill in item 1 under 'Production and sales' (maximum output 100).

2 Fill in the 'Costs' column in order to calculate the cost of each item.

3 Decide on a price.

4 Show your decision form to the teacher, who will fill in the sales (item 4 under 'Production and sales'). Remember, the lower the price the higher the sales, and vice versa.

5 Fill in the 'Revenue' column. In period 1, starting cash is £4000. (How can you work out whether you have made a profit in this period?)

6 Complete item 5 in the 'Production and sales' column.

7 Turn to the next 'Quarterly Decision Form'.
   a) Fill in the stock brought forward (item 2), which is the unsold goods (item 5) from the previous form.
   b) Fill in 'Starting cash', which is the 'Cash in hand' from the previous form.

8 Carry on as from number 1 above.

You will continue to play this game for a number of 'years', and the aim is to make as much profit as possible.

## Quarterly Decision Form

Company.................... Year ........................ Quarter .....................

Price ...........................

### Company Balance Sheet

| COSTS | £ | REVENUE | £ |
|---|---|---|---|
| Total Fixed Costs | 1000 | Starting cash | |
| Total Variable Costs (£20 per article) | ______ | Income from sales (price × sales) | ______ |
| TOTAL COSTS | ______ | TOTAL INCOME | |
| Average costs, i.e. | | ← Less costs | ______ |
| $\frac{\text{Total Costs}}{\text{Output}} =$ | ______ | CASH IN HAND (becomes starting cash on the next decision form) | ______ |

### Production and Sales

(1) Output this period (determines total variable costs)

(2) Stock brought forward (output not sold last quarter) ______________

(3) TOTAL GOODS FOR SALE ______________ (1+2)

(4) Sales this quarter (depends on price charged and found out from teacher) ______________

(5) Unsold goods (becomes stock brought forward on next decision sheet) ______________ (3−4)

# Part 2 Expanding the company

# Shall we expand our firm? 8

In Part 1 we considered how we might set up a small manufacturing firm.

Let us assume that we have now done this successfully and we are now wondering whether or not to expand our firm. What do you think are the advantages and disadvantages of expansion? If we decide to expand, how might we do this?

Suppose we decide to expand. We shall have to raise more money to build a larger factory, and one way of doing this would be to turn our private limited company into a public limited company – 'going public' – so that we could raise money on the Stock Exchange. We shall look at this in Section 9.

When we build our larger factory we shall have to consider very carefully where to put it. It is important not only to us but also to the people in the areas where we might build it, and we shall go into this in more detail in Section 10.

A big factory is organised very differently from a small one – for example, in the variety of jobs available. This will be the topic of Section 11.

In a small factory all the workers can easily have direct contact with the managing director – they probably see him every day and know him personally. In a large factory this is not the case, and labour relations have to be organised very carefully. All kinds of difficulties can arise. We shall be looking at some of these in Section 12.

# 9 'Going public'

### 9.1 The launching

If we wish to expand our firm, one way of doing this is to change from being a private limited company to being a public limited company so that we can raise more capital by selling shares to the public on the Stock Exchange.

Use either Document 9A or the book supplied by your teacher to obtain the following information.

1 Name a private limited company.

2 Name a public limited company.

3 Why doesn't a company wishing to go public draw up its own prospectus without the aid of a sponsor?

4 Why does the Council of the Stock Exchange check the financial records of a company before allowing it to go public?

5 Why is it made so difficult for companies to go public?

6 What are the four ways of issuing shares? What are the advantages and disadvantages of each method?

7 What is underwriting? Why do companies arrange for the underwriting of their share issues?

8 How do members of the public apply to buy shares in a new public company before it is quoted on the Stock Exchange?

9 Write an introduction to your prospectus, outlining the reasons why your company should go public. Explain particularly why you have chosen to borrow equity rather than fixed-interest capital.

10 Write a letter to the Council of the Stock Exchange explaining why your company should be granted a quotation. Outline the growth potential of your particular company.

11 Imagine you are a journalist. Write an article about the company, outlining the advantages and disadvantages of going public. Show how the directors, the current shareholders, and the workers in the company will be affected.

12 The bulk of the shares in public companies are often owned by so-called institutional shareholders – pension funds, insurance companies, trade unions, etc. Find out what you can about institutional investment.

13 As a shareholder, how can you influence the policy of the company?

## 9.2 The Stock Exchange

We have seen that one reason for the existence of the Stock Exchange is to enable large companies to raise large amounts of capital from a large number of shareholders, each of whom might contribute only a small proportion of the total capital.

One reason why people buy shares is because every year they can expect to be paid a dividend from the profits which they expect their company to make.

However, very few people would buy shares if they could not sell them again at a later date, and another reason for the existence of the Stock Exchange is to provide this facility.

Use either Document 9B or the book provided by your teacher to answer the following questions.

1. Why is there a branch of the Stock Exchange in most large cities? Which is the most important branch of the Stock Exchange? Why is it so?
2. Why do jobbers specialise in the shares that they handle? Why is it important for jobbers to be in competition with each other?
3. What is the role of stockbrokers on the floor of the Stock Exchange?
4. Explain how share prices are determined on the floor of the Stock Exchange. Why do share prices fluctuate?
5. What is 'the account'? What is the advantage of buying at the beginning of the account?
6. What is the difference between the nominal (or face) value of a share and its market value?

## 9.3 Dividends

When a person buys shares issued by a public company, he becomes one of the owners of that company. This entitles him every year to receive a part of the profits made by the company. The payment of part of the profits to shareholders is made by means of the dividend.

For a public company to calculate its dividend, three pieces of information are required:

1. The number of shares (called ordinary shares or equities) issued by the company.
2. The face value of these shares. This is a figure printed on the share certificate which is used for the calculation of dividends. It has nothing at all to do with the market price of the company's shares.
3. The amount of the profit that is to be given out to shareholders.

When this information is available, two simple calculations have to be made:

a) The amount of the profit has to be divided by the number of shares. This tells you how much profit is to be distributed per share.
b) The profit given out per share is expressed as a percentage of the face value of the shares.

For example, the company wishes to give 10p profit per share. The face value of the shares is 20p. The calculation is

$$\frac{10}{20} \times 100 = 50\%$$

The dividend would be 50%.

Great care has to be taken in this second calculation to make sure that the two figures used are both pounds or both pence. You must not have one figure in pounds and one in pence.

Example

A company has issued 1 million shares, each with a face value of 25p. It decides to distribute £200 000 profit to shareholders. What will be the dividend?

$$\text{Dividend per share} = \frac{200\,000}{1\,000\,000} = £0{\cdot}20$$

$$\therefore \quad \text{Percentage dividend} = \frac{£0{\cdot}20}{£0{\cdot}25} = 80\%$$

**1** Calculate the percentage dividends of companies A, B, and C:

| | *A* | *B* | *C* |
|---|---|---|---|
| Number of shares | 2 000 000 | 500 000 | 1 000 000 |
| Face value of share | 20p | 20p | 50p |
| Distributed profit | £100 000 | £50 000 | £20 000 |

**2** I own 500 ordinary shares of £1 each. The dividend is 20% How much shall I receive?

# Document 9A *'Going public'*

Imagine that a successful private limited company called ABC Co. Ltd wishes to go public. The rules it must obey are laid down by the Council of the Stock Exchange (see later). ABC Co. Ltd will have to follow this procedure:

a) Its directors must find a *sponsor*. This will usually either be a merchant bank or a firm of stockbrokers. Merchant banks are rather special banks which offer advice and will lend money to large companies.

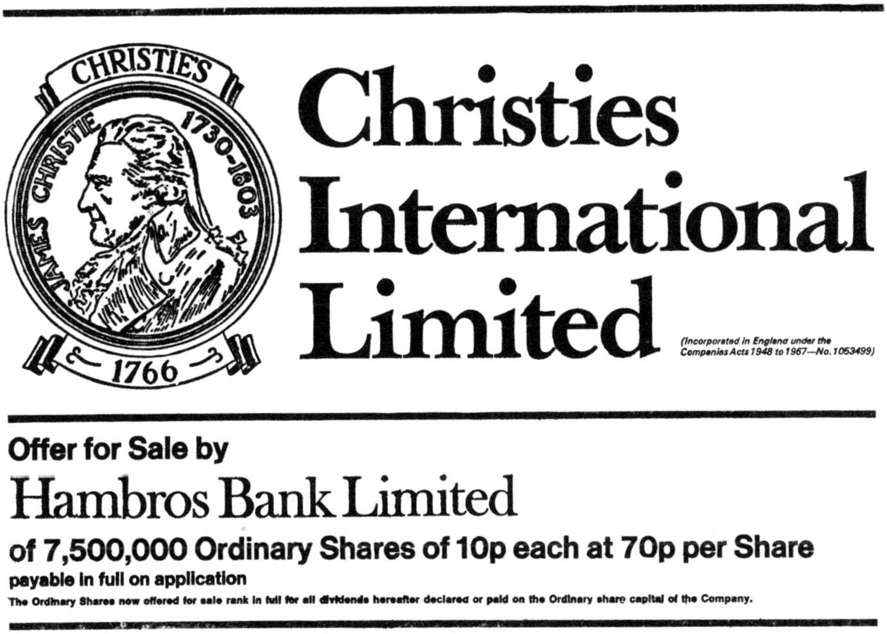


An advertisement for shares in *The Financial Times*

They do not have much to do with ordinary members of the public. Stockbrokers are experts in all matters concerned with shares in public companies.

The sponsor performs two tasks. He advises ABC Co. Ltd about the rules that have to be obeyed by companies going public, and he investigates ABC Co. Ltd to make sure that it is a reliable and well-run business and is worthy of the privilege of going public.

b) The results of the investigations of the sponsor have to be included in a prospectus. This is a small book that has to be published which tells people who are considering buying shares in ABC Co. Ltd all about the company: the company's history, its directors, its recent sales record, its recent profits, its future prospects – these and other items have to be included.

c) The *Council of the Stock Exchange* checks through the prospectus very carefully before it is published. There is very little about ABC Co. Ltd that the Council will not want to know if it is to allow it to go public. The most important job of the Council is to protect those people who may consider buying shares in ABC Co. Ltd. If ABC Co. Ltd is not a most excellent company then the Council of the Stock Exchange will not let it go public.

d) When the Council is sure that ABC Co. Ltd is a sound company, it sets a date for its shares to be available for sale and purchase on the Stock Exchange. ABC Co. Ltd is said to have been 'granted a quotation on the Stock Exchange'.

e) The Sponsor now places advertisements in newspapers encouraging people to buy shares in ABC Co. Ltd. The number of shares to be sold and the price that is to be asked will have been decided, and the task is now to persuade people to invest in the company. As many shares as possible will be sold before the shares are made available for sale on the Stock Exchange; people will buy their shares by filling in an application form and sending off the money. All the money received from the sale of the shares, minus the sponsor's fee and various other costs, will go to ABC Co. Ltd.

# Document 9B *The Stock Exchange*

Trading floor of the London Stock Exchange

The most important branch of the Stock Exchange is in London. There are other branches in Glasgow, Liverpool, Manchester, Birmingham, Bristol, Cardiff, Dublin, and Belfast. The Council of the Stock Exchange meets in London, and it is the work of the London Stock Exchange that we will describe.

Every branch of the Stock Exchange is an indoor market. Most people have been to an open-air street market. The stall-holders sell their goods to the people who go to shop. Customers 'shop around' and buy from the stall where the goods are cheapest. Sometimes stall-holders have to lower their prices to sell all their goods.

The sellers in a street market are the stall-holders. The sellers on the Stock Exchange are called *jobbers*. Stall-holders and jobbers do not do exactly the same kind of work. The stall-holder only sells his goods. The jobber buys as well as sells his goods, which are shares. Nevertheless, the jobber and the street-market trader earn their living in a very similar way.

Members of the public are not allowed into that part of the Stock Exchange where the buying and selling of shares takes place. They cannot do their own shopping like customers in a street market. *Stockbrokers* do the actual buying and selling of shares, and anyone who wants to buy shares on the Stock Exchange has to have a stockbroker.

The work of the Stock Exchange proceeds as follows. Jobbers are free to buy and sell shares at any price they like. Stockbrokers are free to deal with any jobber that they like. Competition between jobbers ensures that prices are fair. Jobbers who ask unreasonably high prices when they try to sell shares will find that they do no business. Jobbers who offer very low prices when stockbrokers try to sell to them will suffer a similar fate.

Stockbrokers 'shop around' to obtain the best possible prices for their clients. If they are selling shares, they obtain the highest price possible. If they are buying shares, they go to the jobber selling at the lowest price.

No money changes hands when stockbrokers and jobbers do business. Both make a note of the deal that they have made, and all exchanges of money take place later. Stockbrokers and jobbers trust one another completely – that is why the motto of the Stock Exchange is, 'My word is my bond.'

Jobbers and stockbrokers thus decide between them the prices of all shares bought and sold on the Stock Exchange. The companies whose shares are being bought and sold have no say at all in deciding their price. The price that any share will fetch on the Stock Exchange is called its *market price*.

How do jobbers and stockbrokers earn a living? Jobbers always try to sell shares for more money than they had to pay for them. The difference between the buying and selling prices is called the 'jobber's turn'. It is usually quite small, a matter of a few pence per share, and it is the income of the jobber. The stockbroker charges his customers a fee on small transactions, this might be as little as £2. Often it is a percentage of the value of this transaction, usually $1\frac{1}{4}\%$. Thus, if shares worth £1000 are bought for a client by a stockbroker, his fee would be £12·50.

# Where shall we build our new factory? 10

## 10.1 Factors affecting our choice

If a firm finds it necessary to expand because of increasing sales, the directors may decide to enlarge their existing factory. However, this is often impossible because no adjoining land is available, and they must decide on a new site for the larger factory.

In making their decision, the directors will try to choose a site where the costs are as low as possible, and the following factors must be taken into account.

### 1 The source of raw material or components, and the location of the market

When manufacturing a product, a firm must obtain suitable raw materials and components, but it must also transport the finished products to their final selling point or market. Often the market and the source of raw materials or components are in different places. In this case the businessman must choose whether to situate his factory near the source of the raw materials, near the market, or somewhere in-between. When making the decision he will try to choose a point where his overall transport costs are lowest. He has either to manufacture the product at the site of the raw materials and transport the final product to the market, or to move the raw materials to the market and manufacture the product there.

The costs of transport are mainly determined by the bulk or volume of the product. Where bulky raw materials are involved, the production process may reduce their volume and thus reduce transport costs. Products of this type are said to be 'bulk-reducing', and their manufacture usually takes place at the site of the raw material.

Other types of products, however, increase in bulk or volume during the manufacturing process and are therefore relatively expensive to transport in their final stage. These products are said to be 'bulk-increasing', and their manufacture tends to be situated near the market.

Which of the following products are bulk-increasing and which bulk-reducing in their manufacture?

a) Metal boxes
b) Furniture
c) Steel manufacture
d) Bread
e) Lemonade
f) Canning of peas

Are there any industries in your area which are bulk-increasing or bulk-reducing?

## 2 Transport

What are the possible methods of transport for our raw materials and finished products? What developments in recent years have made transport from one part of the country to another easier?

Will access to transport facilities be an important factor in determining the location of our factory? Consider two different cases: (a) where we have a few large customers widely distributed, (b) where we distribute direct to many small shops.

## 3 Labour with appropriate skills

In many cases, firms require workers with certain specific types of skills, and the availability of those workers varies from area to area. In order to obtain information about this, we consult statistics produced by various government departments which give us an occupational analysis of wholly (as distinct from temporarily) unemployed adults and unfilled job vacancies for adults. Document 10A is the analysis for June 1966 and Document 10B is the analysis for December 1968. In June 1966 there were in the country as a whole less unemployed than there were unfilled vacancies, whereas in December 1968 the opposite was the case. To arrive at any definite conclusions we should study the more recent statistics over a period of time, but we can draw some tentative conclusions from these two tables. Suppose we require mainly machine-tool operators and miscellaneous engineering workers.

Let us look first at the figures for machine-tool operators in December 1968. At this time, unemployed exceeded vacancies in the country as a whole. Were there any regions in which vacancies exceeded unemployed? Where was the highest ratio of unemployed to vacancies?

Now look at the figures for machine-tool operators for June 1966, when in the country as a whole vacancies exceeded unemployed. Was there any region in which unemployed still exceeded vacancies? Which region gave the most favourable conditions of labour supply for an employer? Considering both the 1968 and 1966 figures, where is the best pool of labour of machine operators? What conclusions do you draw from the figures for miscellaneous engineering workers?

Where is the best pool of labour for (a) a furniture manufacturer, (b) a firm manufacturing electronic equipment, (c) a precision-instrument manufacturer, (d) a shoe manufacturer? Is there a clear case for one region rather than another in all these cases?

## 4 Cost of land

The firm can either buy or rent the land it requires. Land varies in cost from place to place. Where would you expect to find the most expensive land? Why would it be so expensive?

The importance of the cost of land will vary from industry to industry. If a factory requires a lot of land the firm will need to find cheap land, but if the factory can be relatively small (compared to the price of the product) the firm may decide to use more expensive land in order to have access to other amenities.

In which of the following industries do you consider that the cost of land would be relatively important?

a) Motor-car manufacturing
b) Shoe manufacturing
c) Radio manufacturing
d) Bread baking
e) Steel manufacturing
f) Cloth weaving

### 5 Power

Make a list of all the possible sources of power for driving the machinery in a factory.

Prior to 1920, the most readily available source of power was coal. If we had chosen this as our source of power, in what regions should we have built our factory? Why?

Why do we have a wider choice of location for our factory today than we would have had in 1920?

A few industries use very large amounts of power and may need to be located near the source of power. Can you name one of these?

### 6 Other factors

In the past, the economic factors we have been discussing were not so important, and many centres of industry owe their origin to 'other factors' – the owner's mother-in-law lived there (or did not live there), or his wife liked the scenery, etc. As we shall see in Section 10.2, once an industry has become established in an area, other similar firms tend to go to the same area.

Since the 1939–45 war, government policy has been an important factor in determining the location of industry, and we shall also look at this in Section 10.2.

## 10.2 Government intervention in the location of industry

When a particular type of industry has become established in an area, other firms of the same nature tend to cluster in the same locality. What reasons can you give for this? (Refer back to Section 5.)

Plot the following towns on an outline map of Great Britain, and use the book *Britain: an official handbook* to discover the main industry of each.

1 London
2 Luton
3 Southampton
4 Bristol
5 Ipswich
6 Birmingham
7 Stoke-on-Trent
8 Leicester
9 Bolton
10 Bradford
11 Newcastle-upon-Tyne
12 Glasgow

Document 10C shows how the number of persons engaged in various industries changed between 1923 and 1938. Can you think of any explanation why certain industries declined and others expanded?

Where are the declining industries in Britain located?
What will be the problems caused by this?
What could a government do to try to alleviate these problems?

### 10.3 Making our choice

Read Document 10D, which examines some of the reasons why the Ford Motor Company factory is located at Dagenham.

Your teacher will now divide the class into groups. Each group elects a chairman and secretary and one director to be responsible for each of the factors which influence choice of location (see Section 10.1). Each group decides the best location for a fairly large factory manufacturing:

1 petroleum products,
2 motor cars,
3 furniture,
4 plastic kitchen equipment.

## Document 10A (from *Statistics on Income, Prices, Employment and Production*)

**Occupational Analysis of Wholly Unemployed Adults and Unfilled Vacancies for Adults, June 1966** **E.10**

**MEN**

| Occupation | Great Britain | | Region: London and South Eastern* | | Eastern and Southern* | | South Western | | Midlands* | | Yorkshire and Humberside* | | North Western | | Northern | | Scotland | | Wales | |
|---|---|---|---|---|---|---|---|---|---|---|---|---|---|---|---|---|---|---|---|---|
| | Wholly unemployed | Unfilled vacancies | Wholly unemployed | Unfilled vacancies | Wholly unemployed | Unfilled vacancies | Wholly unemployed | Unfilled vacancies | Wholly unemployed | Unfilled vacancies | Wholly unemployed | Unfilled vacancies | Wholly unemployed | Unfilled vacancies | Wholly unemployed | Unfilled vacancies | Wholly unemployed | Unfilled vacancies | Wholly unemployed | Unfilled vacancies |
| **Farm workers, fishermen, etc.** | **3,044** | **2,386** | **160** | **514** | **388** | **728** | **380** | **246** | **235** | **378** | **464** | **124** | **148** | **123** | **166** | **63** | **970** | **131** | **133** | **79** |
| Regular farm, market garden workers | 1,607 | 819 | 67 | 103 | 247 | 226 | 202 | 122 | 160 | 147 | 69 | 44 | 53 | 43 | 94 | 37 | 635 | 42 | 80 | 55 |
| Gardeners, nursery workers, etc. | 548 | 1,457 | 84 | 399 | 96 | 488 | 99 | 120 | 68 | 225 | 29 | 56 | 38 | 77 | 47 | 24 | 61 | 45 | 26 | 23 |
| Forestry workers | 76 | 76 | 8 | 12 | 5 | 13 | 7 | 4 | 5 | 6 | 1 | 4 | 1 | 2 | 7 | 2 | 30 | 32 | 12 | 1 |
| Fishermen | 813 | 34 | 1 | — | 40 | 1 | 72 | — | 2 | — | 365 | 20 | 56 | 1 | 18 | — | 244 | 12 | 15 | — |
| **Miners and quarrymen** | **242** | **4,621** | **1** | **1** | **2** | **8** | **5** | **30** | **16** | **1,217** | **21** | **1,287** | **10** | **367** | **26** | **53** | **99** | **15** | **62** | **1,643** |
| Colliery workers | 179 | 4,471 | — | — | — | — | — | — | 11 | 1,193 | 19 | 1,275 | 7 | 366 | 19 | 14 | 74 | 11 | 49 | 1,612 |
| Other miners and quarrymen | 63 | 150 | 1 | 1 | 2 | 8 | 5 | 30 | 5 | 24 | 2 | 12 | 3 | 1 | 7 | 39 | 25 | 4 | 13 | 31 |
| **Gas, coke and chemicals makers** | **126** | **545** | **15** | **57** | **6** | **55** | **2** | **51** | **3** | **101** | **6** | **28** | **49** | **101** | **16** | **11** | **22** | **135** | **7** | **6** |
| **Glass workers** | **47** | **219** | **17** | **61** | **3** | **48** | **1** | **5** | **3** | **49** | **4** | **20** | **5** | **24** | **1** | **7** | **10** | **3** | **3** | **2** |
| **Pottery workers** | **63** | **105** | **1** | **5** | **3** | **1** | **2** | **4** | **43** | **89** | **2** | — | **1** | **6** | **5** | — | **5** | — | **1** | — |
| **Furnace, forge, foundry, rolling mill workers** | **518** | **1,751** | **40** | **139** | **41** | **209** | **10** | **57** | **96** | **743** | **75** | **207** | **41** | **149** | **59** | **57** | **134** | **175** | **22** | **15** |
| Moulders and coremakers | 251 | 1,098 | 21 | 100 | 26 | 162 | 2 | 39 | 52 | 439 | 18 | 81 | 26 | 104 | 28 | 27 | 76 | 136 | 2 | 10 |
| Smiths, forgemen | 109 | 337 | 5 | 15 | 11 | 20 | 5 | 13 | 10 | 166 | 10 | 56 | 5 | 15 | 19 | 17 | 28 | 30 | 16 | 5 |
| Other workers | 158 | 316 | 14 | 24 | 4 | 27 | 3 | 5 | 34 | 138 | 47 | 70 | 10 | 30 | 12 | 13 | 30 | 9 | 4 | — |
| **Electrical and electronic workers** | **2,006** | **5,014** | **440** | **1,089** | **219** | **1,151** | **147** | **322** | **162** | **885** | **147** | **401** | **270** | **413** | **174** | **250** | **319** | **271** | **128** | **232** |
| Electronic equipment manufacture and maintenance workers | 575 | 1,689 | 162 | 557 | 80 | 551 | 60 | 133 | 35 | 138 | 34 | 36 | 71 | 109 | 48 | 63 | 54 | 55 | 31 | 47 |
| Electricians | 1,069 | 1,531 | 223 | 262 | 102 | 396 | 55 | 64 | 75 | 269 | 78 | 110 | 139 | 126 | 89 | 78 | 231 | 132 | 77 | 94 |
| Electrical fitters, etc. | 362 | 1,794 | 55 | 270 | 37 | 204 | 32 | 125 | 52 | 478 | 35 | 255 | 60 | 178 | 37 | 109 | 34 | 84 | 20 | 91 |
| **Engineering and allied trades workers** | **9,076** | **36,653** | **1,501** | **8,271** | **937** | **7,065** | **560** | **1,768** | **1,202** | **6,971** | **504** | **2,755** | **1,248** | **4,867** | **971** | **1,660** | **1,575** | **2,144** | **570** | **1,152** |
| Constructional fitters and erectors | 613 | 165 | 52 | 15 | 32 | 62 | 43 | 7 | 61 | 49 | 66 | 19 | 82 | 11 | 80 | — | 107 | 2 | 90 | — |
| Platers | 171 | 1,057 | 16 | 171 | 19 | 125 | 8 | 23 | 6 | 249 | 7 | 145 | 21 | 125 | 38 | 78 | 37 | 110 | 19 | 31 |
| Riveters and caulkers | 126 | 110 | 10 | 3 | 14 | 9 | 9 | — | — | 13 | — | 6 | 5 | 52 | 26 | 5 | 47 | 20 | 15 | 2 |
| Shipwrights | 166 | 252 | 7 | 28 | 20 | 73 | 17 | 9 | 1 | 1 | 2 | 20 | 40 | 30 | 23 | 4 | 43 | 87 | 13 | — |
| Miscellaneous boilershop and shipbuilding workers | 263 | 149 | 24 | 7 | 36 | 18 | 6 | 7 | 8 | 38 | 5 | 7 | 60 | 28 | 42 | 15 | 73 | 11 | 9 | 18 |
| Sheet metal workers | 279 | 2,154 | 54 | 592 | 28 | 502 | 13 | 115 | 25 | 255 | 9 | 138 | 34 | 283 | 32 | 62 | 72 | 139 | 12 | 68 |
| Welders | 750 | 1,869 | 124 | 281 | 70 | 357 | 40 | 119 | 116 | 331 | 42 | 142 | 98 | 235 | 84 | 155 | 116 | 145 | 60 | 104 |
| Toolmakers | 53 | 509 | 13 | 157 | 8 | 135 | 9 | 28 | 4 | 93 | 3 | 5 | 6 | 39 | 1 | 13 | 4 | 24 | 5 | 15 |
| Press tool makers | 38 | 454 | 7 | 136 | 7 | 98 | 2 | 8 | 8 | 95 | — | 4 | 8 | 37 | 3 | 7 | 1 | 11 | 2 | 58 |
| Mould makers | 10 | 157 | 2 | 41 | 2 | 60 | — | 1 | 1 | 40 | — | 4 | — | 2 | 2 | 8 | 2 | — | 1 | 1 |
| Precision fitters | 911 | 3,860 | 135 | 893 | 122 | 845 | 92 | 227 | 96 | 749 | 35 | 290 | 104 | 485 | 167 | 96 | 114 | 171 | 46 | 104 |
| Maintenance fitters, erectors | 621 | 2,524 | 91 | 387 | 48 | 251 | 33 | 56 | 53 | 664 | 30 | 368 | 101 | 323 | 102 | 222 | 102 | 87 | 61 | 166 |
| Fitters (not precision), mechanics | 927 | 4,416 | 181 | 1,215 | 93 | 886 | 65 | 255 | 89 | 681 | 47 | 291 | 157 | 478 | 86 | 146 | 157 | 340 | 52 | 124 |
| Turners | 188 | 2,403 | 38 | 452 | 22 | 453 | 10 | 105 | 27 | 431 | 9 | 192 | 19 | 332 | 19 | 170 | 37 | 233 | 7 | 35 |

*Note.*– Wholly unemployed figures relate to 13th June and unfilled vacancy figures to 8th June.
* See page 161 of the April 1965 issue of the *Ministry of Labour Gazette* for details of changes in regional organisation.

Source: Ministry of Labour

## Occupational Analysis of Wholly Unemployed Adults and Unfilled Vacancies for Adults, June 1966—*continued*

### MEN

| Occupation | Great Britain | | Region: London and South Eastern* | | Eastern and Southern* | | South Western | | Midlands* | | Yorkshire and Humberside* | | North Western | | Northern | | Scotland | | Wales | |
|---|---|---|---|---|---|---|---|---|---|---|---|---|---|---|---|---|---|---|---|---|
| | Wholly unem-ployed | Unfilled vacancies | Wholly unem-ployed | Unfilled vacancies | Wholly unem-ployed | Unfilled vacancies | Wholly unem-ployed | Unfilled vacancies | Wholly unem-ployed | Unfilled vacancies | Wholly unem-ployed | Unfilled vacancies | Wholly unem-ployed | Unfilled vacancies | Wholly unem-ployed | Unfilled vacancies | Wholly unem-ployed | Unfilled vacancies | Wholly unem-ployed | Unfilled vacancies |
| **Engineering and allied trades workers**—*continued* | | | | | | | | | | | | | | | | | | | | |
| Machine-tool setters, setter operators | 513 | 6,581 | 83 | 1,122 | 45 | 1,322 | 26 | 342 | 96 | 1,557 | 38 | 454 | 60 | 1,163 | 57 | 242 | 84 | 268 | 24 | 111 |
| Machine-tool operators | 880 | 3,112 | 165 | 876 | 69 | 605 | 43 | 191 | 247 | 568 | 53 | 230 | 93 | 288 | 26 | 28 | 147 | 174 | 37 | 152 |
| Electro platers | 29 | 137 | 10 | 44 | 6 | 39 | 1 | 2 | 6 | 33 | 2 | 3 | 3 | 13 | — | — | — | — | 1 | 3 |
| Plumbers, pipe fitters | 671 | 1,686 | 152 | 302 | 69 | 315 | 51 | 72 | 62 | 183 | 44 | 112 | 94 | 210 | 28 | 263 | 135 | 149 | 36 | 80 |
| Miscellaneous engineering workers | 1,251 | 2,576 | 205 | 903 | 124 | 485 | 58 | 98 | 226 | 518 | 66 | 84 | 178 | 363 | 119 | 31 | 209 | 67 | 66 | 27 |
| Watch makers and repairers | 66 | 68 | 21 | 25 | 2 | 12 | 6 | 5 | 5 | 13 | 5 | 2 | 7 | 6 | 12 | 2 | 7 | 2 | 1 | 1 |
| Instrument makers and repairers | 154 | 677 | 39 | 218 | 25 | 195 | 11 | 44 | 14 | 79 | 9 | 13 | 17 | 48 | 10 | 45 | 18 | 24 | 11 | 11 |
| Goldsmiths, jewellers, etc. | 24 | 61 | 10 | 23 | 2 | 6 | 2 | 3 | 4 | 22 | 1 | — | 1 | 2 | — | 5 | 3 | — | 1 | — |
| Vehicle and cycle chassis and body building | 129 | 794 | 32 | 119 | 13 | 115 | 6 | 43 | 14 | 165 | 15 | 118 | 25 | 134 | 5 | 44 | 17 | 30 | 2 | 26 |
| Aircraft body building | 90 | 233 | 8 | 88 | 49 | 57 | 7 | 3 | 5 | 6 | 2 | 4 | 9 | 25 | 2 | 3 | 5 | 40 | 3 | 7 |
| Miscellaneous metal goods workers | 153 | 649 | 22 | 173 | 12 | 40 | 2 | 5 | 28 | 138 | 14 | 104 | 26 | 155 | 7 | 16 | 38 | 10 | 4 | 8 |
| **Woodworkers** | **1,680** | **5,082** | **597** | **1,210** | **144** | **1,110** | **84** | **421** | **129** | **784** | **79** | **304** | **203** | **379** | **156** | **251** | **213** | **387** | **75** | **236** |
| Carpenters, joiners | 1,244 | 3,637 | 438 | 688 | 99 | 810 | 70 | 311 | 103 | 553 | 60 | 231 | 131 | 282 | 121 | 222 | 159 | 331 | 63 | 209 |
| Cabinet makers | 139 | 381 | 66 | 157 | 15 | 69 | 6 | 26 | 6 | 49 | 2 | 10 | 28 | 30 | 6 | 12 | 6 | 22 | 4 | 6 |
| Sawyers, wood cutting machinists | 145 | 544 | 51 | 200 | 14 | 124 | 1 | 49 | 15 | 52 | 5 | 29 | 22 | 48 | 17 | 10 | 16 | 14 | 4 | 18 |
| Pattern makers | 39 | 189 | 2 | 29 | 8 | 44 | 2 | 10 | 1 | 70 | 2 | 11 | 6 | 3 | 6 | 2 | 9 | 10 | 3 | — |
| Other woodworkers | 113 | 331 | 40 | 126 | 8 | 63 | 5 | 25 | 4 | 60 | 10 | 23 | 16 | 16 | 6 | 5 | 23 | 10 | 1 | 3 |
| **Leather workers** | **316** | **279** | **87** | **91** | **32** | **46** | **7** | **12** | **50** | **78** | **16** | **9** | **27** | **20** | **21** | **6** | **60** | **9** | **16** | **8** |
| Tanners, fellmongers, etc. | 56 | 103 | 25 | 45 | 4 | 22 | — | 3 | 3 | 23 | 2 | 2 | 9 | 6 | 4 | — | 6 | 1 | 3 | 1 |
| Boot and shoe makers, repairers | 260 | 176 | 62 | 46 | 28 | 24 | 7 | 9 | 47 | 55 | 14 | 7 | 18 | 14 | 17 | 6 | 54 | 8 | 13 | 7 |
| **Textile workers** | **435** | **1,245** | **24** | **26** | **11** | **47** | **3** | **31** | **92** | **120** | **101** | **403** | **105** | **539** | **4** | **9** | **87** | **63** | **8** | **7** |
| Textile spinners | 61 | 285 | — | — | — | 4 | — | 1 | 2 | 3 | 11 | 69 | 31 | 194 | — | 3 | 14 | 11 | 3 | — |
| Textile weavers | 54 | 227 | — | — | — | 15 | — | 10 | 4 | 6 | 17 | 95 | 15 | 82 | — | — | 17 | 15 | 1 | 4 |
| Other textile workers | 320 | 733 | 24 | 26 | 11 | 28 | 3 | 20 | 86 | 111 | 73 | 239 | 59 | 263 | 4 | 6 | 56 | 37 | 4 | 3 |
| **Clothing, etc. workers** | **614** | **1,297** | **332** | **735** | **48** | **163** | **17** | **48** | **21** | **92** | **22** | **52** | **67** | **123** | **43** | **21** | **51** | **47** | **13** | **16** |
| Retail bespoke tailoring workers | 78 | 138 | 29 | 76 | 9 | 21 | 3 | 9 | 2 | 13 | 7 | 7 | 11 | 4 | 4 | 3 | 12 | 4 | 1 | 1 |
| Wholesale heavy clothing workers | 190 | 536 | 143 | 368 | 6 | 42 | 1 | 11 | 4 | 18 | 6 | 9 | 15 | 61 | 1 | 5 | 11 | 19 | 3 | 3 |
| Other clothing workers | 112 | 346 | 58 | 181 | 12 | 49 | 5 | 8 | 8 | 29 | — | 27 | 9 | 30 | 7 | 7 | 11 | 11 | 2 | 4 |
| Upholstery workers, etc. | 234 | 277 | 102 | 110 | 21 | 51 | 8 | 20 | 7 | 32 | 9 | 9 | 32 | 28 | 31 | 6 | 17 | 13 | 7 | 8 |
| **Food, drink and tobacco workers** | **477** | **900** | **84** | **143** | **31** | **131** | **25** | **109** | **46** | **117** | **22** | **99** | **83** | **196** | **28** | **32** | **145** | **43** | **13** | **30** |
| Workers in food manufacture | 433 | 855 | 76 | 127 | 28 | 117 | 24 | 106 | 35 | 114 | 21 | 99 | 78 | 194 | 24 | 30 | 135 | 43 | 12 | 25 |
| Workers in drink manufacture | 32 | 20 | 7 | 9 | 1 | 3 | 1 | 2 | 10 | 2 | 1 | — | 1 | 2 | 1 | 2 | 10 | — | — | — |
| Workers in tobacco manufacture | 12 | 25 | 1 | 7 | 2 | 11 | — | 1 | 1 | 1 | — | — | 4 | — | 3 | — | — | — | 1 | 5 |

*Note.*—Wholly unemployed figures relate to 13th June and unfilled vacancy figures to 8th June.
* See footnote on page 88.

Source: Ministry of Labour

E.10

## Occupational Analysis of Wholly Unemployed Adults and Unfilled Vacancies for Adults, June 1966—*continued*

### MEN

| Occupation | Great Britain | | Region: London and South Eastern* | | Eastern and Southern* | | South Western | | Midlands* | | Yorkshire and Humberside* | | North Western | | Northern | | Scotland | | Wales | |
|---|---|---|---|---|---|---|---|---|---|---|---|---|---|---|---|---|---|---|---|---|
| | Wholly unem-ployed | Unfilled vacancies | Wholly unem-ployed | Unfilled vacancies | Wholly unem-ployed | Unfilled vacancies | Wholly unem-ployed | Unfilled vacancies | Wholly unem-ployed | Unfilled vacancies | Wholly unem-ployed | Unfilled vacancies | Wholly unem-ployed | Unfilled vacancies | Wholly unem-ployed | Unfilled vacancies | Wholly unem-ployed | Unfilled vacancies | Wholly unem-ployed | Unfilled vacancies |
| **Paper and printing workers** | **330** | **696** | **135** | **227** | **31** | **205** | **17** | **49** | **23** | **63** | **12** | **24** | **40** | **77** | **7** | **16** | **53** | **28** | **12** | **7** |
| Paper and paper products workers | 73 | 252 | 18 | 84 | 3 | 49 | 2 | 18 | 1 | 24 | 2 | 16 | 12 | 38 | 1 | 5 | 32 | 14 | 2 | 4 |
| Printing workers | 257 | 444 | 117 | 143 | 28 | 156 | 15 | 31 | 22 | 39 | 10 | 8 | 28 | 39 | 6 | 11 | 21 | 14 | 10 | 3 |
| **Building materials workers** | **87** | **620** | **14** | **42** | **10** | **270** | **7** | **10** | **5** | **103** | **6** | **32** | **12** | **66** | **9** | **17** | **18** | **49** | **6** | **31** |
| Brick and tile production workers | 56 | 475 | 10 | 28 | 8 | 226 | 2 | 4 | 3 | 78 | 5 | 22 | 5 | 43 | 5 | 12 | 16 | 38 | 2 | 24 |
| Other building materials workers | 31 | 145 | 4 | 14 | 2 | 44 | 5 | 6 | 2 | 25 | 1 | 10 | 7 | 23 | 4 | 5 | 2 | 11 | 4 | 7 |
| **Makers of products not elsewhere specified** | **238** | **1,012** | **88** | **302** | **22** | **198** | **13** | **70** | **21** | **229** | **7** | **42** | **37** | **139** | **8** | **6** | **35** | **4** | **7** | **22** |
| Rubber workers | 35 | 227 | 6 | 15 | 2 | 9 | 1 | 7 | 6 | 112 | — | 19 | 8 | 61 | — | — | 10 | 1 | 2 | 3 |
| Plastics workers | 92 | 564 | 49 | 214 | 9 | 139 | 3 | 52 | 10 | 90 | 3 | 16 | 5 | 41 | 4 | 5 | 7 | — | 2 | 7 |
| Other workers | 111 | 221 | 33 | 73 | 11 | 50 | 9 | 11 | 5 | 27 | 4 | 7 | 24 | 37 | 4 | 1 | 18 | 3 | 3 | 12 |
| **Construction workers** | **2,449** | **4,439** | **550** | **726** | **198** | **890** | **172** | **297** | **246** | **845** | **135** | **407** | **370** | **386** | **187** | **361** | **402** | **301** | **189** | **226** |
| Bricklayers | 546 | 2,594 | 102 | 395 | 66 | 507 | 47 | 166 | 73 | 550 | 40 | 254 | 66 | 197 | 53 | 206 | 70 | 174 | 29 | 145 |
| Masons | 89 | 125 | 7 | 2 | 3 | 21 | 23 | 43 | 8 | 16 | 3 | 2 | 6 | 7 | 1 | 3 | 30 | 23 | 8 | 8 |
| Slaters | 129 | 136 | 21 | 32 | 7 | 10 | 3 | 3 | 19 | 8 | 7 | 15 | 22 | 10 | 7 | 22 | 34 | 34 | 9 | 2 |
| Plasterers | 279 | 321 | 67 | 49 | 22 | 80 | 28 | 31 | 31 | 38 | 21 | 29 | 37 | 36 | 18 | 19 | 35 | 21 | 20 | 18 |
| Others | 1,406 | 1,263 | 353 | 248 | 100 | 272 | 71 | 54 | 115 | 233 | 64 | 107 | 239 | 136 | 108 | 111 | 233 | 49 | 123 | 53 |
| **Painters and decorators** | **2,076** | **3,647** | **671** | **1,217** | **223** | **776** | **127** | **177** | **196** | **451** | **104** | **240** | **287** | **331** | **145** | **172** | **223** | **149** | **100** | **134** |
| Painters | 1,739 | 3,041 | 556 | 934 | 188 | 675 | 120 | 157 | 154 | 353 | 95 | 217 | 232 | 280 | 119 | 159 | 192 | 140 | 83 | 126 |
| Decorators (excluding pottery and glass decorators) | 337 | 606 | 115 | 283 | 35 | 101 | 7 | 20 | 42 | 98 | 9 | 23 | 55 | 51 | 26 | 13 | 31 | 9 | 17 | 8 |
| **Drivers, etc. of stationary engines, cranes, etc.** | **1,132** | **1,139** | **167** | **192** | **74** | **267** | **34** | **53** | **118** | **221** | **66** | **97** | **144** | **146** | **132** | **57** | **298** | **56** | **99** | **50** |
| **Transport and communication workers** | **10,696** | **18,969** | **1,544** | **8,055** | **954** | **2,388** | **719** | **502** | **1,002** | **4,249** | **795** | **774** | **1,554** | **1,284** | **935** | **713** | **2,235** | **693** | **958** | **311** |
| Railway workers | 261 | 1,193 | 19 | 220 | 16 | 151 | 14 | 26 | 22 | 307 | 32 | 120 | 17 | 157 | 39 | 59 | 78 | 118 | 24 | 35 |
| Motor drivers (except P.S.V.) | 8,596 | 5,693 | 1,151 | 2,134 | 767 | 1,072 | 608 | 318 | 916 | 769 | 657 | 321 | 1,273 | 462 | 766 | 231 | 1,612 | 264 | 846 | 122 |
| P.S.V. drivers, conductors | 176 | 9,692 | 28 | 5,027 | 39 | 746 | 9 | 107 | 16 | 2,292 | 8 | 258 | 22 | 505 | 8 | 393 | 29 | 253 | 17 | 111 |
| Seamen | 1,102 | 67 | 162 | 3 | 76 | 54 | 38 | 3 | 16 | — | 68 | — | 184 | 2 | 78 | — | 445 | 2 | 35 | 3 |
| Harbours and docks workers | 82 | 91 | 17 | 9 | 6 | 16 | 9 | 3 | 1 | 1 | 7 | 9 | 8 | 49 | 16 | 3 | 10 | — | 8 | 1 |
| Other transport workers | 204 | 1,442 | 71 | 418 | 23 | 130 | 15 | 22 | 12 | 762 | 7 | 31 | 27 | 32 | 16 | 16 | 25 | 14 | 8 | 17 |
| Communications workers | 275 | 791 | 96 | 244 | 27 | 219 | 26 | 23 | 19 | 118 | 16 | 35 | 23 | 77 | 12 | 11 | 36 | 42 | 20 | 22 |
| **Warehousemen, packers, etc.** | **2,491** | **2,477** | **589** | **1,107** | **219** | **412** | **217** | **129** | **272** | **309** | **126** | **149** | **313** | **170** | **166** | **58** | **447** | **97** | **142** | **46** |
| Warehouse workers | 2,106 | 1,780 | 400 | 687 | 202 | 360 | 206 | 108 | 230 | 233 | 117 | 116 | 253 | 113 | 155 | 45 | 406 | 76 | 137 | 42 |
| Packers, bottlers | 385 | 697 | 189 | 420 | 17 | 52 | 11 | 21 | 42 | 76 | 9 | 33 | 60 | 57 | 11 | 13 | 41 | 21 | 5 | 4 |

Note Wholly unemployed figures relate to 13th June and unfilled vacancy figures to 8th June.
* See footnote on page 88.

Source: Ministry of Labour

Occupational Analysis of Wholly Unemployed Adults and Unfilled Vacancies for Adults, June 1966—*continued* **E.10**

MEN

| Occupation | Great Britain | | Region: London and South Eastern* | | Eastern and Southern* | | South Western | | Midlands* | | Yorkshire and Humberside* | | North Western | | Northern | | Scotland | | Wales | |
|---|---|---|---|---|---|---|---|---|---|---|---|---|---|---|---|---|---|---|---|---|
| | Wholly unemployed | Unfilled vacancies | Wholly unemployed | Unfilled vacancies | Wholly unemployed | Unfilled vacancies | Wholly unemployed | Unfilled vacancies | Wholly unemployed | Unfilled vacancies | Wholly unemployed | Unfilled vacancies | Wholly unemployed | Unfilled vacancies | Wholly unemployed | Unfilled vacancies | Wholly unemployed | Unfilled vacancies | Wholly unemployed | Unfilled vacancies |
| **Clerical workers** | **23,584** | **7,394** | **5,831** | **3,054** | **3,594** | **1,228** | **2,991** | **326** | **1,745** | **1,070** | **1,461** | **416** | **2,959** | **624** | **1,403** | **262** | **2,187** | **250** | **1,413** | **164** |
| Clerks | 21,584 | 5,814 | 5,210 | 2,432 | 3,339 | 951 | 2,849 | 221 | 1,579 | 869 | 1,297 | 319 | 2,685 | 453 | 1,278 | 217 | 2,004 | 217 | 1,343 | 135 |
| Book-keepers, cashiers | 1,820 | 1,366 | 573 | 523 | 218 | 241 | 129 | 61 | 137 | 188 | 162 | 96 | 254 | 159 | 107 | 41 | 174 | 32 | 66 | 25 |
| Other clerical workers | 180 | 214 | 48 | 99 | 37 | 36 | 13 | 44 | 29 | 13 | 2 | 1 | 20 | 12 | 18 | 4 | 9 | 1 | 4 | 4 |
| **Shop assistants** | **3,176** | **4,501** | **641** | **1,577** | **404** | **941** | **294** | **274** | **265** | **552** | **194** | **236** | **439** | **413** | **207** | **141** | **512** | **228** | **220** | **139** |
| **Service, sport and recreation workers** | **7,489** | **11,427** | **2,732** | **3,875** | **660** | **2,300** | **377** | **778** | **403** | **1,141** | **317** | **907** | **1,157** | **924** | **473** | **445** | **1,084** | **658** | **286** | **399** |
| Police, etc. | 404 | 2,216 | 98 | 433 | 63 | 630 | 24 | 144 | 31 | 316 | 19 | 254 | 63 | 198 | 24 | 92 | 44 | 32 | 38 | 117 |
| Hotels and catering: | | | | | | | | | | | | | | | | | | | | |
| Kitchen staff | 784 | 1,900 | 274 | 632 | 91 | 372 | 53 | 174 | 50 | 139 | 36 | 167 | 130 | 98 | 41 | 60 | 76 | 193 | 33 | 65 |
| Bar staff | 639 | 643 | 168 | 233 | 56 | 117 | 48 | 56 | 46 | 40 | 21 | 32 | 66 | 37 | 27 | 38 | 185 | 68 | 22 | 22 |
| Waiters, etc. | 443 | 1,041 | 196 | 254 | 48 | 221 | 39 | 156 | 12 | 73 | 6 | 29 | 66 | 64 | 19 | 51 | 39 | 142 | 18 | 51 |
| Others | 512 | 1,187 | 154 | 520 | 49 | 191 | 44 | 44 | 34 | 115 | 37 | 120 | 58 | 70 | 34 | 45 | 68 | 53 | 34 | 29 |
| Hairdressers | 245 | 280 | 65 | 79 | 29 | 62 | 14 | 26 | 20 | 24 | 9 | 16 | 29 | 27 | 17 | 13 | 45 | 19 | 17 | 14 |
| Laundry and dry cleaning workers | 54 | 224 | 27 | 86 | 5 | 49 | 6 | 14 | 1 | 15 | 1 | 15 | 11 | 31 | 1 | 2 | — | 6 | 2 | 6 |
| Domestics | 103 | 228 | 16 | 89 | 15 | 53 | 19 | 24 | 10 | 29 | 9 | 7 | 11 | 10 | 3 | 7 | 14 | 6 | 6 | 3 |
| Attendants | 1,456 | 1,342 | 181 | 412 | 87 | 229 | 31 | 51 | 108 | 151 | 82 | 135 | 274 | 161 | 217 | 80 | 412 | 73 | 64 | 50 |
| Porters, messengers | 1,050 | 1,326 | 404 | 724 | 37 | 182 | 37 | 46 | 24 | 90 | 59 | 63 | 324 | 167 | 52 | 22 | 98 | 28 | 15 | 4 |
| Entertainment workers | 1,394 | 67 | 1,024 | 25 | 94 | 8 | 34 | 2 | 37 | 4 | 15 | 1 | 87 | 8 | 18 | 12 | 59 | 5 | 26 | 2 |
| Others | 405 | 973 | 125 | 388 | 86 | 186 | 28 | 41 | 30 | 145 | 23 | 68 | 38 | 53 | 20 | 23 | 44 | 33 | 11 | 36 |
| **Administrative, professional, technical workers** | **13,577** | **17,887** | **3,935** | **4,689** | **1,838** | **3,419** | **1,225** | **786** | **1,169** | **3,548** | **786** | **1,122** | **1,690** | **1,906** | **900** | **927** | **1,445** | **1,098** | **589** | **392** |
| Laboratory assistants | 258 | 805 | 61 | 200 | 36 | 265 | 17 | 14 | 17 | 90 | 15 | 20 | 57 | 95 | 24 | 96 | 16 | 6 | 15 | 19 |
| Draughtsmen | 514 | 1,940 | 142 | 445 | 89 | 447 | 68 | 85 | 34 | 519 | 47 | 65 | 57 | 198 | 23 | 40 | 32 | 98 | 22 | 43 |
| Nurses | 109 | 3,548 | 25 | 852 | 9 | 483 | 9 | 176 | 9 | 819 | 3 | 247 | 18 | 503 | 7 | 136 | 16 | 277 | 13 | 55 |
| Other administrative, professional and technical workers | 12,696 | 11,594 | 3,707 | 3,192 | 1,704 | 2,224 | 1,131 | 511 | 1,109 | 2,120 | 721 | 790 | 1,558 | 1,110 | 846 | 655 | 1,381 | 717 | 539 | 275 |
| **Labourers** | **104,725** | **26,587** | **11,808** | **6,695** | **6,617** | **5,814** | **5,610** | **1,365** | **10,747** | **4,611** | **7,916** | **2,506** | **15,801** | **2,825** | **13,826** | **1,003** | **21,898** | **843** | **10,502** | **925** |
| General labourers (heavy) | 40,209 | 5,612 | 3,065 | 1,130 | 1,646 | 1,489 | 1,428 | 326 | 3,683 | 836 | 3,007 | 369 | 7,320 | 744 | 5,915 | 298 | 10,756 | 271 | 3,389 | 149 |
| General labourers (light) | 41,755 | 758 | 4,360 | 213 | 2,938 | 236 | 2,932 | 36 | 4,519 | 164 | 3,869 | 41 | 5,438 | 33 | 5,665 | 11 | 7,821 | 21 | 4,213 | 3 |
| Factory hands | 9,148 | 4,369 | 2,214 | 1,768 | 798 | 1,478 | 387 | 149 | 860 | 421 | 183 | 26 | 993 | 236 | 745 | 50 | 1,066 | 54 | 1,902 | 187 |
| Other labourers | 13,613 | 15,848 | 2,169 | 3,584 | 1,235 | 2,611 | 863 | 854 | 1,685 | 3,190 | 857 | 2,070 | 2,050 | 1,812 | 1,501 | 644 | 2,255 | 497 | 998 | 586 |
| **GRAND TOTAL** | **190,694** | **160,892** | **32,004** | **44,100** | **16,709** | **29,870** | **13,046** | **7,920** | **18,310** | **29,016** | **13,388** | **12,641** | **27,060** | **16,598** | **20,068** | **6,598** | **34,527** | **7,877** | **15,582** | **6,272** |

*Note.*—Wholly unemployed figures relate to 13th June and unfilled vacancy figures to 8th June.
* See footnote on page 88.

Source: Ministry of Labour

# Document 10B (from *Statistics on Income, Prices, Employment and Production*)

Occupational Analysis of Wholly Unemployed Adults and Unfilled Vacancies for Adults, December 1968 **E.10**

MEN

| Occupation | Great Britain | | Region: London and South Eastern | | Eastern and Southern | | South Western | | Midlands | | Yorkshire and Humberside | | North Western | | Northern | | Wales | | Scotland | |
|---|---|---|---|---|---|---|---|---|---|---|---|---|---|---|---|---|---|---|---|---|
| | Wholly unemployed | Unfilled vacancies | Wholly unemployed | Unfilled vacancies | Wholly unemployed | Unfilled vacancies | Wholly unemployed | Unfilled vacancies | Wholly unemployed | Unfilled vacancies | Wholly unemployed | Unfilled vacancies | Wholly unemployed | Unfilled vacancies | Wholly unemployed | Unfilled vacancies | Wholly unemployed | Unfilled vacancies | Wholly unemployed | Unfilled vacancies |
| **Farm workers, fishermen, etc.** | **6,403** | **1,193** | **392** | **233** | **909** | **428** | **920** | **122** | **605** | **167** | **1,183** | **61** | **261** | **64** | **370** | **26** | **304** | **42** | **1,459** | **50** |
| Regular farm, market garden workers | 2,807 | 527 | 154 | 56 | 497 | 189 | 359 | 60 | 377 | 94 | 198 | 39 | 73 | 23 | 175 | 18 | 189 | 28 | 785 | 20 |
| Gardeners, nursery workers, etc. | 1,429 | 629 | 217 | 155 | 297 | 238 | 181 | 55 | 214 | 71 | 106 | 21 | 114 | 41 | 77 | 8 | 68 | 14 | 155 | 26 |
| Forestry workers | 91 | 36 | 7 | 22 | 6 | 1 | 8 | 6 | 8 | 2 | 6 | 1 | 3 | — | 7 | — | 6 | | 40 | 4 |
| Fishermen | 2,076 | 1 | 14 | — | 109 | — | 372 | 1 | 6 | — | 873 | — | 71 | — | 111 | — | 41 | — | 479 | — |
| **Miners and quarrymen** | **834** | **2,076** | **11** | **6** | **8** | **2** | **15** | **3** | **140** | **763** | **180** | **620** | **65** | **66** | **83** | **7** | **67** | **399** | **265** | **210** |
| Colliery workers | 673 | 1,959 | 3 | 2 | 2 | 1 | 2 | — | 107 | 754 | 168 | 618 | 50 | 62 | 51 | 6 | 53 | 356 | 237 | 160 |
| Other miners and quarrymen | 161 | 117 | 8 | 4 | 6 | 1 | 13 | 3 | 33 | 9 | 12 | 2 | 15 | 4 | 32 | 1 | 14 | 43 | 28 | 50 |
| **Gas, coke and chemicals makers** | **364** | **360** | **67** | **40** | **33** | **46** | **4** | **1** | **66** | **42** | **34** | **46** | **92** | **91** | **15** | **8** | **15** | **16** | **38** | **70** |
| **Glass workers** | **6,832** | **191** | **49** | **20** | **7** | **47** | **—** | **1** | **13** | **25** | **18** | **10** | **6,717** | **61** | **9** | **3** | **4** | **16** | **15** | **8** |
| **Pottery workers** | **117** | **80** | **5** | **1** | **1** | **11** | **6** | **2** | **95** | **59** | **1** | **5** | **4** | **1** | **—** | **—** | **—** | **—** | **5** | **1** |
| **Furnace, forge, foundry, rolling mill workers** | **1,707** | **1,518** | **110** | **106** | **49** | **209** | **17** | **30** | **558** | **651** | **368** | **182** | **136** | **163** | **215** | **64** | **52** | **12** | **202** | **101** |
| Moulders and coremakers | 687 | 776 | 50 | 69 | 18 | 155 | 9 | 21 | 273 | 247 | 83 | 95 | 74 | 72 | 75 | 38 | 17 | 11 | 88 | 68 |
| Smiths, forgemen | 400 | 228 | 22 | 11 | 18 | 21 | 2 | 8 | 77 | 92 | 72 | 42 | 30 | 27 | 100 | 14 | 22 | 1 | 57 | 12 |
| Other workers | 620 | 514 | 38 | 26 | 13 | 33 | 6 | 1 | 208 | 312 | 213 | 45 | 32 | 64 | 40 | 12 | 13 | — | 57 | 21 |
| **Electrical and electronic workers** | **6,286** | **3,173** | **1,244** | **818** | **729** | **860** | **374** | **196** | **757** | **480** | **565** | **172** | **879** | **249** | **650** | **105** | **338** | **118** | **750** | **175** |
| Electronic equipment manufacture and maintenance workers | 1,355 | 1,355 | 393 | 425 | 201 | 464 | 107 | 78 | 155 | 158 | 90 | 26 | 179 | 82 | 73 | 21 | 49 | 38 | 108 | 63 |
| Electricians | 3,422 | 854 | 647 | 173 | 326 | 239 | 217 | 55 | 336 | 124 | 367 | 25 | 402 | 109 | 391 | 33 | 223 | 37 | 513 | 59 |
| Electrical fitters, etc. | 1,509 | 964 | 204 | 220 | 202 | 157 | 50 | 63 | 266 | 198 | 108 | 121 | 298 | 58 | 186 | 51 | 66 | 43 | 129 | 53 |
| **Engineering and allied trades workers** | **31,009** | **23,755** | **4,367** | **5,294** | **2,541** | **5,511** | **1,478** | **1,265** | **5,782** | **4,886** | **2,618** | **1,837** | **3,754** | **2,250** | **5,001** | **676** | **1,654** | **673** | **3,814** | **1,363** |
| Constructional fitters and erectors | 2,383 | 84 | 262 | 3 | 173 | 15 | 87 | | 387 | 25 | 335 | 10 | 288 | 1 | 408 | 13 | 222 | 13 | 221 | 4 |
| Platers | 632 | 682 | 43 | 54 | 24 | 118 | 11 | 22 | 36 | 198 | 26 | 101 | 52 | 58 | 286 | 54 | 32 | 14 | 122 | 63 |
| Riveters and caulkers | 394 | 70 | 22 | 7 | 16 | 12 | 9 | 1 | 5 | — | 13 | 12 | 19 | 6 | 210 | — | 44 | 3 | 56 | 29 |
| Shipwrights | 395 | 162 | 20 | 26 | 32 | 35 | 22 | 6 | 4 | — | 10 | 3 | 14 | — | 191 | 7 | 39 | 3 | 63 | 82 |
| Miscellaneous boilershop and shipbuilding workers | 604 | 78 | 75 | 8 | 29 | 14 | 12 | 1 | 37 | 14 | 39 | 5 | 130 | 6 | 190 | 14 | 18 | 3 | 74 | 13 |
| Sheet metal workers | 942 | 1,442 | 154 | 349 | 79 | 385 | 43 | 70 | 153 | 179 | 49 | 70 | 135 | 134 | 183 | 33 | 34 | 50 | 112 | 172 |
| Welders | 3,323 | 1,155 | 362 | 193 | 254 | 317 | 122 | 58 | 499 | 270 | 285 | 95 | 310 | 101 | 773 | 48 | 226 | 29 | 492 | 44 |
| Toolmakers | 187 | 386 | 41 | 80 | 21 | 149 | 14 | 37 | 40 | 58 | 4 | 15 | 18 | 27 | 18 | 8 | 11 | 4 | 20 | 8 |
| Press tool makers | 117 | 356 | 16 | 149 | 13 | 39 | 6 | 9 | 43 | 69 | 4 | 22 | 17 | 13 | 4 | 5 | 9 | 23 | 5 | 27 |
| Mould makers | 33 | 113 | 2 | 28 | 7 | 52 | 5 | | 11 | 25 | 2 | 2 | 2 | 5 | 2 | — | 2 | 1 | — | — |
| Precision fitters | 2,914 | 2,333 | 385 | 535 | 315 | 763 | 226 | 112 | 467 | 435 | 133 | 135 | 364 | 153 | 645 | 38 | 128 | 75 | 251 | 87 |
| Maintenance fitters, erectors | 2,362 | 1,540 | 289 | 253 | 146 | 240 | 72 | 37 | 318 | 373 | 258 | 212 | 359 | 168 | 419 | 69 | 174 | 70 | 327 | 118 |
| Fitters (not precision), mechanics | 3,311 | 2,715 | 536 | 709 | 305 | 680 | 223 | 179 | 506 | 429 | 279 | 130 | 428 | 235 | 358 | 94 | 187 | 111 | 489 | 148 |
| Turners | 587 | 1,448 | 105 | 262 | 37 | 241 | 36 | 94 | 122 | 353 | 47 | 127 | 55 | 148 | 73 | 40 | 24 | 36 | 88 | 147 |

*Note.* Wholly unemployed figures relate to 9th December and unfilled vacancy figures to 4th December.

Source: Department of Employment and Productivity

## Occupational Analysis of Wholly Unemployed Adults and Unfilled Vacancies for Adults, December 1968—*continued*

### MEN

| Occupation | Great Britain | | London and South Eastern | | Eastern and Southern | | South Western | | Midlands | | Yorkshire and Humberside | | North Western | | Northern | | Wales | | Scotland | |
|---|---|---|---|---|---|---|---|---|---|---|---|---|---|---|---|---|---|---|---|---|
| | Wholly unemployed | Unfilled vacancies | Wholly unemployed | Unfilled vacancies | Wholly unemployed | Unfilled vacancies | Wholly unemployed | Unfilled vacancies | Wholly unemployed | Unfilled vacancies | Wholly unemployed | Unfilled vacancies | Wholly unemployed | Unfilled vacancies | Wholly unemployed | Unfilled vacancies | Wholly unemployed | Unfilled vacancies | Wholly unemployed | Unfilled vacancies |
| **Engineering and allied trades workers**—*continued* | | | | | | | | | | | | | | | | | | | | |
| Machine-tool setters, setter operators | 1,869 | 4,324 | 290 | 895 | 157 | 889 | 71 | 263 | 487 | 1,150 | 143 | 323 | 229 | 462 | 205 | 102 | 66 | 108 | 221 | 132 |
| Machine-tool operators | 2,510 | 2,078 | 334 | 515 | 168 | 471 | 88 | 184 | 957 | 500 | 251 | 162 | 268 | 148 | 100 | 19 | 49 | 13 | 295 | 66 |
| Electro platers | 120 | 103 | 20 | 43 | 10 | 22 | 4 | 5 | 47 | 21 | 2 | 2 | 17 | 4 | 3 | 5 | 3 | 1 | 14 | — |
| Plumbers, pipe fitters | 2,940 | 1,252 | 462 | 367 | 232 | 286 | 169 | 59 | 292 | 152 | 231 | 171 | 453 | 106 | 548 | 17 | 171 | 39 | 382 | 55 |
| Miscellaneous engineering workers | 3,655 | 1,717 | 535 | 462 | 357 | 441 | 169 | 52 | 1,024 | 352 | 364 | 92 | 372 | 182 | 283 | 11 | 155 | 24 | 396 | 101 |
| Watchmakers and repairers | 107 | 48 | 26 | 7 | 14 | 9 | 8 | 5 | 6 | 16 | 10 | 3 | 7 | 3 | 11 | 1 | 3 | 1 | 22 | 3 |
| Instrument makers and repairers | 397 | 451 | 111 | 113 | 39 | 169 | 31 | 28 | 40 | 28 | 18 | 14 | 49 | 40 | 41 | 34 | 14 | 11 | 54 | 14 |
| Goldsmiths, jewellers, etc. | 68 | 33 | 34 | 13 | 4 | 10 | 2 | — | 19 | 5 | 2 | 1 | 3 | 3 | — | — | 1 | — | 3 | 1 |
| Vehicle and cycle chassis and body building | 421 | 523 | 86 | 94 | 40 | 75 | 10 | 27 | 94 | 107 | 28 | 35 | 57 | 99 | 26 | 44 | 30 | 23 | 50 | 19 |
| Aircraft body building | 268 | 145 | 71 | 41 | 45 | 17 | 20 | 7 | 61 | 11 | 13 | 25 | 39 | 22 | 6 | — | 6 | 7 | 7 | 15 |
| Miscellaneous metal goods workers | 470 | 517 | 86 | 88 | 24 | 62 | 18 | 9 | 127 | 116 | 72 | 70 | 69 | 126 | 18 | 20 | 6 | 11 | 50 | 15 |
| **Woodworkers** | **5,892** | **2,715** | **1,059** | **747** | **650** | **596** | **352** | **185** | **743** | **309** | **743** | **144** | **680** | **226** | **814** | **123** | **305** | **90** | **546** | **295** |
| Carpenters, joiners | 4,944 | 1,621 | 828 | 362 | 543 | 331 | 318 | 139 | 628 | 162 | 658 | 86 | 562 | 133 | 715 | 103 | 271 | 64 | 421 | 241 |
| Cabinet makers | 208 | 239 | 69 | 119 | 19 | 39 | 7 | 14 | 16 | 23 | 17 | 12 | 33 | 13 | 11 | 5 | 11 | 4 | 25 | 10 |
| Sawyers, wood cutting machinists | 405 | 476 | 99 | 159 | 47 | 135 | 11 | 21 | 46 | 47 | 35 | 27 | 42 | 47 | 65 | 10 | 12 | 9 | 48 | 21 |
| Pattern makers | 108 | 135 | 9 | 19 | 12 | 37 | 7 | 3 | 21 | 35 | 10 | 11 | 22 | 11 | 16 | 5 | 2 | 8 | 9 | 6 |
| Other woodworkers | 227 | 244 | 54 | 88 | 29 | 54 | 9 | 8 | 32 | 42 | 23 | 8 | 21 | 22 | 7 | — | 9 | 5 | 43 | 17 |
| **Leather workers** | **604** | **271** | **154** | **96** | **53** | **49** | **21** | **16** | **128** | **68** | **79** | **9** | **60** | **12** | **33** | **5** | **14** | **5** | **62** | **11** |
| Tanners, fellmongers, etc. | 155 | 130 | 54 | 44 | 18 | 25 | 3 | 13 | 20 | 28 | 31 | 6 | 12 | 4 | 5 | 3 | 2 | 4 | 10 | 3 |
| Boot and shoe makers, repairers | 449 | 141 | 100 | 52 | 35 | 24 | 18 | 3 | 108 | 40 | 48 | 3 | 48 | 8 | 28 | 2 | 12 | 1 | 52 | 8 |
| **Textile workers** | **1,000** | **1,404** | **58** | **27** | **18** | **114** | **13** | **18** | **179** | **113** | **318** | **284** | **246** | **623** | **10** | **31** | **22** | **4** | **136** | **190** |
| Textile spinners | 127 | 164 | 1 | — | — | — | — | — | — | — | 44 | 40 | 52 | 84 | 3 | 12 | 5 | — | 22 | 28 |
| Textile weavers | 94 | 416 | 3 | — | 3 | 49 | 2 | 13 | 1 | 7 | 25 | 98 | 33 | 188 | — | — | — | — | 27 | 71 |
| Other textile workers | 779 | 824 | 54 | 27 | 15 | 65 | 11 | 5 | 178 | 106 | 249 | 156 | 161 | 351 | 7 | 19 | 17 | 4 | 87 | 91 |
| **Clothing, etc. workers** | **1,165** | **740** | **525** | **397** | **82** | **102** | **31** | **20** | **66** | **30** | **97** | **55** | **170** | **74** | **68** | **20** | **25** | **11** | **101** | **31** |
| Retail bespoke tailoring workers | 158 | 59 | 86 | 23 | 12 | 12 | 6 | 5 | 4 | 1 | 9 | 3 | 19 | 10 | 3 | — | 7 | 1 | 12 | 4 |
| Wholesale heavy clothing workers | 331 | 339 | 208 | 215 | 6 | 31 | 2 | — | 12 | 9 | 28 | 39 | 48 | 26 | 7 | 9 | 1 | — | 19 | 10 |
| Other clothing workers | 282 | 200 | 115 | 120 | 38 | 30 | 9 | 8 | 20 | 11 | 15 | 1 | 44 | 13 | 9 | 3 | 5 | 6 | 27 | 8 |
| Upholstery workers, etc. | 394 | 142 | 116 | 39 | 26 | 29 | 14 | 7 | 30 | 9 | 45 | 12 | 59 | 25 | 49 | 8 | 12 | 4 | 43 | 9 |
| **Food, drink and tobacco workers** | **1,064** | **479** | **215** | **83** | **87** | **95** | **61** | **52** | **99** | **73** | **121** | **36** | **185** | **62** | **66** | **18** | **41** | **17** | **189** | **43** |
| Workers in food manufacture | 983 | 444 | 190 | 76 | 76 | 93 | 57 | 51 | 88 | 64 | 118 | 31 | 176 | 53 | 63 | 18 | 39 | 17 | 176 | 41 |
| Workers in drink manufacture | 52 | 17 | 16 | 1 | 6 | 2 | 3 | — | 6 | 9 | 1 | 5 | 5 | — | 2 | — | — | — | 13 | — |
| Workers in tobacco manufacture | 29 | 18 | 9 | 6 | 5 | — | 1 | 1 | 5 | — | 2 | — | 4 | 9 | 1 | — | 2 | — | — | 2 |

*Note.*—Wholly unemployed figures relate to 9th December and unfilled vacancy figures to 4th December.

Source: Department of Employment and Productivity

E.10

## Occupational Analysis of Wholly Unemployed Adults and Unfilled Vacancies for Adults, December 1968—*continued*

### MEN

| Occupation | Great Britain | | London and South Eastern | | Eastern and Southern | | South Western | | Midlands | | Yorkshire and Humberside | | North Western | | Northern | | Wales | | Scotland | |
|---|---|---|---|---|---|---|---|---|---|---|---|---|---|---|---|---|---|---|---|---|
| | Wholly unemployed | Unfilled vacancies | Wholly unemployed | Unfilled vacancies | Wholly unemployed | Unfilled vacancies | Wholly unemployed | Unfilled vacancies | Wholly unemployed | Unfilled vacancies | Wholly unemployed | Unfilled vacancies | Wholly unemployed | Unfilled vacancies | Wholly unemployed | Unfilled vacancies | Wholly unemployed | Unfilled vacancies | Wholly unemployed | Unfilled vacancies |
| **Paper and printing workers** | **1,070** | **534** | **474** | **164** | **138** | **138** | **67** | **41** | **55** | **51** | **33** | **12** | **113** | **72** | **29** | **14** | **20** | **4** | **141** | **38** |
| Paper and paper products workers | 199 | 206 | 58 | 83 | 22 | 27 | 7 | 4 | 7 | 23 | 8 | 4 | 26 | 36 | 9 | 4 | 4 | — | 58 | 25 |
| Printing workers | 871 | 328 | 416 | 81 | 116 | 111 | 60 | 37 | 48 | 28 | 25 | 8 | 87 | 36 | 20 | 10 | 16 | 4 | 83 | 13 |
| **Building materials workers** | **206** | **315** | **17** | **12** | **27** | **155** | **19** | **17** | **36** | **24** | **24** | **25** | **18** | **25** | **17** | **28** | **11** | **7** | **37** | **22** |
| Brick and tile production workers | 71 | 224 | 4 | 9 | 8 | 127 | 7 | 6 | 21 | 13 | 8 | 24 | 3 | 17 | 4 | 3 | 4 | 4 | 12 | 21 |
| Other building materials workers | 135 | 91 | 13 | 3 | 19 | 28 | 12 | 11 | 15 | 11 | 16 | 1 | 15 | 8 | 13 | 25 | 7 | 3 | 25 | 1 |
| **Makers of products not elsewhere specified** | **779** | **759** | **245** | **172** | **64** | **160** | **27** | **34** | **187** | **202** | **44** | **28** | **113** | **143** | **35** | **5** | **13** | **6** | **51** | **9** |
| Rubber workers | 132 | 272 | 31 | 28 | 4 | 9 | — | 9 | 36 | 142 | 5 | — | 38 | 80 | 1 | — | 2 | 3 | 15 | 1 |
| Plastics workers | 309 | 348 | 105 | 106 | 37 | 118 | 4 | 19 | 108 | 50 | 4 | 21 | 34 | 23 | 6 | 4 | 4 | 1 | 7 | 6 |
| Other workers | 338 | 139 | 109 | 38 | 23 | 33 | 23 | 6 | 43 | 10 | 35 | 7 | 41 | 40 | 28 | 1 | 7 | 2 | 29 | 2 |
| **Construction workers** | **11,347** | **1,793** | **1,935** | **343** | **1,158** | **338** | **699** | **130** | **1,674** | **221** | **1,492** | **86** | **1,322** | **214** | **1,197** | **77** | **716** | **101** | **1,154** | **283** |
| Bricklayers | 3,544 | 774 | 465 | 131 | 378 | 155 | 186 | 68 | 641 | 118 | 600 | 39 | 381 | 71 | 489 | 25 | 185 | 38 | 219 | 129 |
| Masons | 261 | 70 | 25 | 9 | 15 | 12 | 72 | 17 | 10 | 5 | 25 | 5 | 19 | — | 22 | 1 | 20 | 12 | 53 | 9 |
| Slaters | 449 | 138 | 94 | 17 | 45 | 13 | 32 | 4 | 49 | 3 | 47 | 9 | 50 | 34 | 35 | 4 | 32 | 4 | 65 | 50 |
| Plasterers | 1,169 | 191 | 218 | 27 | 142 | 41 | 115 | 11 | 171 | 17 | 114 | 6 | 154 | 29 | 50 | 14 | 111 | 29 | 94 | 17 |
| Others | 5,924 | 620 | 1,133 | 159 | 578 | 117 | 294 | 30 | 803 | 78 | 706 | 27 | 718 | 80 | 601 | 33 | 368 | 18 | 723 | 78 |
| **Painters and decorators** | **9,829** | **1,041** | **2,772** | **335** | **1,131** | **253** | **612** | **77** | **1,266** | **117** | **892** | **57** | **1,225** | **64** | **718** | **45** | **442** | **15** | **771** | **78** |
| Painters | 8,929 | 681 | 2,525 | 195 | 1,059 | 178 | 579 | 47 | 1,097 | 64 | 836 | 36 | 1,096 | 39 | 635 | 39 | 409 | 11 | 693 | 72 |
| Decorators (excluding pottery and glass decorators) | 900 | 360 | 247 | 140 | 72 | 75 | 33 | 30 | 169 | 53 | 56 | 21 | 129 | 25 | 83 | 6 | 33 | 4 | 78 | 6 |
| **Drivers, etc. of stationary engines, cranes, etc.** | **4,217** | **687** | **463** | **129** | **260** | **130** | **151** | **21** | **665** | **167** | **503** | **54** | **489** | **85** | **557** | **45** | **390** | **27** | **739** | **29** |
| **Transport and communication workers** | **30,959** | **19,598** | **5,384** | **3,621** | **3,048** | **1,267** | **2,036** | **3,166** | **3,784** | **2,089** | **2,991** | **582** | **3,836** | **3,215** | **3,014** | **552** | **2,705** | **360** | **4,161** | **4,746** |
| Railway workers | 325 | 753 | 56 | 563 | 31 | 87 | 17 | 11 | 67 | 32 | 30 | 6 | 47 | 20 | 24 | 8 | 16 | 9 | 37 | 17 |
| Motor drivers (except P.S.V.) | 24,533 | 2,540 | 3,569 | 768 | 2,513 | 453 | 1,714 | 203 | 3,489 | 337 | 2,645 | 119 | 2,910 | 284 | 2,288 | 89 | 1,984 | 66 | 3,421 | 221 |
| P.S.V. drivers, conductors | 512 | 4,733 | 81 | 1,836 | 67 | 483 | 56 | 57 | 61 | 1,092 | 46 | 211 | 53 | 564 | 54 | 221 | 41 | 80 | 53 | 189 |
| Seamen | 3,237 | 65 | 655 | 2 | 236 | 4 | 137 | — | 17 | 1 | 215 | 49 | 695 | — | 541 | 4 | 226 | 3 | 515 | 2 |
| Harbours and docks workers | 161 | 36 | 60 | — | 18 | — | 2 | — | 3 | — | 3 | 1 | 26 | 9 | 30 | 25 | 2 | — | 17 | 1 |
| Other transport workers | 686 | 382 | 276 | 192 | 102 | 83 | 61 | 11 | 71 | 47 | 23 | 5 | 61 | 18 | 26 | 8 | 18 | 7 | 48 | 11 |
| Communications workers | 1,505 | 11,089 | 687 | 260 | 81 | 157 | 49 | 2,884 | 76 | 580 | 29 | 191 | 44 | 2,320 | 51 | 197 | 418 | 195 | 70 | 4,305 |
| **Warehousemen, packers, etc.** | **5,693** | **1,317** | **1,416** | **541** | **568** | **262** | **423** | **46** | **762** | **202** | **514** | **46** | **626** | **75** | **320** | **49** | **278** | **42** | **786** | **54** |
| Warehouse workers | 4,826 | 1,013 | 1,001 | 371 | 505 | 208 | 404 | 41 | 636 | 162 | 469 | 36 | 523 | 54 | 296 | 48 | 269 | 42 | 723 | 51 |
| Packers, bottlers | 867 | 304 | 415 | 170 | 63 | 54 | 19 | 5 | 126 | 40 | 45 | 10 | 103 | 21 | 24 | 1 | 9 | — | 63 | 3 |

*Note.*—Wholly unemployed figures relate to 9th December and unfilled vacancy figures to 4th December.

Source: Department of Employment and Productivity

**Occupational Analysis of Wholly Unemployed Adults and Unfilled Vacancies for Adults, December 1968**—*continued*

**MEN**

| Occupation | Great Britain | | London and South Eastern | | Eastern and Southern | | South Western | | Midlands | | Yorkshire and Humberside | | North Western | | Northern | | Wales | | Scotland | |
|---|---|---|---|---|---|---|---|---|---|---|---|---|---|---|---|---|---|---|---|---|
| | | | Region | | | | | | | | | | | | | | | | | |
| | Wholly unemployed | Unfilled vacancies | Wholly unemployed | Unfilled vacancies | Wholly unemployed | Unfilled vacancies | Wholly unemployed | Unfilled vacancies | Wholly unemployed | Unfilled vacancies | Wholly unemployed | Unfilled vacancies | Wholly unemployed | Unfilled vacancies | Wholly unemployed | Unfilled vacancies | Wholly unemployed | Unfilled vacancies | Wholly unemployed | Unfilled vacancies |
| **Clerical workers** | **43,120** | **4,457** | **10,744** | **1,486** | **6,078** | **806** | **5,333** | **193** | **4,165** | **820** | **3,158** | **277** | **4,898** | **459** | **2,671** | **149** | **2,492** | **96** | **3,581** | **171** |
| Clerks | 38,866 | 3,359 | 9,290 | 1,070 | 5,601 | 611 | 5.060 | 154 | 3,685 | 661 | 2,853 | 200 | 4,404 | 332 | 2,436 | 120 | 2,355 | 77 | 3,182 | 134 |
| Book-keepers, cashiers | 3,730 | 951 | 1,270 | 367 | 406 | 149 | 245 | 27 | 392 | 141 | 290 | 69 | 449 | 117 | 219 | 27 | 115 | 18 | 344 | 36 |
| Other clerical workers | 524 | 147 | 184 | 49 | 71 | 46 | 28 | 12 | 88 | 18 | 15 | 8 | 45 | 10 | 16 | 2 | 22 | 1 | 55 | 1 |
| **Shop assistants** | **8,105** | **2,560** | **1,803** | **955** | **1,049** | **524** | **762** | **138** | **952** | **316** | **808** | **134** | **852** | **218** | **541** | **90** | **448** | **56** | **890** | **129** |
| **Service, sport and recreation workers** | **18,171** | **4,564** | **6,257** | **1,698** | **2,030** | **870** | **1,416** | **340** | **1,282** | **463** | **1,051** | **218** | **2,307** | **469** | **1,041** | **126** | **677** | **169** | **2,110** | **211** |
| Police, etc. | 1,108 | 833 | 249 | 184 | 177 | 168 | 62 | 53 | 127 | 127 | 92 | 49 | 140 | 117 | 94 | 19 | 58 | 67 | 109 | 49 |
| Hotels and catering: | | | | | | | | | | | | | | | | | | | | |
| Kitchen staff | 3,117 | 933 | 915 | 380 | 438 | 184 | 398 | 78 | 198 | 77 | 176 | 38 | 379 | 53 | 167 | 33 | 147 | 54 | 299 | 36 |
| Bar staff | 1,772 | 243 | 437 | 90 | 175 | 46 | 190 | 16 | 126 | 34 | 94 | 12 | 208 | 21 | 93 | 6 | 64 | 4 | 385 | 14 |
| Waiters, etc. | 1,410 | 390 | 445 | 84 | 215 | 76 | 212 | 93 | 69 | 40 | 50 | 20 | 158 | 36 | 65 | 9 | 68 | 8 | 128 | 24 |
| Others | 1,399 | 467 | 444 | 217 | 156 | 76 | 154 | 29 | 111 | 34 | 91 | 20 | 108 | 49 | 69 | 16 | 85 | 4 | 181 | 22 |
| Hairdressers | 605 | 169 | 207 | 57 | 63 | 48 | 47 | 9 | 48 | 21 | 36 | 7 | 51 | 17 | 35 | 1 | 24 | 2 | 94 | 7 |
| Laundry and dry cleaning workers | 209 | 70 | 99 | 34 | 20 | 15 | 10 | 1 | 23 | 5 | 12 | 3 | 21 | 8 | 4 | 1 | 6 | 2 | 14 | 1 |
| Domestics | 272 | 152 | 78 | 40 | 42 | 39 | 43 | 9 | 27 | 21 | 13 | 14 | 15 | 7 | 13 | 9 | 11 | 7 | 30 | 6 |
| Attendants | 2,600 | 488 | 447 | 165 | 210 | 79 | 80 | 26 | 257 | 44 | 155 | 21 | 538 | 90 | 309 | 21 | 103 | 14 | 501 | 28 |
| Porters, messengers | 1,941 | 507 | 784 | 310 | 91 | 67 | 67 | 8 | 90 | 24 | 203 | 23 | 417 | 52 | 96 | 7 | 34 | 2 | 159 | 14 |
| Entertainment workers | 2,549 | 21 | 1,707 | 10 | 247 | 5 | 74 | 4 | 91 | 1 | 81 | — | 149 | — | 55 | — | 44 | 1 | 101 | — |
| Others | 1,189 | 291 | 445 | 127 | 196 | 67 | 79 | 14 | 115 | 35 | 48 | 11 | 123 | 19 | 41 | 4 | 33 | 4 | 109 | 10 |
| **Administrative, professional, technical workers** | **27,288** | **13,850** | **7,845** | **3,236** | **4,039** | **2,705** | **2,149** | **639** | **3,488** | **2,209** | **1,775** | **1,167** | **3,024** | **1,666** | **1,591** | **961** | **1,064** | **390** | **2,313** | **877** |
| Laboratory assistants | 670 | 476 | 169 | 78 | 104 | 175 | 46 | 36 | 86 | 66 | 61 | 35 | 81 | 53 | 46 | 8 | 34 | 13 | 43 | 12 |
| Draughtsmen | 1,323 | 1,267 | 416 | 191 | 183 | 352 | 110 | 80 | 163 | 326 | 109 | 87 | 180 | 106 | 70 | 33 | 32 | 31 | 60 | 61 |
| Nurses | 426 | 2,456 | 77 | 635 | 44 | 311 | 39 | 112 | 33 | 287 | 24 | 194 | 35 | 455 | 12 | 161 | 30 | 41 | 132 | 260 |
| Other administrative, professional and technical workers | 24,869 | 9,651 | 7,183 | 2,332 | 3,708 | 1,867 | 1,954 | 411 | 3,206 | 1,530 | 1,581 | 851 | 2,728 | 1,052 | 1,463 | 759 | 968 | 305 | 2,078 | 544 |
| **Labourers** | **220,544** | **10,827** | **27,209** | **2,955** | **14,723** | **2,344** | **11,348** | **734** | **29,340** | **1,485** | **24,711** | **745** | **24,808** | **1,196** | **33,970** | **473** | **18,959** | **275** | **35,476** | **620** |
| General labourers (heavy) | 89,451 | 2,249 | 8,163 | 484 | 4,622 | 468 | 4,045 | 169 | 10,280 | 346 | 11,799 | 110 | 8,954 | 247 | 15,013 | 122 | 7,438 | 91 | 19,137 | 212 |
| General labourers (light) | 75,322 | 400 | 7,712 | 111 | 5,017 | 119 | 4,437 | 14 | 10,075 | 79 | 9,168 | 20 | 9,009 | 19 | 12,958 | 9 | 6,233 | 6 | 10,713 | 23 |
| Factory hands | 20,901 | 2,695 | 5,392 | 1,245 | 1,974 | 848 | 757 | 190 | 2,702 | 158 | 410 | 39 | 2,089 | 58 | 2,283 | 62 | 3,273 | 49 | 2,021 | 46 |
| Other labourers | 34,870 | 5,483 | 5,942 | 1,115 | 3,110 | 909 | 2,109 | 361 | 6,283 | 902 | 3,334 | 576 | 4,756 | 872 | 3,716 | 280 | 2,015 | 129 | 3,605 | 339 |
| **GRAND TOTAL** | **444,605** | **100,257** | **74,820** | **23,515** | **39,480** | **18,022** | **28,334** | **7,487** | **56,887** | **16,032** | **44,321** | **6,892** | **56,880** | **11,843** | **53,035** | **3,700** | **31,056** | **2,951** | **59,792** | **9,815** |

*Note.*—Wholly unemployed figures relate to 9th December and unfilled vacancy figures to 4th December.

Source: Department of Employment and Productivity

# Document 10C *Industrial distribution of employment in the United Kingdom, 1923-38**

| Industry | Estimated number of insured persons aged 16 to 64 in employment in June 1938 | Percentage increase (+) or decrease (−) since June 1923 |
|---|---|---|
| *Expanding:* | | |
| Distributive trades | 1 911 218 | + 64·5 |
| Building and contracting | 1 141 203 | + 63·2 |
| General engineering | 591 430 | + 16·8 |
| Hotel, restaurant, etc., service | 394 877 | + 71·7 |
| Road transport | 385 312 | + 73·1 |
| Motor and aircraft engineering | 360 836 | +109·4 |
| Local government service | 317 323 | + 49·8 |
| Electrical manufacturing | 275 120 | +128·7 |
| Printing, publishing and bookbinding | 268 564 | + 27·6 |
| Gas, water and electricity supply | 205 177 | + 34·2 |
| Tailoring | 190 776 | + 8·5 |
| Laundries, dyeing, etc. | 168 629 | + 69·5 |
| Professional services | 165 608 | + 61·7 |
| Bread, biscuit and cake-making | 163 446 | + 15·7 |
| Furniture making | 132 422 | + 57·3 |
| Entertainments, sport, etc. | 127 731 | \| 150·5 |
| *Contracting:* | | |
| Coal mining | 701 713 | − 41·5 |
| Cotton manufacturing | 251 184 | − 43·2 |
| Woollen and worsted manufacturing | 164 731 | − 32·3 |
| Iron and steel | 152 965 | − 17·7 |
| Railway service (non-permanent workers) | 149 508 | − 14·0 |
| Shipbuilding | 139 968 | − 4·8 |
| Dock, harbour, etc. service | 118 270 | − 14·6 |
| Boot and shoe manufacturing | 111 792 | − 11·9 |
| All industries | 12 075 268 | + 21·5 |

* *Ministry of Labour Gazette*, December 1938, pp. 486, 487.

# Document 10D *The Ford Motor Company, Dagenham*

The Ford Motor Company of the United States purchased 294 acres of land at Dagenham in 1924, including a water-front on the River Thames, for £150000. The first vehicle was produced on the site in 1931.

The site was away from the centre of London and there was plenty of cheap and relatively flat land available for future expansion. Today the site consists of 665 acres. The wharf facilities on the River Thames will accommodate ships of 15000 tons. This enables the easy import of raw materials of about 14500 tons a day. In 1972, 274 ships and nearly 1000 barges docked to unload raw materials such as iron ore and coal, and to ship out vehicles and spare parts. These are exported down the River Thames to Europe and the rest of the world. The company's blast furnace and power station provide the factory with some of its own steel and electricity, and the River Thames provides plenty of water for cooling purposes.

In the 1950's the London County Council was building a very large housing estate on the outskirts of what was then Dagenham Village. The workers who moved into these houses provided the company with a ready supply of suitably skilled labour. Today the Dagenham works employs some 29000 people.

# 11 How is a big factory different from a small one?

When we have raised the money to expand our business, and decided where to locate our new factory, we must plan it in a very different way from our original small works. The reasons for this will become clear when we make a detailed study of a medium-sized factory.

Read through Document 11A, 'The Northern Domestic Appliance Co. Ltd', then refer back to Section 5 and read through the document on the Wyre Co. Ltd. We shall be making some comparisons between the two factories.

Now answer the following questions.

1 How many directors does the Northern Domestic Appliance Co. Ltd have? Make a list of the departments in the company for which each director is responsible.

2 What duties are performed by the personnel-and-training department?

3 Make a list of five people in the firm who do jobs similar to those in the Wyre Co. Ltd. Make another list of five people who have no counterpart in the smaller firm. Why should the larger firm require the skills of workers of this type, but not the smaller firm?

4 What training and career experience would each of the following require: (a) the chief work-study engineer, (b) the purchasing manager, (c) the financial director, (d) the senior shop steward?

5 Draw a 'flow diagram' of the production line of the factory. Start your diagram by showing the raw materials and components as they enter the factory, and finish it by showing the completed goods leaving the factory.

6 What influence might the shop stewards in the factory have over the organisation and running of the production line? How might the management of the company make use of the experience and advice of the shop stewards to make the production line run efficiently?

7 Seven different trade unions have members employed by the company, and we are told that 'the wage-bargaining procedure is somewhat complex'. What does this mean? Make a list of all the difficulties that might be created for both management and workers by the existence of so many unions.

**8** The Wyre Co. Ltd would have to stop work if there were strikes in the firms which produced wire, electroplating, or electric power. Make a list of the industries on which the Northern Domestic Appliance Co. Ltd is reliant. Is this firm more or less in danger from strikes in other factories than the Wyre Co. Ltd?

**9** What welfare and social facilities are available to the workers in the larger firm which are not available to the workers in the smaller firm? Can you think of any reasons why a worker might prefer to join a works social club rather than a club in the district where he lives?

**10** Suppose a simple new process were to be invented for giving metal a cheap, durable ceramic coat suitable for cookers, and the firm decided to introduce this instead of enamelling. Describe how you might view this change from the point of view of (a) the director of manufacturing, (b) a worker in the enamelling department.

**11** In Section 5 we saw that small firms have the advantage of flexibility – they can change the production line relatively easily to do short runs of production. What is the corresponding advantage of large firms? Document 11B may help you.

**12** In the Wyre Co. Ltd, which is a private company, the managing director, Mr Wyre, has a substantial portion of the shares and therefore receives a substantial portion of the profits. The company we are now studying is a public company with a much greater number of shares owned by a large number of different people. The managing director and the other four working directors own some shares, but most of their income is made up from their salaries as directors: if the firm makes higher profits, most of the money goes to the other shareholders.

Presumably Mr Wyre's aim is to make as much profit as possible. If you were a working director of the Northern Domestic Appliance Co. Ltd, would your aims be in any way different?

**13** The Northern Domestic Appliance Co. Ltd faces strong competition from other firms making similar products. What effect might this competition have on (a) the prices it charges, (b) the quality of the goods it produces?

**14** What steps might the Northern Domestic Appliance Co. Ltd take to increase demand for its products?

**15** How might the decisions mentioned in questions 10 and 14 be taken within the firm? Think about who might have the idea, and who would be concerned in each of these decisions.

# Document 11A *The Northern Domestic Appliance Co. Ltd*

This is a public company with an issued ordinary-share capital of £750 000. The shares are widely distributed among shareholders, and no one shareholder has more than £10 000 worth. The turnover is about £5 million, and there are about 1000 employees. About 400 000 people live within travelling distance of the factory, and the proportion engaged in engineering trades is above the national average.

The company produce mainly cookers and fires. The raw materials are iron castings (the foundry is a subsidiary company), sheet steel, and a very wide variety of bought-in components such as thermostats, wooden surrounds for fires, wire shelves, knobs, nuts and bolts, etc.

The home market for domestic appliances is very competitive, because in the showrooms of the gas board and the electricity board a customer has the opportunity to compare the products of many manufacturers. The firm must therefore try to produce cookers and fires which are better than those of its rivals at a price which is the same or slightly lower. They therefore employ three research-and-development teams (cookers, fires, and future products) consisting of scientists and engineers and their assistants, about 25 people in all, whose job it is to design the required product. They work in close co-operation with draughtsmen in the design department (about 18 people) under the general direction of the technical manager, who is in turn responsible to the technical director.

If they come up with a design which has possibilities, then the marketing executive carries out market research to find out what the demand will be, and if the product appears to

Figure 11A. Plan of factory of the Northern Domestic Appliance Co. Ltd

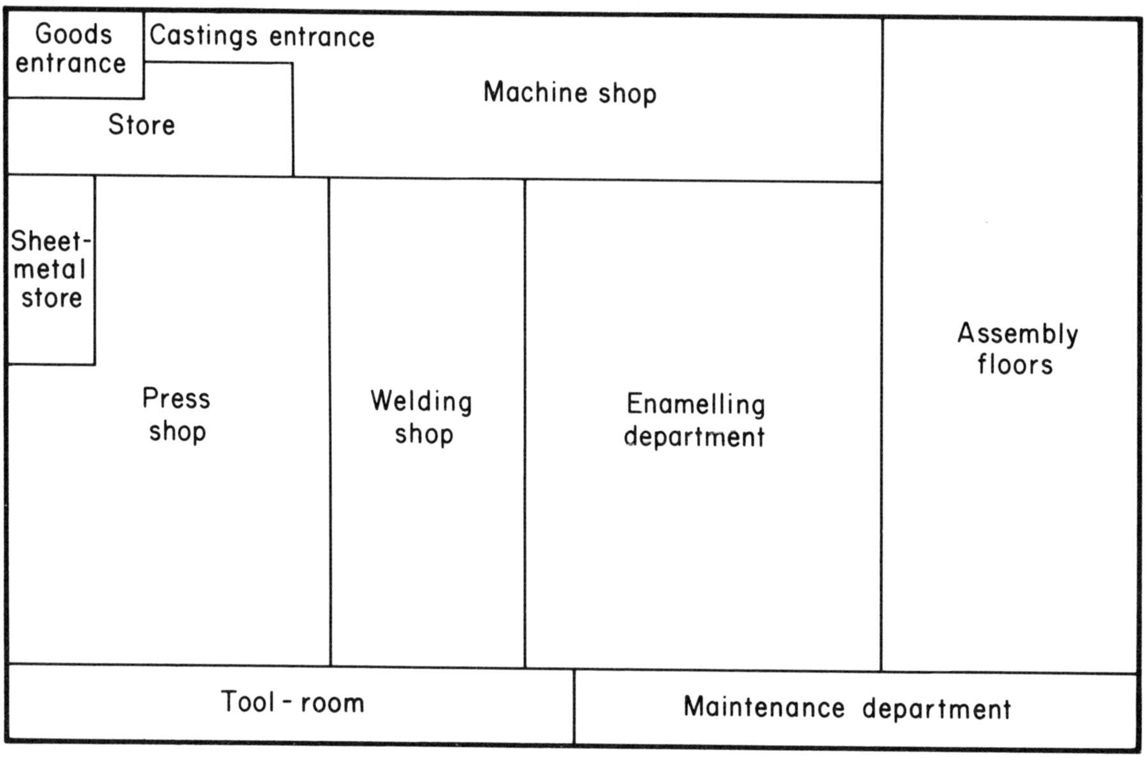

have a good sale then a production line is organised.

The production-planning department decides how the product will be made and organises the flow of work through the factory. The purchasing department makes arrangements for the purchase of raw material and components. Usually the details are put on the firm's computer (at present an ICL 1901) so that immediately an order is received the computer will work out how many of each component needs to be ordered. The tool-room (about 30 highly skilled technicians) produces the jigs and tools. The planning and purchasing departments, the tool-room, and the factory itself come under the manufacturing director.

Refer now to figure 11A, the plan of the factory. Sheet steel, castings, and bought-in components enter at A. Castings and bought-in components are inspected. Castings pass to the machine shop, where milling and drilling takes place. Some of this work must be done to very close tolerances, and about 8 of the men in this department are highly skilled, whereas the other 30 are only semi-skilled and require relatively little training. The finished castings pass to the assembly floors.

The sheet steel passes first to the press shop, where it is guillotined to size and stamped into shape. The smaller parts are done in hand presses, worked mainly by women, and the larger parts are stamped by powerful hydraulic presses worked by men. Altogether there are 75 people in this department. Any parts which require electroplating are sent out to a specialist firm.

The pressed steel parts then go into the welding shop, where they are assembled on jigs and fixed together by electric spot welding. About 20 men work in this department.

After inspection and correction of faults, the parts are cleaned and degreased, given a carbon coating, and then enamelled by hand-dipping or spraying. They are then dried, inspected, and baked in ovens through which they pass on a conveyor line. About 90 men and women work in this department. After inspection, the parts pass to the assembly floors.

There are separate assembly lines for the cookers and the fires, employing about 160 people in all. There is an extensive overhead conveyor system to get all the parts from the stores to the various parts of the factory where they are required, including the final assembly line. After assembly, there is extensive inspection before the product is packed for transportation.

The foremen of the machine shop, press shop, and welding shop are responsible to the assistant works manager, who together with the managers of the enamelling department and the assembly floor is responsible to the works manager. The production-control department is responsible for chasing the progress of work through the factory, and the work-study engineers are responsible for tasks such as improving the flow of work through the factory and fixing the standard times for jobs. The works manager, the production controller, and the chief work-study engineer are responsible to the manufacturing director, as is also the maintenance department. The inspectors, of whom there are over 50, are responsible to the technical director. The transport department comes under the marketing director.

There are four main sections of the accounts office. One section deals with the accounts for raw materials and components – the 'bought ledger' – another deals with the 'sales ledger', and a third deals with wages. All these three sections, about 50 people in all, are responsible to the chief accountant, who is in turn responsible to the financial director (who is also the company secretary). The fourth section is the computer section: the systems analyst and the programmers and operators work under the data-processing manager, who is again responsible to the financial director. The security department is also responsible to the financial director.

The hiring and training of all employees is the responsibility of the personnel-and-training department, the head of which reports directly to the chief executive.

A sample of employees gave the following descriptions of their careers.

### A spot welder

Short on-the-job training.

### A tool-room craftsman

Joined the firm at 16+ with five good grades in CSE subjects. The first year was full-time at the college of further education, followed by three years further training with day release.

### An assembly-line operator

Joined the firm as a married woman. Received a few weeks training in the firm's 'school'.

(The firm had introduced this schooling period because before this there had been a high rate of turnover among assembly-line operators during their first few weeks of employment.)

### A junior secretary

Joined the firm at 16+ with two or three subjects at CSE. Had taken day release to follow a typing and commercial-studies course, and had made junior secretary by the age of 20.

### Section manager 'sales ledger'

Left school at 16+ with four GCE O-levels, had then taken a two-year OND Business Studies course at the college of further education and joined the firm at 18+ as a ledger clerk. His OND gave him exemption from part of the Institute of Cost and Works Accountants examination, and he had taken the rest of the examination by spare-time study over a period of four years. (The minimum period is five years from the age of 16+, but few people pass every stage the first time.) He was earning over £2500 per annum by the age of 30 (in 1968).

### Technical manager

A good honours graduate in physics who took a post-graduate apprenticeship with a firm of heating engineers. Later he did research and development with another manufacturer of domestic appliances, and he also spent some time as a marketing executive.

### Works manager

Left school at 18+ with two A-levels (physics and chemistry) and did a student apprenticeship, after which he took a four-year sandwich course at the local polytechnic to give him a CNAA degree in engineering. After being in charge of the machine shop for some time, he transferred to production control, and he then had a period in work study with another firm. He came back as assistant works manager, and later succeeded as works manager.

The training to be given for each type of job is now determined by the Industrial Training Board for the engineering industry. The Industrial Training Boards, one for each industry, raise a levy from employers and make grants to those firms who provide training which they approve, the purpose being that all firms should in one way or another make a contribution towards training. As well as financing the training organised by larger firms, the boards also arrange for various organisations to provide training for workers in those firms which do not have schemes of their own.

It is the aim of the personnel department to ensure that there are always one or two people being 'groomed' to succeed to each post in middle or senior management. For example, if the production controller is due to retire in three or four years time, one or two of the work-study engineers might be sent on production-control courses and then given the necessary experience, even if it meant creating a post of assistant production controller (in parallel with the deputy production controller, who is an older man due to retire himself a few years after the controller).

About 80% of the workers are members of the General and Municipal Workers' Union. The other 20% belong to a variety of unions – Transport and General Workers' (TGW), the Amalgamated Union of Engineering Workers (AUEW), the Electrical Trades Union (ETU), the draughtsmen's union TASS, and the Association of Scientific, Technical and Managerial Staff (ASTMS).

There being such a variety of different jobs, the wage-bargaining procedure is somewhat complex, as in the rest of the engineering industry. A group of workers who are dissatisfied with the rate they are receiving for a particular job might take the following course of action. The bargaining would stop at the stage when both workers and management were satisfied that a fair solution had been reached.

a) Workers discuss their dissatisfaction with their foreman.
b) Workers and the shop steward of their union talk to the foreman.
c) The shop steward talks to the foreman and the departmental manager.
d) The shop steward and the factory convenor (the chairman of the committee of the shop stewards from all the unions in the factory) talk to the departmental manager and the personnel manager.
e) The factory convenor talks to the personnel manager and the director.
f) The factory convenor and the union district organiser talk to the director and officials from the employers' federation.

The firm has an extensive range of welfare and social services. There is a surgery with a full-time nurse, and there is a works canteen and a staff canteen which serve subsidised meals. There is a social club which has two dance halls, facilities for indoor games, bars, and playing fields.

All matters other than those concerning pay can be discussed at meetings of the Joint Consultative Committee, which consists of five representatives of the workers and five representatives of the management, under the chairmanship of the personnel manager.

## Document 11B *Percentage of total sales obtained by the largest five firms in each industry* (*from* 1968 Census of Production)

| *Commodity* | *Percentage* | *Commodity* | *Percentage* |
|---|---|---|---|
| Biscuits | 71·0 | Cars | 99·2 |
| Margarine | 93.8 | Jewellery | 49·5 |
| Cigarettes | 99·9 | Underwear | 53·1 |
| Petrol | 97·5 | Woven carpets | 51·7 |
| Detergents | 79·9 | Women's tailored outer wear | 20·1 |
| Television sets | 92·7 | Wooden domestic furniture | 15·0 |
| Record players | 75·7 | Toys | 58·2 |

# 12 'What about my share of the profits?'

## 12.1 Joining a trade union

In a firm with about fifty workers, many of them will know the managing director as a person, and negotiations over wages, conditions of work, etc. can often be conducted face-to-face. In the much larger firm, however, the relations between management and workers are usually much more complicated.

Imagine that you are a worker in a large firm, and you get to know that the firm has substantially increased its profits. You and your mates naturally decide that you would like some of the increased profits as increased wages.

There are three groups of workers in the firm, and their weekly wages are as follows:

skilled workers (e.g. maintenance engineers), £40;
semi-skilled workers (e.g. assembly-line workers), £35;
unskilled workers (e.g. packers, cleaners), £30.

There is a shortage of skilled and semi-skilled workers in the area, but a number of unemployed unskilled workers. The employers say that they intend to pay increased wages to the skilled and semi-skilled workers, but nothing more to the unskilled workers.

Your teacher will divide you into three groups representing each of the groups of workers in the factory.

Discuss what you are going to do about the wage offer.

In order to protect your position you may decide to join a trade union. There are three types of union which you must consider:

an *industry union*, which seeks to represent all the workers in a particular industry whatever their type of job;
a *craft union*, which represents a particular kind of skilled worker whichever industry he may be in;
a *general union*, which represents semi-skilled and unskilled workers doing many different kinds of jobs in a wide variety of industries.

Examine Document 12A. Decide which are (a) industry unions, (b) craft unions, (c) general unions.

What is a 'white collar' union?

In most factories there are members of more than one union. For example, in 1969 the Ford Motor Co. had to deal with fifteen unions in their pay negotiations. If there is more than one union in a factory, this is referred to as 'multiunionism'.

What problems do you think multiunionism might cause in a factory?

What are the benefits of multiunionism to the workers?

From the literature provided by your teacher, make a list of the benefits provided by trade unions.

In most European countries there are 'dirty jobs' which the Europeans do not want to do themselves and which are done by 'guest workers' from other countries. For example, thousands of men from Turkey do unskilled jobs in West Germany, sending money home to their families in Turkey. Most of these men live in hostels. Very few belong to trade unions.

What difficulties could arise if there were severe unemployment in West Germany?

## 12.2 The organisational structure of a trade union

### 1 The factory floor

The workers in a particular union in each part of the factory are represented by a shop steward. He is elected by the workers each year and, although he continues with his job, he devotes much of his time to his duties as shop steward. He looks after all the interests of the workers and helps to solve any problems they may have in the factory.

Much of his time is taken up 'trouble-shooting', e.g. a worker may object to being moved by the foreman from one job to another and the shop steward will be called in to represent the worker in discussions with the management.

In very large factories, one senior shop steward will act as convenor of meetings for all the shop stewards from that union, and there may be a convenor of meetings for all the shop stewards from all the unions represented in the firm. The shop stewards and management frequently work out together the application of wage negotiations agreed at national level.

In most large firms, representatives of management and shop stewards meet from time to time as a Consultative Committee to discuss matters such as conditions of work, safety regulations, social facilities, and dates of holidays.

1 Write an imaginary diary of a day in the life of a shop steward.

### 2 The structure of a union

This varies from one union to another, but the following is fairly typical.

From time to time all the members of a union in a particular area will meet together – the branch or 'lodge' meeting. This local meeting will elect representatives to a district committee. Sometimes the local lodge or district has a permanent headquarters and paid full-time staff.

The local lodge or district elects representatives to the national committee, which usually has a full-time president and general secretary. The national committee is the most powerful force in controlling the affairs of the union, and many national presidents and secretaries are well known names.

A local branch union meeting

The national committee elects representatives to the general council of the Trades Union Congress (TUC).

The local branch also elects representatives to a local district meeting of all trade unions – the Trades Council – which in turn elects representatives to a national Federation of Trades Councils.

The annual meeting of the Trades Union Congress

2 Draw a diagram representing clearly the structure of a union and its various connections with other organisations.

3 The Trades Union Congress and the Confederation of British Industry

Most trade unions in Britain are affiliated to the Trades Union Congress (TUC), which therefore represents some ten million members. The TUC represents the trade-union movement in discussions with the government, employers, and unions overseas.

Employers too have their organisations, usually on an industrial basis, e.g. many of the employers in the engineering industry belong to the Engineering Employers Association. These associations too have district and national committees. Most employers associations are affiliated to the Confederation of British Industries (CBI) which represents the employers' point of view in talks with government, trade unions, and other organisations.

3 Suppose a government minister wished to introduce legislation in Parliament to make it compulsory for firms to give details of their costs and profits to their employees. What discussions would probably take place before he drafted the Bill for Parliament?

4 Wage negotiations

In most industries, wage negotiations are very complicated.

Many industries have a Joint National Council which consists of representatives of the union national committees and representatives of the national committee of the appropriate employers association. The Joint National Council negotiates a basic wage structure which is further modified by negotiations at factory level.

A member of your local Trades Council will be invited to the school to talk to you, and you should question him in detail about machinery for negotiating wages and settling disputes.

You will then write an account of the machinery which is used in an important local industry.

## 12.3 Industrial disputes

In all industries, differences of opinion occur between workers and management and among the workers themselves. Some of these differences concern pay, but many are concerned with other matters, such as the number of men required to operate a machine, or alleged victimisation.

In many factories a 'disputes procedure' has been established whereby a problem is discussed by trade-union and management representatives at a number of levels until a solution is found. If a solution is not found easily, the workers may take some form of industrial action.

Your teacher will show you a film about two disputes in a Coventry firm.

Imagine that you work in a factory where a dispute has occurred over the manning of a new machine. Six men were required to man the old machine, but the manager maintains that only four men are required for the new machine. The workers object.

Divide into groups to discuss the way in which the problem might be dealt with. If, as workers, you are not happy about the solution proposed, what forms of industrial action might you take?

Sometimes disputes lead to strike action. If the strike has the support of the union headquarters it is called an 'official' strike, but if the men stop work without union support the strike is called 'unofficial', and the men do not receive strike pay from the union.

From the workers' point of view, many factors will affect the likely success of a strike. Ideally, the workers should have official union support, be united, have sufficient union funds to pay strike pay over a long period if necessary, and provide a product or service the lack of which will produce immediate hardship to a large number of people.

Document 12B gives the background to two industrial disputes. Discuss whether the workers are likely to be successful in achieving their demands.

The effects of industrial action can be widespread. What would be the effects of the disputes described in Document 12B?

Document 12C shows the strike record of this country and compares it with that of other countries.

Can you account for the increase in the number of days lost through strikes in Britain?

Can you account for the relative strike records of various countries?

## 12.4 Industrial-relations problems

From watching TV news items and from the work you did on previous sections of this course you will have learnt something about the kind of disputes which can arise in industry.

It is important that we should learn to look at problems from several different points of view, so in each of the following case studies you will act out a different part. When you have been told which character you will act, try to think yourself into being that person, and behave in the discussion as you think he or she would behave.

### **Case 1** A question of commission

Characters: Van driver
Union district organiser
Shopkeeper
Managing director of bread company

### Background to the case

The workers in question are van drivers who sell bread and cakes to shops. They earn a basic wage plus a commission based on sales. The more they sell, the more they earn. It has been the practice of the bread company to accept back unsold bread without charge. The cost of producing bread is rising, so the makers decide to charge the shopkeepers the full price for bread whether it is sold or unsold.

Shopkeepers have to be more careful, and order less bread. The take-home pay of the bread salesmen falls. The union district organiser demands that the management increase the men's basic wage to compensate for the loss of commission. The management refuse, saying that the present wage agreement has another year to run. The men come out on official strike.

*Van driver.* My wages have dropped by nearly £5 per week. I have a wife and two children to support, and £5 is a lot of money to me. The management caused the trouble by refusing to sell bread on a sale-or-return basis. My wages are being sacrificed to increase their profits, and I am prepared to stay out on strike for a long time to obtain the extra money.

*Union district organiser.* The management did not consult me at all when they changed their arrangements for selling bread, yet they must have known that it would cost my members money. I was suspicious about the idea of payment by commission in the first place, and I intend to obtain a high basic wage for my members as soon as possible. The management must learn to take the union more seriously.

*Shopkeeper.* I am receiving no bread at present, and I am in danger of going bankrupt. I have told the bread manufacturers that I will buy bread from another bakery if this drags on much longer, and I know some other shopkeepers who will do the same. The bread manufacturers were right to refuse to accept back unsold bread, because it did encourage wasteful ordering, but the union should have been consulted. Why should the van drivers suffer a drop in pay?

*Bread manufacturer.* It is true that we have made a mess of our labour relations here. We should have consulted the union. However, I object strongly to the union telling us what to do. I also suspect that they want to get rid of the commission element in the men's wages and want a high basic wage instead. This I will not accept. I am willing to compromise because I am losing business, but there are matters of principle at stake here which I don't intend to sacrifice.

### **Case 2** An unofficial strike

Characters: A worker
Shop steward
Union district organiser

### Background to the case

A dispute arose because a worker was moved from one department to another against his will. The union district organiser told the men to keep calm until he had settled the case with the management, but the shop steward was put under pressure by the worker who had been moved, a mate of his, and he called an unofficial one-day strike. A few of the workers did not come out on strike, and afterwards the shop steward and the other workers claimed that these workers ought to pool the money they had earned on that day with the workers who *had* come out. Most of the non-strikers agreed, but one of them objected to union headquarters. There is now to be a discussion between the worker who objected, the shop steward, and the union district organiser.

*The worker.* My wife has just had a baby, and I cannot afford to lose any money. The whole thing could have been settled by the union and, if the man who was moved hadn't happened to be a mate of the shop steward, there would never have been a strike. I am going to hang on to my pay, but I want the district organiser to know all about it to make sure I don't get victimised in the future.

*Shop steward.* This lad's a troublemaker. If I don't make him knuckle under on this one, I shall look a right fool and there's no telling the trouble I may have in future.

*Union district organiser.* The lad's in the right, but what good will it do if he persists? The other workers may get their own back on him later, and I shall be at cross-purposes with the shop steward and the workers who went on strike. Perhaps the best thing I can do is to say, 'The strike was unofficial, settle it among yourselves.'

### **Case 3** A demarcation dispute

Characters: Shop steward of the general union
Full-time official of the general union
Shop steward of the craft union
Full-time official of the craft union
Work-study engineer
Works manager

#### Background to the case

At this particular firm, all skilled work with plastics is done by members of a craft union, but packaging is done by members of a general union. Packaging normally consists of just wrapping the products in plastic sheet, but the firm are now starting to export to a country with a humid climate, and they have decided that the plastic bags must be heat-sealed. The management and the general union are happy that this job should be done by the packaging workers, but the craft workers' union are claiming that this is a skilled job and their workers must be introduced into the packaging department to operate the heat-sealing machine.

*Shop steward and full-time official of the general union.* The packaging department is a 'closed shop' for our union, and we would like to keep it that way. This job isn't really as skilled as the jobs the craft workers normally do, and our men could easily do it. But because it is a little more skilled than the normal packaging, we shall be able to get higher rates of pay than usual for it, and in future negotiations we shall be able to edge up these rates to approach those of the craft workers (after all, they are now claiming it is a craft worker's job). Then we shall be able to edge up the rates of pay of the rest of the packaging workers on the grounds that the differentials must not be allowed to grow too large. There is a lot in this case for us.

*Shop steward and full-time official of the craft union.* This job isn't as skilled as the jobs our men normally do, and to that extent we are demeaning ourselves by taking it on. On the other hand, as these new materials are introduced we have had to fight hard to keep our hold on the skilled jobs, and if we let this one go there is no telling where it will end. Surely we can persuade our brothers in the general union that it does no good to the workers as a whole to let the management get away with paying general rates for this job.

*Management team.* It suits us to have the packaging department as a closed shop – we have only one union to deal with. If we let in another union, there will be no end to the demarcation disputes. Also, we don't see why we should pay craft rates for a job which isn't all that skilled.

## **Case 4** A question of promotion

Characters: Skilled worker
Graduate trainee
Shop steward
Full-time union official
Personnel officer
Works manager
Managing director

### Background to the case

This firm have in the past recruited their foremen from among their skilled workers, and for the present vacancy there is a suitable candidate among these workers. He is very good at his job, he is respected by his fellow workers, and he would probably make a good foreman. However, he has no educational qualifications, and he probably wouldn't get any higher than foreman.

There is another man in the firm who is a graduate engineer and came in as a graduate trainee. He has done the training specified by the Industrial Training Board, and worked on the shop floor for a short time. He is a member of the same trade union. He is good at his job, and popular with the workers. The union have known all about him, but thought this was a new and better way of getting experience on the way to one of the 'professional' posts such as production-planning engineer or assistant departmental manager. They are dismayed to find him coming in as foreman, and they have objected strongly.

*Skilled worker.* I would quite like to be a foreman, but I am not very bothered. The pay isn't very different, and the responsibility is much greater. I am certainly not going to swot for any exams to get the job. The other chap's all right. Why all the fuss?

*Graduate trainee.* I would have liked one of the 'professional' jobs, but there are a lot more graduates about these days, and this is a step in the right direction. I am sorry for the other man, but that's life.

*Shop steward.* They are both OK by me and the rest of the workers. Who wants to be foreman, anyway?

*Full-time official.* There aren't many chances of promotion for our men, and it's important to keep them open. This graduate's all right, but he isn't really one of 'us'. Anyway, the non-graduate's got more experience, and the important thing is whether you can do the job, not whether you've got a bit of paper.

*Management team.* We must make it quite clear that we can promote who we like to whatever job we like, and this is a good case in which to establish the principle. Foremen jobs are becoming a great deal more responsible, and it will suit us very well if we can get into these jobs some sound and popular men with a wider horizon than the usual foreman: someone who when it comes to a crunch will be on our side, not the workers'.

## **Case 5** Consultation

Characters: Personnel manager, acting as chairman of consultation committee
Four representatives of management
Four representatives of workers

### Background to the case

The firm has gradually increased in size, and there have been a number of troubles which could have been avoided if the workers had been fully aware of all the reasons for the decisions which were made. The management have therefore established this consultation committee, which can discuss all matters except those relating to pay. It is not yet clear whether this committee is only advisory, or whether all their findings will be acted upon.

Recently the workers in one department agreed to shorten their lunch break so that they could leave earlier in the afternoon. The workers' representatives on this committee are now claiming that this matter should have been referred to this committee before a decision was taken.

*Workers' representative.* If this committee is to do any good, we must make sure that all matters of this sort are referred to this committee, and that our findings are acted upon. This particular matter has implications outside the particular department concerned, so there is every reason why we should have discussed it.

*Management representatives.* This matter concerned only one department, so there was no need for it to be referred to this committee. If every matter of this kind were referred to this committee, the delays would be endless. Also, we must get it understood that this committee is only advisory.

*Personnel manager.* This committee could do a lot of good in improving communications, but we must keep off dangerous matters like whether or not it is only advisory. It is best to let 'understandings' evolve. Also, I am not satisfied that the workers' representatives are in fact in close communication with the workers. I think they are keeping things to themselves, and see themselves as becoming a new source of power similar to the shop stewards. This would defeat the whole object of the exercise.

### **Case 6** Trade-union recognition

Characters: Works manager
Shop steward
Full-time union official

#### Background to the case

Because of high unemployment in certain industries, the government have instituted emergency retraining schemes for the workers made redundant. Nationally, the craft union has promised recognition to the workers trained in this way.

One of the retrained workers has now applied to this firm for a job at a time when there is at least temporarily some unemployment in the area, even in his new trade. The shop steward is maintaining that the vacancy should go to one of the apprentice-trained unemployed, and not to this newly trained worker.

Describe the attitude which each of the above characters might adopt, and write a summary of the discussion which might take place.

## 12.5 Job satisfaction

An adult spends nearly half his waking hours at work. For most people their job is their only source of income, and their standard of living depends on it. Nevertheless, people have very different attitudes towards their work, as you will see by reading the following case studies.

### 1 Bill Gregory

Bill left school at fifteen and took a job as a clerk in a small manufacturing firm. After a year as a 'tea-boy' he was given some more varied and interesting work, and eventually he was helping to deal with customers' queries and complaints. But when he was twenty-one he wanted to get married. He found he wasn't saving fast enough and he didn't see much chance of promotion, so he took his present job as a machine operator – 'for the money'.

He is now thirty-six, is married, and has two children. He lives in a small private semi-detached house and he has a car. He has spent a lot of time improving the house, and he has an allotment where he grows most of his own vegetables. He goes fishing with a club on Sundays. He says he is very happily married, and his wife has a part-time job as a shop assistant which brings them in enough to go on a package holiday to Spain each year.

He makes no secret of the fact that he does the job entirely for the money. He is often bored, and he day-dreams a lot. He misses the friendly contacts which he had in his clerical job. Although he is a union member, he has never been to a branch meeting. He is not a member of the social club, and he never sees his workmates outside work. The only people he recognises as friends are in the angling club, and the only people he visits, or is visited by, are relations.

## 2 Jenny Wright

Jenny Wright is a social worker in her mid twenties, married to a schoolteacher. She describes her salary as 'inadequate', and the hours she works as 'excessive'. She works in a large city, dealing with the old, the sick, the down-and-out, the dishonest. Her job is often depressing, and she worries about the effect that her experiences are having on her personality. Nothing shocks her any more, and her husband complains that she has become unsympathetic.

Jenny went into social work as a vocation, because she felt that she would be helping the community. She still holds this attitude to some extent, but admits that often she doesn't feel particularly useful, because the problems are so great and her efforts are so small. She enjoys the independence that she has at work, and enjoys making decisions. She sees the job as a challenge, and would not readily give it up.

## 3 Jack Belcher

Jack Belcher is a retired, self-employed grocer, and tells his own story.

'My shop was situated in a densely populated suburb of a large city. I became the owner of the shop in 1957, buying out my partner who retired. Even then I worked long hours – a minimum of 60 hours per week. In the early 1960's, competition from supermarkets badly affected my business. I sacked my full-time assistant and managed with two part-time assistants instead. I started to work about 75 hours per week, and had no holidays at all.

'I worked hard so that I could afford to educate my three children. I had little formal education, and I wanted my children to have a start in life which my parents could not give me. All my children have university degrees and are well-established in their careers. None works particularly long hours, and all have good salaries. Ill-health forced me to retire three years ago, but any sacrifice that I have made is worth it. My children will achieve things in life that have been denied to me, and that is all the satisfaction that I require.'

## 4 David Long

David Long is twenty-seven years old, and is unmarried. He is a clerk in the purchase invoice department of a large car factory. His job is to examine invoices (or bills) as they come in to the factory, check that the goods charged for have actually been received, and clear the invoices for payment. It is a routine sort of job. David says he 'doesn't mind it', but also admits that he could and should be doing something better.

His trouble, so he says cheerfully, is that he can't be bothered. He can't be bothered to get to work on time; he can't be bothered to dress smartly; he can't be bothered even to read the newspaper. He is completely unambitious, says he earns enough to live on, and declares that he would never work on the production line even though he could almost double his wages.

David enjoys life outside the factory. He watches the local football team play on Saturday afternoons. He referees football matches on Sunday mornings. He plays cribbage, darts, and dominoes expertly. He says that his wages enable him to do what he wants to do, and that he is perfectly happy.

Write a short paragraph on each of the four characters, explaining what motivates them.

Bill Gregory, in one of our case studies above, said that his job was very boring.

Bill is employed on a mass-production line. As the product (car,

Metal finishers working on a traditional car assembly line

Employees work in small groups at the Kalmar factory

refrigerator, etc.) moves along the line, each man does one very simple job on it – fits a wind-screen wiper, or brake light, or exhaust pipe. A relatively unskilled man soon becomes very proficient at his particular task, but also he may become very bored. Some people say that workers employed on this sort of job are more likely to go on strike just to get some variety out of life. Someone said, 'Most of us spend most of our lives doing jobs we don't really like to produce articles we don't really need.' Ought we to reorganise work so that many more people can have interesting jobs? Attempts to do this are called 'job enrichment'.

The Volvo motor-car company in Sweden has introduced a new experiment in job enrichment. The labour force is divided up into groups of about twenty workers, and each group completes one major stage in the production process, e.g. one group might install the complete electrical system.

The factory building is nothing more than a collection of production bays, and parts and components are moved from one bay to another by a system of electrical trolleys. Each group of workers has its own production bay. Workers swap tasks regularly, discuss the organisation of the work, and can transfer from one work unit to another work unit from time to time to do a different kind of work. The workers can gain some measure of satisfaction from their work, and take a pride in the cars that they are manufacturing.

Volvo have taken something of a risk. Their Kalmar factory cost 10% more to build than a conventional car factory. The production process will probably be more costly than the traditional production line. But Volvo expect to gain in the following ways.

1 Less absenteeism of workers.

2 Fewer industrial disputes.

3 Slower turnover of labour force – in 1969 Volvo had almost exactly one half of its labour force leave to find alternative employment.

4 Easier recruitment of new workers. Sweden has an excellent system of education, and most people enjoy a very high standard of living. It is not easy to find workers to perform dull, monotonous tasks in such a country.

5 High standard of workmanship, resulting in better cars. This should enable Volvo to save money on repairs performed under guarantee, and should boost the company's reputation for making reliable motor cars.

Volvo make the right sort of motor cars to make their experiment work. They make high-quality, high-priced vehicles. If the new production techniques cause prices to rise (which is doubtful), the reliability and reputation of Volvo cars should still ensure high sales.

Volvo expect the new production system to boost their profits in the long run. The company has strictly economic motives – it expects to produce more cars, more efficiently, and more cheaply. It expects to sell more cars. Other motor-car companies will be watching the Volvo experiment with interest. We may be on the verge of a revolution in the motor-car industry.

Both automation and job-enrichment cut out semi-skilled jobs. What would be the effect on the job opportunities available when you leave school?

## Document 12A *Membership of some unions, 1973*

| *Name of union* | *Number of members (October 1973)* |
|---|---|
| Transport and General Workers Union | 1 747 000 |
| Amalgamated Union of Engineering and Foundry Workers | 1 146 000 |
| General and Municipal Workers Union | 848 000 |
| National Union of Teachers | 274 000 |
| National Union of Mineworkers | 271 000 |
| National Society of Metal Mechanics | 43 000 |
| Prison Officers Association | 16 000 |
| Wallpaper Workers Union | 4010 |
| Cigarette Machine Operators Society | 400 |
| Military and Orchestral Musical Instrument Makers Trade Society | 158 |
| Wool Shear Workers Trade Union, Sheffield | 20 |

## Document 12B *The background to two industrial disputes*

### 1 Dock workers

The employers in the docks are trying to introduce machinery to handle the new container traffic. At the same time they wish to reduce the labour force in order to keep costs and prices steady. The dockers are striking to get better redundancy agreements – fewer dockers made redundant, and more compensation for those who have to go.

All the dockers are members of the same union. About a quarter of all the goods we consume come in from abroad, and about a quarter of what we produce is exported. Without the dockers, imports and exports would virtually cease. In an emergency the government could use troops to handle cargoes, but there is a possibility that this would lead to violence.

### 2 Post Office workers

Many Post Office workers are poorly paid, and they are striking for a particularly large pay increase. The strike is official, but the union does not have sufficient funds to give strike pay. They had hoped for financial support from other unions, but this has not been forthcoming.

Nearly all postmen and postwomen are on strike, but most telephone operators and engineers are still working, as they belong to a different union.

## Document 12C *Working days lost through stoppages*

### 1 Stoppages in years 1963–72

| *Year* | *Total number of working days lost through stoppages* |
|---|---|
| 1963 | 1 755 000 |
| 1964 | 2 277 000 |
| 1965 | 2 925 000 |
| 1966 | 2 398 000 |
| 1967 | 2 787 000 |
| 1968 | 4 690 000 |
| 1969 | 6 846 000 |
| 1970 | 10 980 000 |
| 1971 | 13 551 000 |
| 1972 | 23 909 000 |

### 2 International comparison of days lost through industrial disputes: days lost per 1000 employees

| *Country* | *1963* | *1972* | *Average 1963–72* |
|---|---|---|---|
| France | 770 | 290 | 325 |
| Germany | 140 | less than 5 | 54 |
| Italy | 1150 | 1680 | 1481 |
| Japan | 180 | 270 | 213 |
| New Zealand | 160 | 320 | 269 |
| Sweden | 10 | less than 5 | 44 |
| Switzerland | 50 | less than 5 | 6 |
| United Kingdom | 140 | 2080 | 576 |
| United States | 630 | 870 | 1232 |

# Making bigger profits 13

The directors of a firm have many aims, but one of these is certainly to make bigger profits. Sometimes this is because they wish to use the profits as capital to expand the firm, and sometimes it is to distribute them to the shareholders.

We are going to look at the ways in which, as directors of a firm, we might try to make larger profits, and then in Section 14 we are going to ask whether the consumer needs to be protected against any of the actions we might be tempted to take.

*"Well this is the space-saving car of the future, but how are we going to get people that small?"*

## 13.1 Value analysis

One way of increasing our profits would be to manufacture our product more cheaply. In industry, this process is sometimes called 'value analysis'. We examine our product and ask ourselves the following questions:

1. Are we making the product better than the customer really wants? For example, if we are manufacturing a pen-knife with a lot of 'gadgets', does the customer use all the gadgets? If not, we can make it cheaper by leaving off the ones which are never used. Another example: if we are manufacturing paper plates, it is no use giving them a surface finish which will stand up to wiping, because they are thrown away after use.

2. Can cheaper material be used for any part of the product?

3. Can any components be replaced by cheaper standard components? (Examine record-players in shops: you will find that most makes use the same record-changing mechanism.)

4. Would a minor change in design eliminate or reduce wastage of material during manufacture, or eliminate any manufacturing process? For example, a certain cooker used to be manufactured by welding metal sheets together; now a large section of it is stamped out of one sheet of metal, thus eliminating some very time-consuming welding.

5. Are all the surface finishes essential?

Example 1

A shoe manufacturer carried out a value analysis on a pair of women's holiday shoes, with the following results:

| | | *Saving* |
|---|---|---|
| a) | Shoe upper and insole: used less expensive material which passed the same wear test. | 3·78% |
| b) | Heel piece: material used to reinforce heel piece was different from that used for the insole; the new material was used for both. | 0·63% |
| c) | Lace: round lace used instead of flat lace. | 0·80% |
| d) | Eyelets: consequent reduction in size of eyelet. | 0·46% |
| e) | Outsole: change in process of moulding and cutting to give less wastage. | 9·85% |
| | Total | 15·52% |

Example 2

**1** At one time, stools in school laboratories were made entirely out of wood. Modern stools have a metal frame and a plastic seat. Describe the process of value analysis which led to this change. What effect would the change have in the factory where the stools are manufactured?

2 Carry out a value analysis on a typical wooden sideboard.

3 Carry out a value analysis on your own product.

4 In what way might a manufacturer abuse this process of value analysis?

**13.2 Expansion of sales**

Another method of increasing profits is to expand our sales. How can we expand? The obvious ways are (a) by selling more of the same product, (b) by starting to manufacture a similar product which uses the same raw materials (so that we can buy in bulk) and employs similar manufacturing processes (so that we can make economies in our production line).

Suppose we decide to manufacture more of the same product. If there is a good sale for it, we had better expand to satisfy the home market quickly, or some other manufacturer will cut in. So we invest heavily in machinery and set up a mass-production line. But suppose our product is durable or semi-durable, such as electric fires or carpets (as distinct from consumables such as bread or washing-up liquid); what happens when nearly every household has one, so that the market is saturated?

We have had to invest heavily to set up a mass-production line in order to prevent anyone else cutting in on our market, but, when the market is saturated, we have all that investment left on our hands.

There are several methods which we might use to help us out of this dilemma.

1 Persuading people to buy more than one of our product

For example, suppose we manufacture carpets, and families are used to buying a square of carpet for the centre of their main room. We could

Do you need a second set?

persuade them that they need wall-to-wall carpet, and that they need it in every room of the house.

## 2 Making our durable a little less durable

A trade journal reported some time ago that some manufacturers of refrigerators were not using the most durable plastics available at the price. The one used was likely to discolour and crack after a period of normal home use.

Rust marks on the wing of a car

The interior of a transistor radio

3 Making our product difficult to repair

If our product includes an electric light bulb, we could make the part which contains the bulb as a sealed unit so that, if the bulb blew, the whole unit would have to be replaced. By pricing the replacement unit at only slightly less than the complete product, most people would be persuaded to have a new product rather than have it repaired.

4 'Improving' our product

Suppose we manufacture hand-push lawn-mowing machines. We might

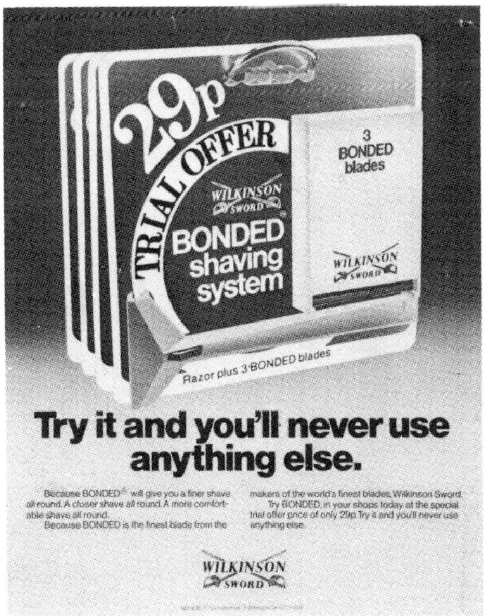

change to manufacturing power mowers, and persuade people they need these instead of their hand mowers. Since gardens are getting smaller and most men say they do not get enough exercise, this might prove a little difficult, but we could try it. Alternatively, we might introduce 'frictionless' bearings on our hand machines. The 'improvement' need not be of great importance.

5 Making fashion changes

Suppose we manufacture lamp shades. We could ring the changes on colours – 'this year's colour is pastel blue' – or style and ornamentation – very plain one year, very ornamental the next. Of all the methods for expanding our sales, fashion changes probably offer the most scope.

A boutique window – full of the latest fashions

1 Imagine you manufacture each of the following products. Devise ways in which you might develop your product.
   a) Tights
   b) Swimsuits
   c) Wrist-watches
   d) Do-it-yourself tools

   Then do the same for the product your class chose to manufacture.

2 Can you think of actual cases, not necessarily with these products, where you think these methods have been applied?

3 In your opinion, have any of these methods been used to expand the sales of motor cars? Explain in as much detail as you can. Read Documents 13A and 13B.

4 As a customer, how do you feel about the practices we have thought about? Find out whether there are any ways in which the customer is protected against these practices.

5 If these practices were pursued to any great extent, what problems might be raised by (a) the exhaustion of our natural resources, (b) the disposal of industrial and household waste?

### 13.3 Advertising

If we wish to expand the sales of our product (or, indeed, to sell our product in any quantity) we must be prepared to advertise it.

Advertising has two functions:

1 to provide information about the product,

2 to persuade people to buy the product.

We have seen in the previous section that a mass-production firm must keep demand for its product at a constant high level in order to justify the large sum of money spent on machinery.

Let us look at the case of a manufacturer of domestic heating appliances (electric fires, gas fires, etc.). He is faced with rising and falling demand depending on the season. This seasonal fluctuation of demand is superimposed on a gradually falling demand for gas and electric fires as more people fit central heating.

As the manufacturer, I might analyse the situation as follows.

What are the limitations of central heating?

1 It may be relatively slow in warming up a room from cold.

2 It may be slow to adapt room temperature to rapidly changing outdoor temperatures, so that there are several months during the spring and autumn when it can cause discomfort by keeping a room too cold or by making it too warm.

3 It may be relatively uneconomic to run under the above conditions.

Therefore as manufacturers we must develop our fire so that it will:

a) give out a lot of heat quickly when needed,
b) turn down to a relatively low level of heat production when necessary.

If we do this, then we may have a strong argument for persuading customers to fit a fire as well as central heating. If we emphasise the spring and autumn use we can stimulate demand at times when it would otherwise be slack.

Having developed our product in the way we think it will be most useful to the public, we must now put our arguments over in such a way that they will buy – we must advertise. At this stage we should probably hire a specialist firm to organise the advertising of our product. This type of firm is called an advertising agency, and the agency will provide us with an advertising campaign suitable for our product.

The important media which carry advertising are television, newspapers, and magazines. A thirty-second item on television costs about the same as a full-page display in a national newspaper, i.e. a half-page or quarter-page display is cheaper than a spot on television. Television is appropriate if we are aiming at all sections of the public, or the majority of the public, but if we are aiming at a particular section then it might be cheaper and just as effective to use one or more of the national newspapers, which are more selective in their readership.

1 Obtain copies of all the national newspapers and decide which of the occupational groups A, B, C1, C2, D, and E are most likely to read each paper (see Table 2A).

2 Which categories are most likely to buy fires in the way we plan?

3 Would you use television or one or more newspapers? If newspapers, which would you use?

4 List other ways by which a manufacturer might advertise his product. Would these methods be suitable for advertising gas or electric fires?

Having decided where to advertise, we must decide on the form of our advertising. We have decided to emphasise that our fire will warm a room quickly, and that in the spring and autumn it is more economic to use a gas or electric fire than central heating, because it can easily be controlled to adapt to varying external temperatures. Now we must do market research to find out whether these arguments will convince the public, and how we can put them across so that they will be convincing. We must also try to find out whether there are any other qualities the public requires in a domestic fire, and if necessary we must adapt our product to incorporate them.

Equally important, we must find out whether the public has any resistances to the purchase of fires. For example, if we manufacture gas fires, we might find that people think gas fires are undesirable because they use up all the air in a room, or because they give off harmful fumes. The difficulty in this kind of market research is that people may not be consciously aware of their prejudices. Advertising agencies often employ psychologists to investigate customers' motives (motivational research), and some of these try to discover unconscious resistances by using word-association tests – the psychologist says a word, and the customer says the first word which comes into his mind. For example, a test might run: apple . . . orange; fork . . . knife; gas fire . . . fumes. If there are any resistances of this kind, then we must frame our advertising to overcome them.

Having drawn up our advertisement, we must check that the public understands it, and that it has no unconscious implications of a detrimental nature. For example, one brewer decided to advertise a brand of beer as low-calorie – less fattening. But on investigation it was found that this implied to the average customer that his other beers were very fattening, and that the low-calorie brand had been in some way denatured, so that it would be less satisfying. None of these implications was much help to the brewer, so the campaign was dropped.

Obviously we must direct our advertising so that not only does the customer go to the gas-board showroom to buy a fire, but when he gets there he buys *our* fire and not that of one of our competitors. So, having found out what the customer desires most in a gas fire, we must create the impression that our fire has it, and by implication the others do not. This is called creating the 'brand image'. For example, our jingle might be, 'Northern – the spring and autumn fire – and for the British summer too!'

To make sure of our effect, we should have literature which emphasises the important features from our advertising on display at the point of sale in the showroom.

Since we are hoping to sell fires in addition to central heating, we might advertise in the trade magazine for heating engineers, suggesting that they might push our product in return for a suitable commission on sales. It is important to co-ordinate all aspects of the marketing operation.

Advertisements appeal in a variety of ways

5 Give examples of 'images' for (a) cigarettes, (b) cars.

6 Give examples of products which you have resisted buying because you did not like the way they were advertised.

Now let us analyse the way in which advertisers use television and the newspapers at present, to discover whether the ideas we have formulated are in fact practised.

We will analyse the television commercials for a particular evening under the following headings.

A What is the duration of the commercial in seconds?
B Does the commercial give information about the product, or reasons for using the product, which seems reasonably reliable?
C Does the commercial make claims for the product which would be impossible to prove, or difficult to prove, or are meaningless?
D Does the commercial make claims which seem grossly exaggerated?
E Is the commercial designed to overcome resistances?
F Is the commercial designed to create a brand image?
G Does it use a jingle to do this (e.g. 'For mash get Smash')?
H Does the commercial seek to create, by implication, a mood of enjoyment (for example, implying that if you smoke our cigars you will feel happy all the time, or if you use our hair-spray you will feel gay and attractive)?

You will probably be surprised to find that each evening between five o'clock and eleven o'clock there are about 100 commercials each lasting from 10 to 30 seconds, so our exercise will require careful organising. It is suggested that you each make out a table like this:

| Time | Name of product | A | B | C | D | E | F | G | H |
|---|---|---|---|---|---|---|---|---|---|
| 17.00 | Peanut Treets | 20 | | | | | √ | √ | √ |
| | Teflon saucepans | 15 | √ | | | | √ | | |
| | PG Tips (tea) | 20 | | | | | √ | √ | √ |

You will then need to operate in teams. Each person fills in the time and the name of the product (which often comes towards the end of the commercial), and scrutinises the commercial for one of the aspects A, B, C, . . . which are ticked where appropriate as in the examples.

In the following lesson, each team can amalgamate its results. Items C, D, E, and H will probably require discussion.

7 How far is our idea that television commercials will be used mainly for products which are bought in quantity by most sections of the public borne out by your analysis?

8 Do you think that advertisers choose the time of showing according to the section of the public they wish to reach?

9 Are there more commercials at some times during the evening? Since there is a rule that commercials can be shown only at 'natural breaks'

in the programme, does this seem to influence the form of the programmes?

**10** Are there any commercials which are shown more than once during the evening? Are there any products which are advertised by two or more different commercials?

**11** Is there any kind of trade 'war' going on (for example, two soap manufacturers each taking a large share of the commercials)?

Now let us analyse the newspaper advertising. Obtain copies of the principal national dailies, and also of the local daily if there is one. Note the price of each, and find out the circulation. For each newspaper, measure the total area of newsprint and the area devoted to advertising. Look through the newspapers and classify the types of advertisement – you might decide on the following classifications.

A Products, e.g. cigarettes.
B Services, e.g. airways, car hire.
C Entertainment.
D Investment.
E Property for sale.
F Jobs vacant.

Measure the area devoted to each. Then complete the following table:

| Name of newspaper | Price | Circulation | Area of newsprint | Area of adverts | % adverts | A | B | C | D | E | F |
|---|---|---|---|---|---|---|---|---|---|---|---|
| *Times* | | | | | | | | | | | |
| *Guardian* | | | | | | | | | | | |
| *Daily Telegraph* | | | | | | | | | | | |
| *Daily Express* | | | | | | | | | | | |
| *Daily Mail* | | | | | | | | | | | |
| *Sun* | | | | | | | | | | | |
| *Daily Mirror* | | | | | | | | | | | |
| Local daily | | | | | | | | | | | |

For each newspaper, list the products advertised in panels of area greater than 16 $cm^2$.

**12** Is there any marked difference between the percentage area devoted to advertising in each paper? Is there any relationship between this and the price and circulation?

**13** Is there any marked difference between the types of advertising in each paper? If so, why do you think this is?

**14** Are the products and services advertised in the newspapers markedly different in any way from those advertised on television?

**15** Do the products and services advertised vary in any way from one newspaper to another? If so, does it bear out our idea that different newspapers are aimed at different sections of the public?

**16** Do you think people would be prepared to pay more for newspapers and magazines which contained no advertising?

We have now looked at advertising in some detail and seen how it fits into the overall concept of 'marketing'. The following questions are concerned with some other aspects of marketing.

**17** Suppose you are given the job of marketing a liquid detergent which you know to be more or less the same as those made by other manufacturers. Describe how you would go about it so that you would gain the largest share of the market.

**18** Go to your local supermarket, make a list of all the detergents and soaps, and look on the packet or wrapper for the name of the manufacturer of each one. You will find that each manufacturer makes several detergents and soaps. Why do you think this is?

**19** Suppose we had created a successful 'brand image' for a brand of clothing, and we were approached by a chain store who asked us to sell them the same article which they would then retail under their own brand name, but cheaper than the price at which we were selling it. Would you agree? Why might they be able to sell it without our brand advertising?

**20** It has been discovered by market research that very few customers in supermarkets go in with a shopping list: they shop on impulse.

Suppose we decide to market fresh fruit juice, and part of our campaign will be to promote impulse buying in supermarkets. Formulate the marketing campaign you would mount, giving reasons for all your decisions.

**21** In what ways do you think the use of advertising could be abused?

**22** Suppose we lived in a planned economy, where a central organisation decided what products should be manufactured, how much of each, and the prices at which they should be sold. Would market research and advertising have any uses? Might they be different in any way?

**23** When we were thinking about the marketing of the liquid detergent which was very little different from our rivals' products, we tried to find out what the public wanted, and to imply in our advertising that our product had these qualities but our rivals' products did not. Could the same techniques be applied to promoting a political party or a political leader at an election? Do you think there is any evidence that these techniques have been so applied? If they have, do you think this is in any way harmful?

**24** Are there any current advertisements which try to persuade people to save money or give it to charities rather than spend it on consumer goods? Which of these do you think are the most persuasive, and why?

Now formulate an advertising campaign for your own product.

# Document 13A *Rust*

(From the AA magazine *Drive,* autumn 1970)

**Rust – the price of apathy**

The creeping menace of rust is costing Britain's motorists something like £250 million a year. It is a massive bill by any reckoning. And there is almost nothing the customer can do about it. *Drive* investigates the causes, the costs and the cures of corrosion – and discovers startling evidence of just where the big savings could begin.

As far as car makers are concerned, rust isn't really a problem. They honestly believe – or make a very good show of honestly believing – that they do their best for the price and that their best is good enough.

Car owners know differently. They know it when the exhaust system rusts away after two winters or less; they know it when the first rust flecks begin to appear on shining bodywork before a year is out. AA engineers and car body repairers also know differently. They know that corrosion can put some cars in danger in less than six years, on the scrap heap in nine or ten.

In fact, the motor industry now stands to be criticised by an independent team of scientists and technicians, set up by the government to examine ways of reducing Britain's £1000-million-a-year national corrosion bill.

In its report, now on the Minister of Technology's desk, the sixteen-man Corrosion and Protection Committee will include evidence of the motor industry's high contribution to the nation's corrosion cost – and also its lack of interest, compared with other industries, in stopping the rot.

*Drive*'s own six-month investigation shows that the rust menace is yearly getting worse for the motorist – and that there are steps manufacturers could take to make cars last longer.

The motor industry claims that it would 'cost too much' to make a longer-lasting product and that, anyway, the public wouldn't pay.

This is hardly true. Savings of up to £100 million a year, or £8 for every car owner, could be achieved simply with pencil, paper and determination at the design stage – and at insignificant cost to the manufacturer. Using better materials, at modest cost, would increase those savings dramatically.

*Drive* also established in two separate surveys that motorists would pay more for cars that rust less. Underbody protection was twice voted top of a list of benefits and improvements that most car owners consider worthwhile at a price [see page 100].

At present rust costs every car owner in Britain at least £20 a year – £12 in body deterioration and £8 or more in exhaust replacements. It is an estimate that is considered to understate the cost rather than exaggerate it.

Rust is one of the main reasons why an £800 car is worth, at most, only £180 after eight years – and why most cars go to the wrecker's yard with many years' toil left in their engines. For good commercial reasons, the short-life car body and exhaust system are stratagems of planned obsolesence.

Policy aside, the cure is twofold: better design, which costs nothing, and better materials – which cost a good deal less than most manufacturers are willing to admit.

No matter how good the paint treatment they are given, cars haven't a chance. Mud and moisture, fed with road salt and aggravated by acid attacks from the atmosphere, are inevitably trapped under the wings, in box sections and in joints – almost everywhere that metal is joined to metal in spot welds and seams. Many of these rust traps could be eliminated, or at least lessened.

Dr Stanley Orman, who headed the Corrosion and Protection Committee's Secretariat, says: 'To design and build a car and only then think about how to protect it is a back-to-front attitude. Unless corrosion protection is part of the design philosophy, you cannot even begin to think about reducing the wastage that is caused.' Many of the corrosion traps are created by the designer trying to give his car 'eye appeal'. In producing an attractive car, he causes problems for the corrosion engineer – and, later, for the buyer he was trying so hard to please.

The advertisement below, setting out the benefits of long-lasting galvanised steel in car bodies, was one of a series planned by the British Steel Corporation to help improve its public image. The campaign was short-lived: the advertisements were withdrawn after pressure from within the motor industry. The copy that offended the industry said:

> 'Making an entire car body of galvanised steel used to be practically impossible. But with Zincote, all things are possible. You can shape it, you can weld it, you can paint it. It comes in 9 different grades. All of them strong. All of them corrosion resistant. But each of them has different characteristics which enable you to do things with it that you wouldn't have dreamed doing before. Zincote seals vulnerable underbody points, wheel arches, sills etc. against corrosion . . .'

The man who admits chief responsibility for 'killing' the campaign is Dr John Wallace, director of manufacturing engineering at the Pressed Steel Fisher body-building division of the British Leyland Motor Corporation. 'It would be impractical to produce a vehicle in the way they illustrated it' he says. 'It is no good leading the public along false lines'. Though upset, the BSC, anxious not to offend one of its biggest customers, agreed to terminate the campaign.

Exhaust systems that need replacing every year or two are a large chunk out of every motorist's budget, adding up to £75 million a year in Britain. It is the form in which the rust problem hits the motorist most often and most directly.

Yet it need cost no more than 8s. to 10s. in materials to treble the life of an exhaust system – a five to ten per cent increase in cost. The extra retail cost per car would be £1 to £2 10s. One of the most promising materials is aluminised steel with a protective aluminium coating on the inside and outside of the mild steel exhaust. It offers strong resistance to most forms of corrosive attack to which an exhaust is prone.

Other materials, such as stainless steel, offer even more substantial improvements, but at a much higher cost. Aluminium paint, which is applied to the outside of many replacement silencers, does not help at all.

The time when the motor industry itself raises the standards for exhaust systems is probably not far off – because while the replacement trade is lucrative and attractive, premature exhaust failures are beginning to rebound on to manufacturers: they can happen within the warranty period.

The unnecessary and misguided short-life exhaust philosophy is serious enough. But AA studies show that many cars are having a short life also in areas which are much more vital – in underbody and subframe sections.

Significant corrosion in these areas can occur in as many as one out of three cars aged from three to five years. It goes unnoticed by most owners, except where it is seen creeping over door sills, and cannot be economically cured once it has begun. The most obvious cure for Britain has already been proven in America and is relatively cheap and effective. It is also the cure which car makers seem least willing to adopt. It is to use steel that has been given a metallic coating of a type known to have high anti-rust properties. The most effective is zinc – and the most effective way of applying it is hot-dip galvanising.

A car underbody given a thousandth of an inch layer of hot-dip galvanised zinc and properly painted will last fifteen to twenty years without serious corrosion – about three times longer than existing finished car bodies.

Its use by the motor industry would be the biggest step forward, on a cost–benefit basis, that could possibly be taken. No other single step would do more to beat the rust problem.

The extra material and process costs are surprisingly low. Hot-dip galvanised steel, used in the stressed frame areas of the Austin 1100 underbody, which includes the sill and cross members, would add only 10s. to the material cost. In a Fiat 600, the extra material cost would be just 8s. 6d.

However, galvanised steel is more difficult to weld with the type of equipment now used in most car plants. Wally Elbers, chief body engineer at Fords, estimates that only 1000 welds can be achieved with a welding tip on galvanised steel compared with 3000 welds on ordinary steel. Other estimates are not so pessimistic.

Assuming a fifty per cent reduction in welding efficiency, only 17s. 6d. is added to the cost of building an Austin 1100 underbody and 10s. to that of a Fiat 600.

Senior engineers at British car plants make much of the welding problem when challenged about their failure to use galvanised steel. They protest too much. The problem has been overcome in America and in Germany – and here in the United Kingdom. Rolls-Royce, the only British saloon car to use some hot-dip galvanised steel on the underbody, is welded at British Leyland's Pressed Steel Fisher plant.

The extra cost for each spot weld is just one farthing on top of the normal penny. On a car like the Morris Oxford, which has about 980 spot welds in its underbody section, this represents an extra underbody welding cost of a little more than £1.

There would, however, be fairly substantial conversion costs on welding equipment as well as the need to find more electricity to run it.

In an effort to meet objections to welding difficulties, the British Steel Corporation developed a differentially-coated hot-dip galvanised steel. The zinc coating is thicker on the side that needs most protection, thinner where the steel has to be welded.

Dr Brian Hundy, director of research for Pressed Steel Fisher, acknowledges that it is probably the ideal material to use, but says that 'the steel industry can't produce it in sufficient quantities. We've been hearing about it for two years, but no-one can deliver it to us'.

Norman Makins, a senior BSC sales executive, has a different angle. 'The motor industry just doesn't want to know', he says. 'How can we build new plants to produce thousands of tons of material just on spec?'

One British manufacturer did, in fact, show a great deal of interest earlier this year – then backed off just as the BSC thought a contract was in the offing.

Undersealing of the black rubber–bitumastic type is only a temporary rust inhibitor; even the best can do more harm than good after two or three years by concealing rust that is slowly destroying the structural steel members underneath it.

Though hot-dip galvanised is undoubtedly the best form of steel for underbodies, there are other kinds available. Ford used 10 000 tons of zinc electroplated steel each year, then dropped it after a new 'electrophoretic' paint plant was introduced.

Wally Ebers defends Ford's decision to drop out of the zinc market by claiming that it was not compatible with the new paint process – and not necessary, anyway, because the new paint technique was so good.

Yet AA inspections of 40 000 vehicles a year show that underbody corrosion is still as serious a problem in Ford cars as in any other make.

Sensitive to competition from foreign suppliers, as well as to pressure from plastics, the British steel industry has made a crusade of producing better corrosion-resistant materials. They have made little headway with Britain's motor industry. Makins says dourly: 'The car manufacturer's reaction is not a desire to improve rust-resistance, but rather a demand that if a material does have better properties, it must not be more expensive'.

Dr Hundy agrees. When discussing plastic bodies, he said: 'Our criterion when adopting new materials or techniques is cheapness, not rust protection. If we also get better anti-rust characteristics, then that is a bonus.'

While it is in the underbody that improvements are most urgently needed, rust is not confined to that area. On many cars the bright trim attachments and light clusters are fixed to the body with fasteners made of a metal that is chemically dissimilar to the trim.

The result is bi-metallic corrosion – rust that arises from the inter-action of two dissimilar metals. Surrounding bodywork is quickly affected.

The cure, long known but adopted on too few cars, is to use plastic fasteners such as nylon. The extra cost is minimal.

In spite of its tendency to rust, ordinary mild steel is still the best material for the body structure of a car. It is a cheap, easily-worked metal that is simple and economical to repair and exhibits good energy-absorbing characteristics in accidents. But it is only as good as the protection it is given.

When mild steel is used for building cars, the most important step in the fight against rust comes before a lick of paint has been applied. The steel is degreased and then phosphating or some similar treatment is given as a rust inhibitor. The process also creates a good 'key' for subsequent paint.

The phosphate layer is a very important and effective one. The paint that an average car, at a cost excluding labour of £3 to £4 – provides some further protection and acts as a beautifier.

Certainly, painting techniques have become more sophisticated and more effective during the past five years (though paint blemishes still account for the highest proportion of warranty claims – £10 million a year for one company alone).

But unless the phosphated steel is rinsed very thoroughly before the primer paint goes on, some phosphate salts remain at critical joints and within eighteen months to four years may become the basis for an acid attack.

While the steel industry goes on fighting with ever more and more new permutations on the zinc theme, plastics are coming up fast. At present, they are economic only on small production lines – an output of about 140 cars a week is the maximum.

Ford's Wally Ebers believes that the plastic-bodied car is still twenty years away. Dr Hundy thinks it could be much closer – 'perhaps ten years'.

At present, and probably for the next decade at least, steel has the advantage of low material cost. A painted bonnet lid costs about £2 to make (£25 retail, with hinges and clips added). Of that £2 only about 10s. is the actual steel cost – one quarter of the total.

The cost of plastics is about three-quarters for material and one-quarter for handling and finishing.

But whether our cars are to be built from plastic or steel, the *Drive* surveys suggest that public pressure is mounting for cars that last longer.

Dr Stanley Orman, who has spent most of his working life studying the corrosion problem in several industries, says: 'The public only put up with rust in their cars because they think nothing can be done about it. The greatest need is to educate the buying public; then the motor industry will quickly follow.'

The Organisation for Economic Co-operation and Development, Paris, which reported last year on vehicle corrosion in Europe, gives an even more uncompromising judgment: 'Corrosion prevention is now one of the major problems facing automobile manufacturers . . . The primary responsibility for solving it remains with the manufacturer . . .'

## Danger ahead on Britain's dead-sea roads

Road salt, industrial fallout and humidity are the biggest causes of rust. Britain has them all in generous doses.

Salt, essential for clearing snow and ice, scourges car bodies the way Dead Sea salt scourges the body of anyone rash enough not to wash after floating in it. The amount used on Britain's roads has more than doubled in only three years. Twenty-five counties were able to provide *Drive* with accurate and detailed figures (see table) that show the density of salt on motorways and trunk roads now exceeds the level (thirty to forty tons a mile) at which American car manufacturers began to use galvanised steel underbodies.

In Kent, motorway salt usage exceeds 118 tons a mile; in Westmorland it is nearly 113 tons. The average for all motorways within the twenty-five counties is more than fifty tons a mile.

With incredible inaccuracy, the Ministry of Transport estimates that, on one million miles of motorway and trunk roads, an average of only 0·2 tons a mile is used.

According to ICI, who supply most of it, only 170 000 tons of salt were used in Britain in 1961. By 1966 this had risen to 800 000 tons, by 1968–69 to 1 300 000 tons and by 1969–70 to 1 600 000 tons.

To find ways of neutralising the corrosive action of salt, the Road Research Laboratory is currently carrying out a two-year programme of tests with a new series of chemicals. But as recently as last year an international road-study group reported: 'The corrosion inhibitors which appear to offer some chance of being effective are very expensive and their use would cause a considerable cost increase for de-icing the roads.' Some of Britain's airports use a mixture of polyglycol and isopropanol. It costs £35 to treat a runway 7500 ft long and 100 ft wide.

Industrial fallout can be almost as serious a problem in car corrosion as salt. Sulphur dioxide from factory chimneys is one of the worst: in 1965, 6 300 000 tons of it – equivalent to 9 800 000 tons of sulphuric acid – were discharged into the air. Many other chemicals also proliferate.

Humidity sharply accelerates the rate of corrosion once it rises over seventy per cent – and in Britain it is more often over seventy per cent than below it, especially in the winter months.

Sea roads

| County | 1966/67 All-roads average* | 1969/70 All-roads average* | 1969/70 Motorway | 1969/70 Trunk |
|---|---|---|---|---|
| Salop | 5·3 | | | |
| Northumberland | 10·9 | | | 57·9 |
| Bucks. | 9·2 | | | |
| Worcs. | 8·7 | | | |
| Mons. | 5·7 | | 107·0 | 24·3 |
| Northants. | 12·5 | | | |
| Cumberland | 9·8 | | 38·4† | |
| Derbyshire | 17·6 | | 3 | |
| Carmarthen | 1·1 | | | |
| Durham | 23·8 | | 61·7 | 72·6 |
| Staffs. | 10·0 | | 69·0† | |
| Banff. | 0·0 | | | 19·4 |
| Surrey | 9·0 | | | 34·2 |
| Westmorland | 5·6 | | 112·7 | 58·9 |
| Huntingdon | 5·0 | | | 18·9 |
| East Yorks | 7·2 | | | 46·6 |
| Herts. | 7·2 | | 58·5† | |
| West Lothian | 27·5 | | 36·1 | 31·3 |
| Sutherland | 0·0 | | | |
| Angus | 1·2 | | | |
| West Suffolk<br>East Suffolk | 2·4 | | | 68·4 |
| Somerset | 3·2 | | | |
| Kent | 7·8 | | 118·2 | 33·6 |
| Caernarvon | 1·4 | | | |
| Average for 25 counties | 6·7 | | 52·4 | 42·7 |

* The 1966/67 figures are based on mileages for all major roads, plus ten per cent of unclassified roads. The 1969/70 figures are based on actual mileages treated with salt as known or estimated by county highways authorities except where asterisked, when the ten per cent figure for unclassified roads has been adopted.

† Average for trunk and motorway roads combined.

**Motorists will pay protection money**

Survey 1:
postal questionnaire to 1075 AA members

Q. If you were buying a new car in the £750–£1000 price range, would you consider paying about £3 extra for any of the following additions or improvements? (Choose as many as you wish, remembering that each would cost £3.)

| *Improvement* | *Total %* | *Rating* |
|---|---|---|
| Underbody rust protection | 88 | 1 |
| Anti-theft device | 57 | 2 |
| Reversing light | 55 | 3 |
| Pair of fog lamps | 45 | 4 |
| Six-year silencer | 43 | 5 |
| Reflective number plates | 33 | 6 |
| Pair of spot lamps | 12 | 7 |
| None of these | 3 | 8 |

Survey 2:
interviews of 477 motorists

Q. If you were buying a new car in the £750–£1000 price range, would you consider paying about £10 more for any of the following additions or improvements? (Choose as many as you wish, remembering that each would cost £10.)

| *Improvement* | *Total %* | *Rating* |
|---|---|---|
| Underbody rust protection | 64 | 1 |
| Collapsible steering column | 59 | 2 |
| Dual-circuit brakes | 52 | 3 |
| Anti-burst door locks | 40 | 4 |
| Six-year silencer | 37 | 5 |
| Laminated windscreen | 35 | 6 |
| Reclining seats | 16 | 7 |
| Vinyl roof | 3 | 8 |

## Document 13B *The 30 000 mile shock absorbers*

(From *The Sunday Times*, May 1970)

Shock absorbers are among the most vital parts of a car – affecting its safety, roadholding and general reliability as well as comfort. But they are well hidden and few people ever check whether they are in working order. Currently, however, shock absorber manufacturers are campaigning through television, posters and leaflets to make people aware that absorbers are often badly worn after 30 000 miles. 'Worn shock absorbers are dangerous', says the publicity.

It seems rather extraordinary that manufacturers should publicise the speed with which their product can wear out. There is, however, as we shall see, a strong commercial motive. But even if the campaign is to the advantage of the motorist as well as to the manufacturers, there is one aspect of the situation which is omitted in the publicity: it is technically possible to mass-produce shock absorbers that would last for 100 000 miles.

The ordinary shock absorber is about a foot long and usually looks something like a bicycle pump with a ring at both ends. There are four on most cars and their job is to damp down the vibration that starts when the car hits a bump or dip in the road. In the trade they are known as 'shocks' or 'shockers'.

Why it is essential to get rid of worn shockers was demonstrated graphically on August 22, 1969. On that day SAMA (the Shock Absorber Manufacturers Association) took six three-year-old cars to the Motor Industry Research Association testing circuit near Nuneaton. There were two Ford Cortinas, two Vauxhall Vivas and two Hillman Minxes. One of each pair of cars was left with its original shock absorbers, and marked, in recognition of this fact, with a skull and crossbones. The other cars were fitted with new ones. Two days earlier, all six cars had successfully negotiated MoT vehicle tests.

For five hours, never travelling at more than 40 m.p.h., the cars went round the circuit, which is specially designed to give in this time the kind of battering a car would receive from 10000 miles of everyday driving on normal roads. By the end of the day, one of the Hillmans was virtually uncontrollable on corners, one of the Fords had a broken half-shaft, and one of the Vauxhalls had parted company with its exhaust pipe. All three cars that went wrong carried the skull and crossbones: the cars with the new shock absorbers came through unscathed.

SAMA had certainly proved its point. Three officers from the Hendon Police Driving School who had come along to watch said they would have booked the three bad cars for being in a dangerous condition.

Significantly, SAMA's demonstration of how troublesome its members' products can be after three years coincided with a drive by the manufacturers to sell shock absorbers as replacements and not just as original equipment for new cars.

One shock absorber manufacturer explained to us in terms of the small family saloon why this should be economically attractive. The manufacturing cost for each shocker – most cars have four – is £1·00. The car manufacturer, after lengthy bargaining, agrees to pay £1·05 each. But in the replacement market the mark-up is very much greater: the selling price to a distributor is often as high as £1·50. And by the time it reaches the motorist, its price tag will be reading at least £3.

The fact that not only the makers of shockers, but the garages which sell them, can do well out of the spares market is stressed in SAMA's promotional material for garages: 'Sell shocks on your accessory counter and catch the DIY motorist as well. It's bouncing business! A new pair of shocks can make more profit than a pair of spotlamps or a pair of tyres or a new battery.'

Nowhere has the effect of selling replacement shock absorbers shown up more clearly on a company's balance sheet than in the case of Armstrong Equipment, one of Britain's largest manufacturers of shockers. Until the mid-1960s, Armstrong almost totally ignored the replacement market. Its profits drifted around the £300000 to £400000 level, dipping in 1966 to £121544. Then Armstrong began to put more emphasis on the replacement market. Profits started to rise dramatically. By last year they had topped the £1 million mark, and two-fifths of all sales were to the replacement market.

It follows that if the SAMA campaign succeeds, and we all get into the habit of checking regularly whether our shockers need replacing (SAMA have recently brought out a machine to make the check), many more will be sold. There will be fewer dangerous cars on the road and the directors of Armstrong, and the other companies, will find their profits soaring as a result.

But it would be perfectly possible to fit longer-lasting shock absorbers in the first place. Armstrong told us it could make them for mass production cars if the car manufacturers wanted them.

A Dutch firm called Koni already makes shockers, which it claims should normally last over 100000 miles, to fit most car models; but except for very expensive cars they are not fitted as original equipment.

Koni and Armstrong agree that to fit long-lasting shockers would add around £20 to the price of a new car – including a far higher profit margin than the car manufacturers allow them. At the moment it costs upwards of £15, including labour charges, for a complete set of new ordinary shockers to be fitted in place of a worn set. If every car had two new sets of shockers during its life, the cost would be £30–£40 more over the whole period. So there would be a financial saving to the motorist if long-lasting shockers were fitted in the first place. And added to this we have the evidence of the experiment at the MIRA circuit and the testimony of the Hendon police officers that worn shock absorbers are dangerous.

The shock absorber makers argue that they are not responsible for this situation since they supply to the specification of car manufacturers who in turn have a natural interest in cutting costs. Indeed, until recently SAMA did not really know how well or badly its members' products performed. As one Armstrong official told us: 'The trouble is that no real research has ever been done. Because shock absorber manufacturers have in the past simply supplied what the car makers wanted, we never had any reason to do research. But now the replacement market is hotting up, we are beginning to examine how long our shock absorbers last.'

Enough is now known to suggest it would be quite feasible for car manufacturers to offer long-lasting shockers, at least as an optional extra on new cars. But according to the Armstrong official, resistance to change may depend on more than the present lack of customer demand. Of the reasons for the present state of affairs, he said: 'Partly it's because of the way our economy works. It needs people to spend money consistently to keep it going. Certainly it may be cheaper in the long run to produce cars with longer-lasting components. But, you know, it may not do the economy much good.'

# Consumer protection 14

In Section 13 we began to understand how manufacturers, for reasons which seem perfectly proper from their point of view, might take actions which look very different from the point of view of the person who buys their products in the shop – the consumer.

We saw that action needs to be taken to ensure that:

a) the goods which the consumer buys are of a reasonable standard, and that he is able to obtain satisfaction from the shopkeeper if they are not;
b) the consumer is not deliberately deceived by advertising;
c) the consumer is aware of all the choices open to him, so that he does not buy one product when a cheaper or better article is available elsewhere.

We shall now look at some of the steps which have been taken to protect the consumer.

## Weights and measures

As long as people buy and sell goods, there must be standard measures of length, weight, and capacity so that consumers are not cheated by receiving less than they expect. Some of our standard measures were the yard, the gallon, and the pound, but we are now 'going metric', i.e. our standard measures have become the metre, the kilogram, the litre, etc.

These weights and measures are supervised by local Trading Standards and Consumer Protection Departments. (They used to be called Weights and Measures Departments, but recently they have been given responsibility for more than this.) Inspectors from these departments check the accuracy of weighing and measuring devices; for example, scales, rulers, and tape measures in shops, the weighing of lorries and their loads, the measurement of a pint of beer, etc. Anyone who is found to be using inaccurate scales or giving short weight or measure can be fined.

The weight of prepacked food (can you think of any examples of prepacked food?) must be clearly stated on the package, and this must be in 'net' terms, not in 'gross' terms. In other words, the actual weight of the contents must be stated, not the weight of the contents and the packaging. Why should net weight be the most important one for the consumer? Even so, many consumers may be persuaded by clever packaging into thinking that they are getting more of the product than they really are; for example, bottles and jars of cosmetics may hold less than they appear to.

A Trading Standards Inspector at work

The law also insists that certain goods must be sold in specific amounts, for example tea can be sold only in 4 oz, 8 oz, or 1 lb quantities, and not in odd amounts which might make it harder for the consumer to calculate the price per ounce.

But there are still problems for the consumer; for example, suppose that there are three brands of toothpaste sold in a shop:

toothpaste A contains 135 cubic centimetres and costs 25p
toothpaste B contains 100 cubic centimetres and costs 20p
toothpaste C contains 125 cubic centimetres and costs 21p

Which of the three is the best value for the money?

Sometimes comparisons between brands are complicated further by the fact that some brands show the quantity in cubic centimetres and others may show it in grams. Thus it may not be easy for consumers to decide which brand gives the best value for money. A law has now been made to ensure that traders show the price of a standard quantity of the goods they are offering for sale (for example, 10p per kilogram or 8p per litre), as well as the selling price. This 'unit pricing', as it is called, will help consumers to compare the prices when the quantities of different brands of the product are dissimilar and difficult to compare arithmetically.

**Food standards**

Public health inspectors visit places such as factories, shops, and restaurants where food is prepared, to ensure that conditions are hygienic. It is most important that businesses concerned with the preparation and sale of food should observe rules regarding cleanliness, because of the danger to the consumer of food poisoning. For example, people working in food shops should not smoke, dogs should not be admitted, and deep freezers should be in good working order.

Any trader who is caught breaking the rules by the public health inspector can be fined.

**The British Standards Institution**

This is an independent organisation which sets minimum standards for many goods. The standards cover quality, safety, and suitability for use. The BSI tests products and, if they reach or are better than the standard set by the BSI, they are awarded the 'Kitemark'.

The Kitemark

The BEAB mark

The product will also be tested regularly after this award has been given, to ensure that the manufacturer is maintaining the standard laid down. Examples of goods that have standards laid down are crash helmets, car safety seats for children, and paraffin heaters. In fact these particular goods must pass the safety standard by law, and it is illegal to sell them if they do not. The Kitemark, therefore, gives the consumer some assurance that at least minimum standards have been met by the manufacturer.

The British Electrotechnical Approvals Board for Household Equipment (BEAB) is another independent authority which deals with the electrical safety of household equipment, basing its tests on British Standards. When it decides that a particular electrical appliance, for example a cooker, meets the standards laid down (especially for safety) it awards its BEAB mark as shown above.

Make a list of the goods which you see carrying

a) the Kitemark,
b) the BEAB mark.

**The Consumers' Association**

In 1957 the Consumers' Association was founded in this country and began to publish a monthly magazine called *Which?*.

The magazine contains detailed information about various products tested for such things as quality, cost, durability, and safety. It recommends 'good value for money' buys, and is critical of poor products. It therefore helps the consumers to decide *which* goods to choose.

*I'll wait and see what Which? says about them.*

The Consumers' Association also publishes specialist magazines such as *Money Which?*, *Motoring Which?*, *Handyman Which?*, and *Holiday Which?* Books are also published on certain other topics, e.g. *The Legal Side of Buying a House*, *How to Sue in the County Court*, *Coping with Disablement*, *Caring for Teeth*, and *Electricity Supply and Safety*.

Here is a list of some of the products which have been investigated by *Which?* recently: electronic calculators, oven cleaners, stereo cassette decks, electric irons, long-life light bulbs, fruit grading, cine projectors, tights, suitcases, toothpaste, detergents.

All the money which is needed to buy and test the products to be investigated comes from subscriptions paid by the Consumers' Association members. No money is received from industry or the government. Why does the Consumers' Association refuse to accept money from these bodies?

No free samples for testing are accepted from manufacturers – in fact the Consumers' Association buys the goods it tests anonymously. Why do you think this should be so?

Your teacher might be able to let you see some reports from *Which?* magazines, or else your parents might be subscribers. If not, you should be able to find the magazines in the reference section of the public library.

**The consumer and the law**

Until the end of the nineteenth century, the rule that was applied to a large extent to the consumer was '*caveat emptor*' ('let the buyer beware'), but, as the products that are bought become more complicated, the consumer has to rely more and more on the advice of the retailer. So the law has been changed in many ways in order to protect the consumer.

One of the most important laws passed was the *Sale of Goods Act* of 1893. This law can be and is used by consumers today. It states that the buyer of an article is entitled to compensation from the seller for one or more of the following reasons:

1 if the article does not correspond to the description the seller has given – for example, if the seller tells you that a refrigerator has a larger cubic capacity than is the case;
2 if the article is not of 'merchantable quality', i.e. if it was not working properly when it was bought and was not therefore worth the price paid for it;
3 if the article is not fit for the purpose for which it was sold; for example if a refrigerator's freezer compartment did not make ice cubes.

When action is taken under this law, the consumer deals with the retailer, not the manufacturer, as the retailer is the seller of the goods. Even though a defective article may not be the fault of the retailer, it is his responsibility. If the customer cannot obtain satisfaction, he takes out a summons for the retailer to appear in the County Court (which is a civil court, not a criminal court). The lawyer's costs, even if the customer wins the case, may be greater than the cost of the faulty article, so many people do not take action, and there are traders who take advantage of this situation. However, a very much simpler procedure for articles costing less than £75 has been introduced, and Citizen's Advice Bureaux will give help to consumers wishing to take advantage of it.

**The Trades Descriptions Act 1968**

This law was passed in order to make it illegal for sellers to mislead the consumer about goods being purchased.

1 If a trader makes an untrue statement, either orally or in writing, about an article or service he is selling, then he can be fined and/or put in prison. In other words a tradesman must not deliberately mislead you with regard to quality, size, when the product was made, or suitability for particular use. For example, if a shirt is described as being non-iron, this must really be so. In a nut-shell, therefore, false advertisements are illegal.
2 A trader must not claim that he has lowered the price of a product unless he has actually charged the old price for at least 28 days in the preceding 6 months. Only then could he show something like the sign on this page. It must also be stated if goods are shop-soiled.
3 Local Departments of Trading Standards and Consumer Protection are responsible for ensuring that traders obey the law.

A trader commits an offence only if he has *deliberately* given false information, but if a consumer feels that a trader is deliberately giving such information then he should contact the Trading Standards and Consumer Protection officers who have the power to enter shops, inspect goods, and take them away.

### The Fair Trading Act 1973

This law created a new office, that of the Director General of Fair Trading. His job is broadly to protect consumers from various practices which may not be in their interests; for example the way in which products are advertised, the methods of salesmanship used, and the way in which goods are packed for sale. He will have to collect information about all these sorts of things and make recommendations for action to the minister in charge of his department.

Find out

a) the name of the present Director of Fair Trading;
b) the name of the minister he must report to.

Incidentally, it is hoped that the Director of Fair Trading will get much of his information from the local trading-standards and consumer-protection departments.

### Live now, Pay later

We often have the choice of buying goods or services either by paying the whole amount immediately or by paying for them over a period of time which may be weeks, months, or years. One way of spreading our payments is known as *hire purchase*.

Few shops finance hire purchase themselves: they ask a finance company which specialises in hire-purchase lending to do it for them. The customer pays the shopkeeper the necessary deposit for the article, and the finance company pays the shopkeeper the rest of the money. The customer then pays his instalments, plus interest charges, to the finance company.

Why do you think that traders prefer finance companies to provide the money for hire-purchase schemes?

1 Work out the difference between the cash price and the total hire-purchase price of the goods shown on page 109.

2 Why should goods cost more when they are bought on credit?

When goods are bought on hire purchase, they do not legally belong to the customer until the last payment has been made. Up to this time, the customer has hired the goods, and the firm to whom the instalments are being paid remains the owner, and therefore the person who is *hiring* the goods cannot sell them to somebody else until the final instalment has been paid.

3 What could the owner of the goods do if the hirer fell behind with his payments?

Hire purchase can be abused by slick door-to-door salesmen who persuade people to buy goods they cannot really afford and then take them back

when the hirer falls behind with the instalments. In 1964 the government passed a law to protect the consumer against this. The law states that when an HP agreement is signed at home, or anywhere else other than at a shop or finance-company office, then the person buying the goods (the hirer) has three days to change his mind and write cancelling his agreement. But, even so, some salesmen now try to get the housewife to an office to sign the agreement.

Another form of instalment buying is known as a *credit sale*. Financially, this method is no different from hire purchase; the difference is a legal one. When something is bought by means of a credit sale, the customer owns the goods as soon as he pays the deposit or the first instalment. If he fails to keep up the payments, the trader cannot reclaim the goods without going to a court of law.

Over £2800 million was borrowed on HP in Great Britain in 1973, and most of this was for the purchase of 'consumer durables', e.g. television sets, washing machines, cars, etc.

**4** What are the advantages and disadvantages of buying goods by hire purchase or credit sale?

When goods are bought on credit, a rate of interest is charged, and this is generally high. For example, when *Money Which?* did a survey of interest rates in December 1972, it was found that, while a personal loan from a

bank cost 14–15%, HP loans could vary between 14 and 27%, and were sometimes even higher! Why do you think that the HP rates of interest are so high?

The shopper should also distinguish between the 'nominal' and the 'true' rate of interest. The most important one for the shopper is the true rate of interest, but he may not be told what this is. Some shops may show only the price of the goods and the amount of each instalment.

Why should the 'nominal' rate of interest differ from the 'true' rate?

The interest charge is calculated on the total amount of money which the buyer borrows and does not take into consideration the fact that, say, over a two-year agreement half the money has been repaid at the end of the first year. Interest during the second year charged is on the full amount of money borrowed, even though only half this figure has still to be repaid. Therefore over two years the true rate of interest is nearly twice the nominal rate of interest. So a consumer should always find out from the trader the true rate of interest.

# 15 A large international company

Your teacher will provide you with a booklet which describes a large international company; the example used will probably be Courtaulds.

You are to imagine that, at about the beginning of this century, the Courtauld family acquired the patents for a method of producing artificial silk, and set up a private limited-liability company on a site in Coventry in order to work this process. Using what you have learnt so far on this course, you are to describe how the firm might have expanded to its present size and constitution, explaining carefully the reasons for each step. It does not matter whether what you describe is the same as the real history, provided that what you describe is reasonably possible. Nor need you explain how every individual factory was acquired, provided you indicate the general line of development.

Why is it do you think that several divisions of the firm now have premises on the large Coventry site?

You will see from the annual report and accounts that Courtaulds owns a majority share in all its major overseas subsidiaries. Another British-based international company, Rio Tinto Zinc, which is concerned mainly with the extraction of minerals in various countries, is only a minority shareholder in its overseas subsidiaries. Can you offer any explanation?

If you were a director of Courtaulds, what lines of expansion would you consider for exploitation, particularly with regard to overseas subsidiaries?

Courtaulds manufactures a wide range of products, and many other large companies have deliberately 'diversified', sometimes into markets quite different from their original products. Why do you think this is?

Examine the job vacancies advertised in the national dailies and Sundays and in at least one local town newspaper. Draw up a chart showing how these jobs might fit in at various levels in a firm like Courtaulds. Using the careers guides which your teacher will provide, map out the careers of one or two people at various levels.

# Part 3 Allocating our resources—the choice before us

# Demand and supply 16

## 16.1 Characteristics of the markets in different products

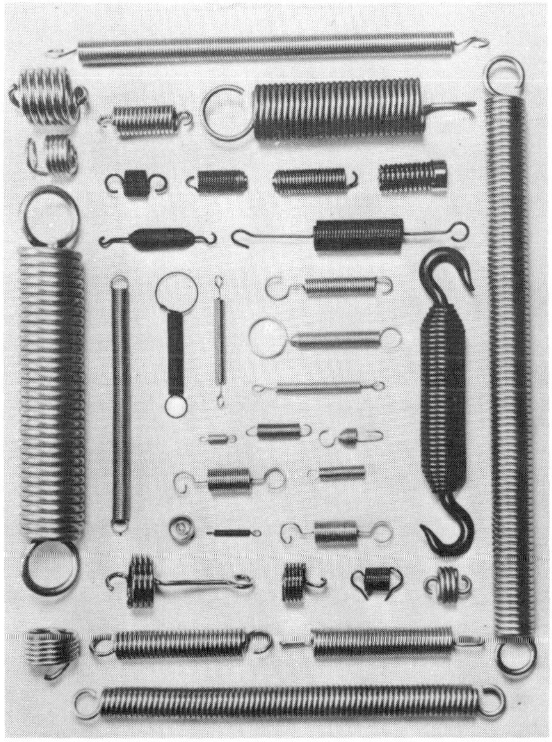

Some manufactured goods – such as ball-bearings, springs, and electric motors – are sold as components to other manufacturers, whereas others are finished products which are sold direct to the consumer, e.g. detergents, washing machines, and motor cars.

Finished products are sometimes further classified as consumables or consumer durables. Consumables are used up soon after purchase, e.g. food, drink, cigarettes, and detergents. Consumer durables are used over a period of time (but not for ever!), e.g. furniture, television sets, and cars. The distinction is not a rigid one, and items such as crockery and clothes might be classified either way.

The total amount of a particular commodity which all the customers together wish to buy *and* have the means to buy is called the 'demand'. Obviously this demand is influenced by various factors such as the price, and we shall be looking into this in more detail below.

A washing machine – a consumer durable

Packets of detergent – consumables

The total amount of a particular commodity which all the suppliers together are prepared to offer for sale is called the supply, and we shall be particularly interested in looking at how the supply of a particular commodity is adjusted to the demand.

As we saw in earlier sections, the term 'market' does not refer to any particular place, but to all the means whereby sellers and buyers come together for the purpose of making transactions.

### a) The market for detergents

One factor which determines the demand for detergents (as for any other product) is customers' habits and preferences. In this case it will depend on how often they wash their clothes. Over a period of time, of course, habits may alter. As more washing machines are bought, people may wash clothes more frequently. People may be persuaded by advertising that they need to wash their clothes more frequently. Both these influences would increase the total demand for detergents.

At any particular time we would expect that if we increased or decreased the price of detergents by moderate amounts it would have little effect on the demand – people's habits would remain the same, and there is no substitute for detergents to which they could switch if the price increased. The demand for detergents is therefore said to be 'inelastic' (or, strictly, 'price-inelastic').

If we look at Table 16A we see that the manufacture of detergents is concentrated in the hands of a few firms – mainly, in fact, Lever Bros and Proctor and Gamble. One reason for this is that detergent is a fairly standardised product which is used in large quantities, and therefore the costs are lower if it is produced in large quantities.

How do manufacturers compete with each other? Those of you who have done experiments on comparing detergents will no doubt have found that all detergents are more or less the same, and it would not be a matter of great inconvenience if there were only one brand on the market.

However, it is the practice of firms to make relatively minor differences between various brands, and then try to persuade us by brand advertising that their particular product is the only one for us. This is called 'product differentiation', and seems to be the main way in which firms compete.

A little research in the grocers will show you that in terms of price per quantity there appears to be little competition between the established brands. What seems to happen is that from time to time a particular firm brings in a new 'improvement', e.g. enzymes. After initial 'introductory offers', to get it established, the new brand is more highly priced. Then other firms bring out similar products, and a common price becomes established. It is easy for this to happen because there are only a small number of firms concerned, and often one firm acts as price-leader and the others follow suit. Later these brands might suffer competition from a new 'improvement', and they might be reduced in price in order to compete.

When earlier in this section we said that the demand for detergents is probably fairly inelastic, we were speaking of the demand for detergents as a whole. The demand for a particular brand of detergent will be much more elastic, because, if it is priced very much higher than its competitors, customers will switch to another brand – unless the manufacturer can persuade us that it has such excellent qualities that it is worth the much higher price.

If there were price competition, it would be very cut-throat. If a particular firm cut its prices, it might get more trade, but because the total demand is inelastic the extra trade must come from its rivals, who would in turn cut their prices, until no-one was making a profit. This is probably why firms behave on a 'do-as-you-would-be-done-by' principle.

### b) The market for margarine

The characteristics of the market for margarine are in many ways similar to those of the market for detergents, the chief difference being that margarine has a competitor in butter.

Until recently, the total demand for yellow fats (margarine together with butter) remained fairly constant for a number of years, but the demand for margarine fell whereas the demand for butter rose. This may be due to the fact that in Britain (but not, apparently, in the USA) margarine still has the image of being a poor-man's butter, so that, as standards of living have risen, housewives have turned to butter.

We would expect that the demand for margarine would be more elastic than the demand for detergents, because there is a close substitute in butter – if the price of margarine rises, customers will switch to butter; if it falls significantly they will switch from butter to some extent.

Again, the manufacture is in the hands of a few large firms who compete by product differentiation and brand advertising rather by charging a lower price than their competitors.

### c) The market for washing machines

Washing machines are consumer durables, so we would expect the demand to be determined not only by the washing habits of customers, but by how many have been sold already. You might like to think about whether firms try to change this situation by the kind of marketing methods we discussed in Section 13.

We would expect the demand for washing machines to be fairly elastic – if the manufacturers can lower the price, it will bring washing machines within the purchasing power of less-wealthy people, and therefore they can sell more.

This being the case, we might expect that there would be price competition, though this would not be so cut-throat as with detergents for example. Experience shows, however, that competition among British makes is again mainly by product differentiation and brand advertising, although there is often some price competition between retailers in the same area. How do you explain that British machines sell in the face of competition from cheaper Italian machines such as Indesit?

### d) The market for beef

The characteristics of the market for beef are very different from those of the other products we have been considering.

In the first place, we would expect the demand to be very elastic, because there are close substitutes in lamb, pork, poultry, and fish.

Secondly, there are many farmers who supply beef cattle, which are sold to butchers by auction, so that the price is very sensitive to changes in demand and supply. If the demand is greater than the supply, auction prices will be high – but not too high or consumers will switch to some other meat. If the supply is greater than the demand, prices will fall – but not too low or consumers will switch from other meats. Nevertheless, there will be greater fluctuations in the price of beef than in that of, say, detergents.

1 In a manner similar to the examples above, describe what you think are the characteristics of the markets for (a) instant coffee, (b) petrol, (c) vacuum cleaners, and (d) eating apples.

## 16.2 Price competition

We see from Table 16A that for many products the market is dominated by a few large firms, and in the previous section we noted that these firms rarely compete directly by cutting prices, especially where the demand is inelastic. What is to prevent these firms from unofficially agreeing a price which will give them very large profits?

The basic reason is said to be competition, or fear of competition. If profits were high on product X then other firms which were not making such high profits on other products would start to make product X and sell it at a slightly lower price, and this would happen until the level of profits came down to a 'normal' level.

Thus when it was thought that Yeoman and Smash were making high profits from instant mashed potato, retailers such as Sainsbury, Tesco and Fine Fare entered the market with their own-label brands at lower prices and soon took a quarter of the market. Similarly, the Metal Box Company, who have a near-monopoly of tin cans for food and drink, told the Monopolies Commission that their profit was fixed by the difference between the cost at which they could manufacture the cans and the cost at which their large customers would be able to manufacture the cans for themselves.

1 How do firms try to maintain a higher price despite potential competition from new entrants to the market?

2 In order to start up production in competition, a firm needs more capital. What means exist for firms to obtain new capital?

3 Why will there be some delay while a firm changes from manufacturing an obsolete product to manufacturing a very different product?

4 If a government felt that there was not sufficient competition among firms in this country to keep the price of a particular product down to a reasonable level, what steps might it take?

5 If a firm were making very high profits, it would be expected to show up as a high profit as a percentage of capital employed. Figures for some large firms are given in *The Times 1000*. On the basis of these, is there any evidence that the large firms which dominate some industries use their position to make 'excessive' profits?

### 16.3 The changing pattern of demand

Consumer preferences change over a period of time, and obviously firms try to change them by advertising. Some experts have maintained that large firms can get us to buy pretty well whatever they choose to make, but read Document 16A and decide how far you think they can go in this.

An important reason for changes in demand is the invention of new products. The demand for wool and cotton declined because of the invention of synthetic fibres such as Nylon and Terylene.

Another reason is population changes. If there is an increase in the birth rate, this will show itself first in an increased demand for baby foods etc., later in a greater demand for teenage products, and finally in a greater demand for housing and household goods.

Change in real income (i.e. allowing for inflation) is another important cause of change in demand, and this will affect different products in different ways. If everyone in the country becomes more affluent, we would not expect them to buy a lot more potatoes and bread, but we would expect them to buy other types of food and more products such as washing machines and cars.

Changes in demand caused by changes in personal income will depend on the way in which the additional income is distributed. If it goes to those who have relatively low incomes it will probably increase the demand for mass-produced non-essential goods such as the cheaper radios, tape-recorders, etc. If it goes to those who already have high incomes, it will alter the demand for a different range of products.

The demand for some products affects the demand for others in a complementary way; thus an increase in the number of cars will increase the demand for petrol. These products are sometimes said to be in joint demand.

1 Look at Table 16B. What are the main items for which demand has fallen? What explanation can you offer?

2 What are the main items for which demand has risen? What explanation can you offer?

## 16.4 How the market responds to the changing pattern of demand

There are a variety of different situations which can arise because of the changing pattern of demand. We shall look at two or three of these.

a) The supply may be greater than a falling demand, so that firms are not able to sell all their production.

In the long run, some of the firms must close down, and the capital and labour be moved to other industries, but this is obviously a situation which is resisted by all concerned: the shareholder and managers will lose money, and the workers will lose their jobs. The workers may be unable to find other jobs in the same trade in the same part of the country, or in any other part of the country. Unemployment which results from this cause is sometimes called 'structural' unemployment. There may be jobs in the same trade in other parts of the country, but there is the difficulty and expense of moving to consider. Those who own houses will have difficulty in selling in an area which has increasing unemployment, and those in council houses are in an even worse position. We referred to this problem of 'geographical' unemployment in Section 10.2; we shall be looking at other causes of unemployment in Section 18.

Because of the way in which new inventions are altering the pattern of demand, many people can expect to have to change jobs at least once during their working life. In order to make this easier, governments have introduced redundancy payments and unemployment benefit which, for a time at least, is related to the earnings in the last job. Advice is available through the employment exchange, and there are government retraining schemes for those who need to learn new trades.

1 How do firms try to resist a falling demand? (Refer to Section 13.)

b) The supply may not be equal to a rising demand.

We might expect that the immediate response to this situation would be a rise in price, but we saw in Section 16.1 that where the market is dominated by a few large firms this is usually not so. One immediate response might be less advertising, which is of course equivalent to an increase in profits just as much as is raising the price. Other responses with consumer durables such as cars might be longer delivery dates and poorer service.

What happens in the long term depends on many factors. In some cases, increased output enables firms to cut the cost per article and therefore make larger profits without raising the price, e.g. the oil industry with larger tankers and larger refineries. The larger profits are used to repay bank loans which were raised to finance the expansion, and to provide funds for further expansion. (In 1973, finance for the expansion of industry came from retained profits 46%, bank loans 32%, government grants etc. 20%, the Stock Exchange 2%.)

In other cases, prices may rise steeply, and this is particularly true of raw materials. For example, if the demand for copper exceeds the supply, the price on the world market will rise rapidly. This has two effects: it encourages consumers to try to find cheaper substitutes, thus decreasing demand, and it makes the mining of low-grade ores a more profitable proposition, thus increasing the supply. Thus the price mechanism helps to ensure the efficient allocation of resources and adjust supply to demand.

**2** Why might firms respond to increased demand by spending less on advertising rather than by increasing the price?

**3** Explain as fully as you can who decides how the market will respond to changes in demand. (Refer to Sections 9 and 15.)

**4** What would you expect to be the short-term and long-term effects of a rise in the demand for beef?

**5** a) What would you expect to be the effect of a rise in the price of oil relative to the price of coal, gas, and electricity?

b) A government might try to keep down the cost of oil to the consumer by a subsidy, i.e. by paying part of the cost of production directly to the producer, from taxes. What would be the effect of a subsidy on oil?

**6** Which of these decisions are made on the basis of choices by individuals as indicated by how they spend their money?

a) That more sweets or more cigarettes will be produced?
b) To produce a car with shock absorbers which last 30 000 miles or produce a car with shock absorbers which last 100 000 miles?
c) To produce more beer and cigarettes, or more roads?
d) Which postal service to use?
e) To have more hospital places or more university places?

### 16.5 The alternative of a planned economy

We have seen that in our 'market' economy the way in which resources are allocated to produce what the consumer demands is achieved mainly through the prices and profits mechanism. There are limitations to this, and we shall be looking at these in Section 17.

However, we have become aware that the operation of the market economy can lead to a number of consequences which we might consider to be undesirable, and we must consider whether there are any other ways in which resources could be allocated?

You may know that in Communist countries the raw materials, factories, and capital are all owned by the State, and the way in which resources are allocated to the production of various types of goods is decided by government planning.

1 What will the planners need to know in order to do their planning?

2 Suppose it is decided that 100 articles 'X' are required each week.

You are the manager who is told to set up a factory to do this. You must calculate your needs in the way of machinery and workers, and these will be provided. If you do not meet your target, you will be transferred to a much lower-paid job. You calculate that, provided there are no breakdowns or other disruptions, you would require either 2 type-A machines, 10 type-B machines and 100 workers, or 1 type-A machine, 15 type-B machines and 75 workers. What will you ask for to *ensure* that you meet your target?

3 Now suppose you are the owner/manager of the same factory under a market economy. The annual cost of type A is £1000, type B £10000, and a worker £1000. In what way will you organise your factory?

4 In what way might resources be 'wasted' in a planned economy which would not happen, or not be so likely to happen, in a market economy?

In what way do you consider resources to be 'wasted' in a market economy which would not happen, or not be so likely to happen, in a planned economy?

## Table 16A *Percentage of total sales of various commodities accounted for by the five leading firms in each trade 1968.* (Census of Production, 1968)

| *Commodity* | *Percentage* | *Commodity* | *Percentage* |
|---|---|---|---|
| Bread | 77·3 | Women's outer clothes | 20·1 |
| Cereals | 93·5 | Upholstered furniture | 17·3 |
| Bacon | 56·9 | Other furniture | 15·0 |
| Fish (frozen) | 91·1 | Cars | 99·2 |
| Butter | 78·4 | TV | 92·7 |
| Margarine | 93·8 | Radios | 74·7 |
| Sugar | 99·3 | Record players | 75·7 |
| Vegetables (frozen) | 97·1 | Records | 95·4 |
| Beer | 64·4 | Cookers | 85·9 |
| Whisky | 91·0 | Vacuum cleaners | 94·5 |
| Cigarettes | 99·9 | Washing machines | 86·9 |
| Other tobacco | 98·1 | Soap | 80·1 |
| Petrol | 97·5 | Detergents | 79·9 |
| Men's outer clothes | 37·6 | | |

# Table 16B (from *National Income and Expenditure 1963–73*)

## Consumers' expenditure at 1970 prices

£ million

| | 1962 | 1963 | 1964 | 1965 | 1966 | 1967 | 1968 | 1969 | 1970 | 1971 | 1972 |
|---|---|---|---|---|---|---|---|---|---|---|---|
| Food (household expenditure): | | | | | | | | | | | |
| Bread and cereals | 852 | 866 | 857 | 852 | 838 | 837 | 828 | 816 | 822 | 795 | 774 |
| Meat and bacon | 1,684 | 1,702 | 1,689 | 1,684 | 1,716 | 1,731 | 1,736 | 1,752 | 1,791 | 1,793 | 1,754 |
| Fish | 221 | 218 | 232 | 233 | 229 | 232 | 228 | 221 | 213 | 199 | 206 |
| Oils and fats | 258 | 254 | 258 | 256 | 262 | 260 | 259 | 264 | 267 | 262 | 247 |
| Sugar, preserves and confectionery | 619 | 606 | 595 | 608 | 615 | 620 | 610 | 590 | 597 | 605 | 625 |
| Dairy products | 848 | 858 | 881 | 881 | 886 | 894 | 909 | 908 | 924 | 957 | 971 |
| Fruit | 331 | 333 | 354 | 353 | 364 | 346 | 363 | 365 | 365 | 378 | 371 |
| Potatoes and vegetables | 620 | 639 | 675 | 683 | 707 | 741 | 749 | 755 | 766 | 771 | 785 |
| Beverages | 326 | 337 | 352 | 345 | 359 | 372 | 378 | 385 | 404 | 396 | 398 |
| Other manufactured food | 172 | 181 | 187 | 186 | 194 | 195 | 200 | 208 | 216 | 203 | 202 |
| Total | 5,931 | 5,994 | 6,080 | 6,081 | 6,170 | 6,228 | 6,260 | 6,264 | 6,365 | 6,359 | 6,333 |
| Alcoholic drink: | | | | | | | | | | | |
| Beer | 1,054 | 1,064 | 1,113 | 1,122 | 1,158 | 1,196 | 1,235 | 1,309 | 1,355 | 1,419 | 1,454 |
| Spirits | 635 | 468 | 508 | 491 | 512 | 524 | 559 | 531 | 620 | 663 | 763 |
| Wines, cider and perry | | 220 | 248 | 242 | 261 | 293 | 325 | 318 | 336 | 390 | 444 |
| Total | 1,689 | 1,752 | 1,869 | 1,855 | 1,931 | 2,013 | 2,119 | 2,158 | 2,311 | 2,472 | 2,661 |
| Tobacco: | | | | | | | | | | | |
| Cigarettes | 1,498 | 1,555 | 1,526 | 1,468 | 1,524 | 1,528 | 1,524 | 1,505 | 1,504 | 1,427 | 1,514 |
| Other | 221 | 219 | 226 | 220 | 218 | 224 | 220 | 218 | 216 | 231 | 234 |
| Total | 1,719 | 1,774 | 1,752 | 1,688 | 1,742 | 1,752 | 1,744 | 1,723 | 1,720 | 1,658 | 1,748 |
| Housing: | | | | | | | | | | | |
| Rent, rates and water charges | 2,784 | 2,843 | 2,888 | 2,965 | 3,044 | 3,129 | 3,236 | 3,317 | 3,396 | 3,464 | 3,547 |
| Maintenance, repairs and improvements by occupiers | 480 | 527 | 536 | 576 | 602 | 661 | 698 | 742 | 737 | 742 | 728 |
| Total | 3,264 | 3,370 | 3,424 | 3,541 | 3,646 | 3,790 | 3,934 | 4,059 | 4,133 | 4,206 | 4,275 |
| Fuel and light: | | | | | | | | | | | |
| Coal and coke | 574 | 574 | 518 | 512 | 488 | 452 | 427 | 408 | 364 | 307 | 263 |
| Electricity | 474 | 514 | 518 | 547 | 562 | 581 | 610 | 640 | 663 | 681 | 724 |
| Gas | 196 | 208 | 214 | 237 | 263 | 287 | 318 | 355 | 381 | 409 | 451 |
| Other | 75 | 82 | 74 | 75 | 74 | 73 | 77 | 81 | 87 | 85 | 97 |
| Total | 1,319 | 1,378 | 1,324 | 1,371 | 1,387 | 1,393 | 1,432 | 1,484 | 1,495 | 1,482 | 1,535 |
| Clothing: | | | | | | | | | | | |
| Footwear | 381 | 393 | 407 | 420 | 414 | 415 | 425 | 432 | 449 | 454 | 470 |
| Other clothing: | | | | | | | | | | | |
| Mens' and boys' wear | 608 | 636 | 662 | 689 | 690 | 686 | 717 | 720 | 748 | 746 | 788 |
| Women's, girls' and infants' wear | 1,164 | 1,214 | 1,267 | 1,317 | 1,321 | 1,342 | 1,413 | 1,425 | 1,469 | 1,484 | 1,598 |
| Total | 2,153 | 2,243 | 2,336 | 2,426 | 2,425 | 2,443 | 2,555 | 2,577 | 2,666 | 2,684 | 2,856 |
| Durable goods: | | | | | | | | | | | |
| Motor cars and motor cycles, new and secondhand | 568 | 747 | 866 | 836 | 833 | 900 | 959 | 855 | 969 | 1,281 | 1,559 |
| Furniture and floor coverings | 610 | 634 | 686 | 713 | 698 | 691 | 729 | 692 | 683 | 704 | 774 |
| Radio, electrical and other durable goods | 515 | 581 | 589 | 594 | 575 | 615 | 649 | 621 | 670 | 745 | 915 |
| Total | 1,693 | 1,962 | 2,141 | 2,143 | 2,106 | 2,206 | 2,337 | 2,168 | 2,322 | 2,730 | 3,248 |
| Other household goods: | | | | | | | | | | | |
| Household textiles and soft furnishings | 240 | 244 | 257 | 259 | 262 | 276 | 306 | 301 | 289 | 304 | 335 |
| Hardware | 275 | 293 | 319 | 336 | 351 | 363 | 390 | 390 | 410 | 436 | 483 |
| Matches, soap and other cleaning materials | 248 | 247 | 248 | 249 | 250 | 256 | 258 | 258 | 259 | 259 | 260 |
| Total | 763 | 784 | 824 | 844 | 863 | 895 | 954 | 949 | 958 | 999 | 1,078 |
| Books, newspapers and magazines: | | | | | | | | | | | |
| Books | 76 | 85 | 86 | 86 | 95 | 97 | 94 | 85 | 95 | 104 | 104 |
| Newspapers | 308 | 302 | 302 | 300 | 302 | 300 | 292 | 283 | 267 | 268 | 270 |
| Magazines | 108 | 103 | 98 | 98 | 104 | 103 | 97 | 104 | 102 | 94 | 99 |
| Total | 492 | 490 | 486 | 484 | 501 | 500 | 483 | 472 | 464 | 466 | 473 |

## Consumers' expenditure at 1970 prices

£ million

| | 1962 | 1963 | 1964 | 1965 | 1966 | 1967 | 1968 | 1969 | 1970 | 1971 | 1972 |
|---|---|---|---|---|---|---|---|---|---|---|---|
| Chemists' goods | 370 | 397 | 420 | 436 | 450 | 456 | 467 | 465 | 471 | 484 | 539 |
| Miscellaneous recreational goods | 519 | 540 | 575 | 604 | 620 | 642 | 686 | 682 | 719 | 743 | 792 |
| Other miscellaneous goods | 370 | 380 | 399 | 412 | 415 | 415 | 407 | 392 | 384 | 391 | 462 |
| Running costs of motor vehicles: | | | | | | | | | | | |
| Petrol and oil | | 427 | 521 | 600 | 672 | 709 | 787 | 822 | 859 | 889 | 991 |
| Motor vehicles and driving licences | 855 | 159 | 172 | 186 | 207 | 229 | 239 | 235 | 247 | 257 | 271 |
| Other | | 355 | 387 | 402 | 439 | 508 | 543 | 579 | 618 | 646 | 697 |
| Total | 855 | 941 | 1,080 | 1,188 | 1,318 | 1,446 | 1,569 | 1,636 | 1,724 | 1,792 | 1,959 |
| Travel: | | | | | | | | | | | |
| Rail | 227 | 223 | 228 | 219 | 217 | 215 | 211 | 223 | 232 | 226 | 213 |
| Bus, coach and tram | 556 | 553 | 539 | 522 | 507 | 492 | 478 | 470 | 443 | 426 | 432 |
| Other | 171 | 189 | 209 | 225 | 252 | 264 | 270 | 298 | 329 | 359 | 463 |
| Total | 954 | 965 | 976 | 966 | 976 | 971 | 959 | 991 | 1,004 | 1,011 | 1,108 |
| Communication services: | | | | | | | | | | | |
| Postal | 108 | 111 | 112 | 117 | 116 | 115 | 112 | 108 | 110 | 87 | 98 |
| Telephone and telegraph | 109 | 117 | 129 | 147 | 153 | 171 | 185 | 198 | 234 | 262 | 312 |
| Total | 217 | 228 | 241 | 264 | 269 | 286 | 297 | 306 | 344 | 349 | 410 |
| Entertainment and recreational services | | | | | | | | | | | |
| Cinema | 120 | 113 | 109 | 103 | 96 | 85 | 76 | 69 | 61 | 56 | 50 |
| Other | 355 | 390 | 421 | 442 | 454 | 480 | 488 | 487 | 485 | 512 | 574 |
| Total | 475 | 503 | 530 | 545 | 550 | 565 | 564 | 556 | 546 | 568 | 624 |
| Domestic service | 172 | 170 | 167 | 167 | 164 | 160 | 160 | 160 | 158 | 149 | 150 |
| Catering, insurance and other services | 3,253 | 3,361 | 3,428 | 3,434 | 3,474 | 3,506 | 3,562 | 3,561 | 3,609 | 3,632 | 3,792 |
| Income in kind not included elsewhere | 56 | 59 | 59 | 60 | 60 | 58 | 54 | 52 | 44 | 46 | 48 |
| *less* Expenditure by foreign tourists, etc. in the United Kingdom | −350 | −351 | −341 | −327 | −347 | −360 | −405 | −470 | −518 | −525 | −528 |
| Consumers' expenditure in the United Kingdom | 25,840 | 26,940 | 27,770 | 28,182 | 28,720 | 29,365 | 30,138 | 30,185 | 30,919 | 31,696 | 33,563 |
| Consumers' expenditure abroad | 442 | 476 | 504 | 526 | 538 | 476 | 418 | 453 | 485 | 515 | 552 |
| Total | 26,269 | 27,416 | 28,274 | 28,708 | 29,258 | 29,841 | 30,556 | 30,638 | 31,404 | 32,211 | 34,115 |

NOTE: More recent figures can be obtained from the current HMSO publication.

## Document 16A *How du Pont's Corfam took $100m caning*

(From *The Sunday Times*)

When the American chemical giant Du Pont announced on Wednesday that it was dropping its synthetic leather material, Corfam, it did more than write off 18 years' research and $100 million development.

It also destroyed a myth – the myth that the world's most sophisticated chemical company, whose scientific and marketing skills had built it up to £1500 million a year of world-wide sales, could somehow guarantee that these skills would turn a scientific breakthrough into a commercial profit-earner.

What went wrong? In global terms the idea looked a winner. Du Pont made a confident forecast in 1959, four years after its 'new venture' team had begun work, that the world was going to run short of real leather and would urgently need a substitute. The human population was outstripping the number of hide-bearing cattle, and increasing affluence would mean that millions more would be buying shoes.

The market seemed readymade and in a way so was Corfam, for Du Pont had done research in the 1930's which showed that it was possible to make a permeable plastic sheet with leather-like properties. By 1953 two versions were at pilot-plant stage with a better technique using synthetic fibres, and by 1955 a 'semi-works' factory was in production. Up to that point nobody had done a proper market forecast. Du Pont was in the grip of what researchers call 'technology-pull'.

Four years later the company was ready to build the large-scale plant at Old Hickory, Tennessee. The first material to roll off was suede finish, because to make this needed one process stage less than the calf or patent-leather finish. But production costs proved too high and the suede market was swamped overnight when Hush Puppies, made from cheap surplus pig hides, hit the shoe market. That was blow number one.

Undaunted, Du Pont switched to the 'smooth' leather market. Unfortunately when it test-marketed 20000 trial pairs of shoes the material was just not permeable enough for heavy everyday use. The marketing men were terrified of winning a reputation for uncomfortable shoes, so they concentrated on the top end of the market.

Women buy three times as many shoes as men and most of them are for dressy wear. Permeability did not seem to matter so much in fashion shoes, and the profit margin looked better.

Again the marketing effort was tremendous. Sales rose fast initially despite the total lack of interest shown by the shop girls who actually sold the shoes. By 1968 Corfam sales had reached 40 million pairs of shoes a year. And there they stuck.

Once again the market was pulled from under Du Pont's feet. By 1968 what women wanted were PVC-type materials. To the chemist PVC looked the worst possible material for shoemaking. Surely it would create nothing but sweaty feet.

But once the fashion had switched to open heels, toes, and sides – the sandal pattern – the chemistry no longer mattered. PVC shoes were cheap and could be thrown away after a month. Corfam was more durable than leather. But who cared?

Should Du Pont have seen the pattern sooner and saved some of its lost millions? It is easy with hindsight to say yes. Du Pont's marketing preparations were as elaborate as they could have been. Not only had it looked at the world demand, it had commissioned university psychologists to make a 'comfort' study, because Corfam has different qualities from leather.

But the product had run away with the company. And there was one other blow to come, sometimes called the 'sailing ship' effect. The old leather industry invaded by Corfam began to improve its product so that it should have all the advantages of leather and those of Corfam as well.

The best sailing ships were made after the coming of the steamer. If Corfam did nothing else it pushed the tanners into the late 20th century.

# 17 The private sector and the public sector

So far we have been looking at those goods and services which are produced by private individuals or companies and usually offered for sale in shops. We can choose whether or not we want to buy these goods and, if we choose to buy, we can usually choose between different makes. This is called the 'private-enterprise sector' of the economy.

But there are also two other ways in which goods and services are supplied. One way is through public corporations e.g. the gas boards, the Post Office, and the British Broadcasting Corporation. We can choose whether or not to send a letter, but if we decide to send a letter we must use the Post Office. In most cases where there is a public corporation, we can choose whether or not we buy, but, if we decide to buy, we have no choice of supplier.

The other way is through central or local government, e.g. medical services through the central government, or refuse-collection through local government. In these cases we have the service whether we want it or not, and pay for it through taxes or rates.

Public corporations, central government, and local government are called the 'public sector' of the economy.

In some cases, goods or services are provided partly through the private sector and partly through the public sector, e.g. there are houses which are built and sold by private companies and there are also houses which are built and rented out through local government.

1 Using a local rate-demand form, a recent copy of *Britain: an Official Handbook*, and any other sources of information you may choose, find out how the following goods and services are provided:

   Milk
   Water
   Sewage disposal
   Protection of property (from thieves)
   Electricity
   Roads
   Insurance
   Newspapers
   Television programmes

2 Because some public corporations have a monopoly, e.g. the Post Office, it might be thought that they could charge as much as they wished for their goods or services. How are the charges made by public corporations decided? (See *Britain: an Official Handbook*.)

3 Are there any instances in which you think it would be to the consumer's benefit to allow private enterprise to compete with public corporations?

4 Of the services which are provided for all by local or national government, which could not be provided in any other way, and which would it be possible to provide by private enterprise if it were so desired?

5 At present most insurance, including car insurance, is provided by private enterprise. What are the arguments for and against providing it through a public corporation?

6 How is the money raised to pay for the services provided by local government? How is it decided how much money shall be raised and how it shall be allocated to the various services?

7 What are the arguments for and against including a loan service for 'classical' records as part of the public-library service without extra payment by the borrowers?

# 18 How the government tries to manage the economy

Since the 1939–45 war, all British governments have tried to achieve the following aims (although not necessarily in this order of priority):

a) full employment, or at least a low rate of unemployment and a short duration of unemployment for those who become redundant;
b) economic growth at a faster rate;
c) more stable prices, or at least less inflation;
d) a balance of foreign payments, and preferably a surplus for overseas investment and aid.

We shall look at each of these in some detail, and then look at the interaction between them which makes it so difficult (if not impossible) to achieve all of these aims simultaneously.

### 18.1 Full employment

At any time there are a number of people unemployed, for a variety of reasons, such as the following.

a) People who are in process of changing from one job to another, either because they have chosen to do so or because they have been made redundant. In many cases the period of unemployment lasts less than eight weeks. This kind of unemployment is often called 'frictional unemployment'. At most times in recent years this group has accounted for 25 to 35% of all registered unemployed.
b) People who are said to be 'voluntarily unemployed'. Some people choose to live on unemployment benefit, and to go to work only when they feel they need more money – they appear to value leisure more than money. This group also includes the so-called 'seasonally unemployed', such as people who work in seaside towns during the summer (often earning quite high wages) and choose to be unemployed during the rest of the year. (If unemployment statistics are said to be 'seasonally adjusted', this has been allowed for.) Also included are students looking for jobs during the holidays.
c) People who have difficulty finding jobs for reasons such as old age or ill-health (either physical or mental).
d) People who have been unemployed for some time – over eight weeks – and who have been trying hard to find a job but have been unable to do so. This is so-called 'hard-core' unemployment.

1 Why are people made redundant? (Refer back to Sections 10 and 16.)

*"Yes, I have tried the Executive's Register!"*

2 In what ways have governments tried to help people in transferring from one type of employment to another?

3 Can you think of any other group of 'voluntarily unemployed'?

4 In which parts of Britain is there most 'hard-core' unemployment? Why does it occur most in these parts of Britain? What have governments tried to do about it? (Refer back to Section 10.)

When, for a variety of reasons which we shall look at later, the number of unemployed rises to what is considered to be an undesirably high figure (usually considered to be about a million), governments generally respond by trying to stimulate the demand for consumer goods. For example, they might reduce the Value Added Tax (VAT) – see Section 19 – which will make goods in the shops a little cheaper. People can buy more goods with their wages, so firms want to produce more, and therefore they employ more people to produce more goods.

**5** In what other ways can governments try to stimulate demand?

**6** Can you estimate how long the delay might be between the government taking action, e.g. reducing VAT, and a decrease in unemployment?

## 18.2 Economic growth

The usual measure of economic growth is the gross national product (GNP). This is the money value of all the goods and services produced within a nation during the year, plus the net income from abroad.

Details for recent years are given in Table 18A. As can be seen from the table, there are two ways of looking at the gross national product. One is to look at what the money is spent on. The main items here are the value of the goods and service bought by consumers, the value of the goods and services bought by local and national government departments and other public concerns, and the value of new buildings and machinery ('gross domestic fixed capital formation'). Part of the latter is to replace worn-out machinery, and part is for entirely new machinery.

The other way of looking at the GNP is to consider who receives the money spent, and this is given in the lower part of the table.

It is commonly assumed that if there is an increase in the GNP, then each person enjoys more goods and services and therefore has a more enjoyable life. There are many reasons why this is not necessarily so.

In the first place, the money values of goods and services may tend to increase from year to year because of inflation (see Section 18.3), and this must be allowed for when making comparisons. Secondly, there will have been an increase in population, so the more significant comparison is the increase in GNP per head. (In countries such as India which have a rapid increase in population, the GNP can increase while the GNP per head decreases.) Furthermore, even if the average GNP per head increases, the increase may not be evenly distributed. As we shall see in Sections 19 and 20, there is a tendency for the richer people to get the larger share of any increase.

All goods and services which are exchanged for money appear in the GNP, but goods and services which are not exchanged for money do not. Thus a big increase in expenditure on defence would appear as an increase in the GNP, although the average citizen would not enjoy an increase in his standard of living. In the UK some goods, e.g. blood plasma, and some services, e.g. much youth work, are given freely. If there was a change to paying for these, there might be an increase in the GNP, but our welfare would not increase at all.

Another factor which is not taken into account in the GNP is the depletion of our resources. Thus over the next decade or so our GNP will be increased because we will be using our own natural gas and oil from the North Sea instead of buying natural gas and oil from abroad, but of course this does not indicate the fact that we are not replacing the natural gas and oil – it is like living off savings.

Certain aspects of economic growth lead to some losses of amenity which are not counted in the GNP. Thus an increase in motor-car production counts as an increase in GNP, but the increase in frustration due to traffic congestion, noise suffered by people living near main roads, and atmospheric pollution by exhaust fumes is not counted as a decrease in GNP.

Economic growth defined as increase in the GNP is likely to occur if

a) there are more people working,
b) people work longer and/or harder,
c) workers use more equipment and/or more efficient equipment,
d) people work more effectively, e.g. they are working to produce what consumers demand, and they produce goods which can be sold for a high price at home or abroad – rather than products which can be imported more cheaply from other countries.

Which of these do you think the government should try to foster?

### 18.3 Control of inflation

A sudden or sustained rise in prices is called *inflation*. One way of measuring price changes is by the retail price index. Market-research techniques (see Section 2) are used to find out what goods and services are bought by a 'typical' household and at what prices. The total for the period chosen as a starting point is scaled up to 100, and the totals for other periods are scaled up correspondingly. For example, suppose we choose as a starting point the period January 1955 and the total expenditure for a typical household for that period was £20. The total for March 1962 is, say, £25. Then, if the index for January 1955 is 100, the index for March 1962 is 125.

Figure 18A plots the average index for each year since 1955.

The graph also shows how earnings have increased, for both those who are paid weekly and those who are paid monthly (salaries).

**1** Why are average weekly earnings higher than weekly rates of wages?

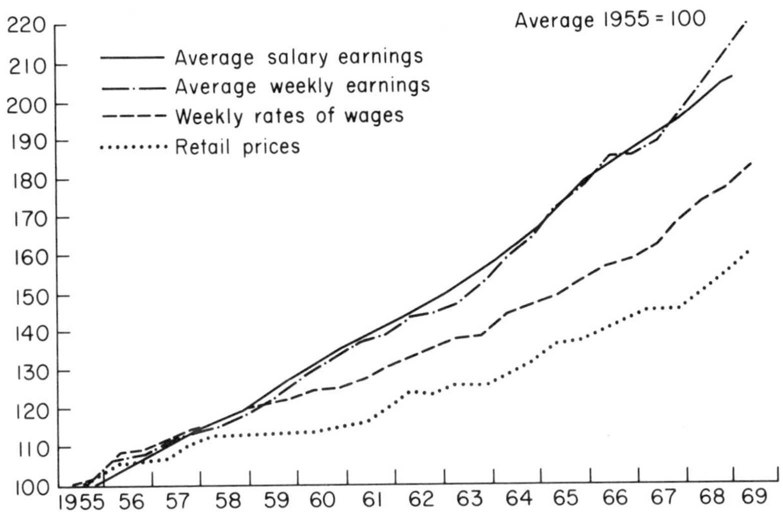


Figure 18A. Inflation between 1955 and 1968

2 In terms of what money will buy, what was the approximate percentage increase in real wages between 1955 and 1968?

3 What are the bad effects of inflation?

4 Which sections of the community will suffer most?

There are a variety of possible causes of inflation – the difficulty is to know which causes are the most important at any one time.

a) Suppose the average household feels able to spend up to £10 a week on food, and the cost of the average family bill is £9. The shopkeepers would be able to push up their prices to £10 before people would start buying less. This is sometimes called 'too much money chasing too few goods', or 'demand-pull' inflation. It can happen in general when the purchasing power of consumers or the money supply rises ahead of the output of producers.

b) Producers' costs might rise. There might be an increase in the price of imported raw materials, or powerful trade unions might obtain wage increases which are not accompanied by more goods being produced, or a fall in demand might result in a higher cost per article (see Section 3). This is often called 'cost-push' inflation.

5 How might the steps which a government takes to cure unemployment cause inflation?

6 In what ways may governments try to control inflation?

## 18.4 The balance of payments

Table 18B gives the value of UK imports for 1972 and 1973, and Table 18C gives the value of exports for the same period. For what types of goods are imports higher than exports, and for what types of goods is the reverse true?

The difference between the value of imported goods and the value of exported goods is called the *balance of trade.*

As well as importing and exporting goods, the UK also pays for services provided by other countries and earns money by the services which it provides, e.g. shipping, civil aviation, insurance, tourism, and interest on investments. These are often called 'invisible items'.

The balance of trade plus the balance on invisible items is called the *balance of payments* on current account.

In a recent year the statistics for the UK showed the following items (+ indicates net income, – indicates net expenditure).

| | *£ million* |
|---|---|
| Imports | 5024 |
| Exports | 4471 |
| Shipping | −71 |
| Civil aviation | +26 |
| Insurance | +134 |
| Tourism | +105 |
| Interest, profits, dividends | +435 |

1 Calculate (a) the balance of trade, (b) the balance of invisible items, (c) the balance of payments on current account.

In addition to the above, capital is coming from other countries into the UK for investment, and capital from the UK is being invested abroad. The net capital flow would have to be added to the balance of payments on current account to give the total balance of payments.

As was stated above, one of the aims of the government is to secure if possible a balance-of-payments surplus on current account for investment abroad, or at least to prevent a deficit. In Section 18.5 we shall see that, in trying to achieve its other aims, a government can easily run into balance-of-payments difficulties, and we shall look at what steps it may be compelled to take to remedy these.

### 18.5 The difficulty of achieving all aims simultaneously

Figure 18B shows how the number of registered unemployed and the number of notified unfilled vacancies have varied from month to month since 1948. (The number of vacancies notified is probably only a proportion of the actual number of vacancies at any time.)

You will notice that, although the number of unemployed varies in a cyclic fashion, there seems to be a long-term trend to higher unemployment. This may be because there is a long-term trend to investment in more sophisticated machinery, so that fewer workers can produce more goods.

Because Britain had such a bitter experience of unemployment during the 1930's, post-war governments have reacted to any increase in unemployment by trying to stimulate demand.

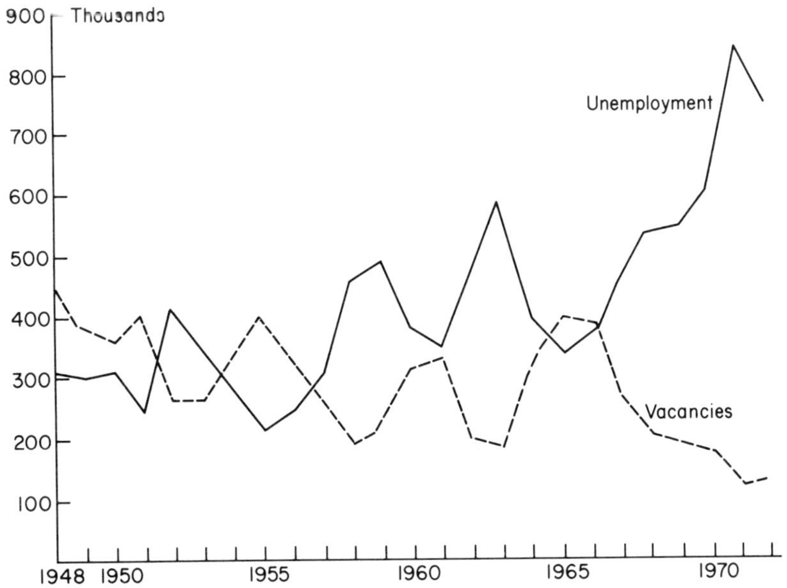


Figure 18B. Unemployment and vacancies

1 How do governments try to stimulate demand?

2 How do the steps taken to increase demand tend to increase inflation?

3 Because of the delay between increased demand and increased output, what effect would a stimulation of demand have on the balance of payments?

Inflation itself tends to cause a balance-of-payments deficit. A particular product, which is manufactured in both Britain and Germany, costs £1 in Britain and 8 deutschmarks (DM) in Germany. At the exchange rate prevailing at a certain time, £1 could be changed for 8 DM. As a result of inflation in Britain, the product some time later costs £2 in Britain but still only 8 DM in Germany. The exchange rate remains the same – British exporters will therefore not wish to export, because they can get £2 in Britain but only the equivalent of £1 in Germany. On the other hand, German exporters will step up their efforts to sell in Britain, because they can get twice as much in Britain as in their own country. The effect of inflation is therefore to increase imports and decrease exports, thus causing a balance-of-payments deficit.

4 Can you suggest possible cures for these difficulties? Are there any disadvantages to the cures you suggest?

Thus we see that the steps which governments take to cure unemployment (and at the same time stimulate investment in new machinery to ensure a faster economic growth) are likely to cause inflation and a balance-of-payments deficit. So, after a time, governments feel forced to take steps to deflate demand, which lead to an increase in unemployment again. This probably partly explains the cyclic variation in unemployment observed in Figure 18B.

In order to try to break out of this vicious circle, various governments have attempted a voluntary or legal prices-and-incomes policy. At the same time as taking steps to increase demand, they have restricted price and wage increases in order to prevent the consequent inflation. Although this may have worked for a short period, over a long period it distorts the function of prices in allocating resources (see Section 16) and it distorts wage differentials (see Section 19), so that eventually it becomes intolerable and is abandoned.

Using the material which you have studied in this section, answer the following questions at some length.

5 Write a general account of the various types of unemployment. In what ways have governments tried to eliminate unemployment? How have governments tried to alleviate the effects of unemployment?

6 Explain what is meant by (a) inflation, (b) balance of trade, and (c) balance of payments on current account.

How may (a) affect (b) and (c), and how do governments try to overcome the difficulties caused?

# Table 18A (from *National Income and Expenditure 1971*)

## Gross national product

£ million

| | Reference number | 1962 | 1963 | 1964 | 1965 | 1966 | 1967 | 1968 | 1969 | 1970 | 1971 | 1972 |
|---|---|---|---|---|---|---|---|---|---|---|---|---|
| **Expenditure** | | | | | | | | | | | | |
| Consumers' expenditure.... | *1* | 18,923 | 20,118 | 21,488 | 22,878 | 24,251 | 25,455 | 27,335 | 28,968 | 31,404 | 34,838 | 39,263 |
| Public authorities' current expenditure on goods and services .................. | *2, 3* | 4,916 | 5,176 | 5,505 | 6,041 | 6,572 | 7,272 | 7,727 | 8,088 | 9,095 | 10,339 | 11,702 |
| Gross domestic fixed capital formation ............... | *4* | 4,820 | 5,018 | 5,983 | 6,438 | 6,844 | 7,438 | 8,055 | 8,458 | 9,223 | 10,101 | 11,214 |
| Value of physical increase in stocks and work in progress ...................... | *5* | −8 | 161 | 734 | 487 | 346 | 322 | 439 | 416 | 257 | 19 | −440 |
| Total domestic expenditure at market prices .... | | 28,651 | 30,473 | 33,710 | 35,844 | 38,013 | 40,487 | 43,556 | 45,930 | 49,979 | 55,297 | 61,739 |
| Exports and property income from abroad .... | *6* | 6,832 | 7,217 | 7,679 | 8,302 | 8,716 | 8,951 | 10,811 | 12,220 | 13,924 | 15,663 | 16,694 |
| *less* Imports and property income paid abroad .... | *7* | −6,599 | −6,956 | −7,888 | −8,167 | −8,430 | −9,035 | −10,861 | −11,549 | −13,026 | −14,372 | −16,347 |
| *less* Taxes on expenditure | *8, 9* | −3,879 | −4,027 | −4,437 | −4,962 | −5,427 | −6,004 | −6,818 | −7,789 | −8,433 | −8,808 | −9,279 |
| Subsidies .......................... | *10, 11* | 608 | 569 | 516 | 574 | 572 | 815 | 910 | 855 | 859 | 895 | 1,133 |
| **Gross national product at factor cost**........................... | *12* | 25,613 | 27,276 | 29,580 | 31,591 | 33,444 | 35,214 | 37,598 | 39,667 | 43,303 | 48,675 | 53,940 |
| **Factor incomes** | | | | | | | | | | | | |
| Income from employment | *13* | 17,306 | 18,195 | 19,717 | 21,291 | 22,786 | 23,706 | 25,341 | 27,033 | 30,179 | 33,331 | 37,138 |
| Income from self-employment (¹)........................... | *14* | 2,148 | 2,207 | 2,324 | 2,519 | 2,679 | 2,843 | 3,090 | 3,298 | 3,662 | 4,167 | 4,764 |
| Gross trading profits of companies (¹) (²) ........... | *15* | 3,595 | 4,103 | 4,544 | 4,741 | 4,610 | 4,663 | 5,275 | 5,143 | 5,279 | 5,756 | 6,584 |
| Gross trading surplus of public corporations(¹)..... | *16* | 745 | 840 | 924 | 988 | 1,042 | 1,132 | 1,363 | 1,451 | 1,395 | 1,464 | 1,612 |
| Gross trading surplus of other public enterprises(¹) | *17, 18* | 84 | 92 | 104 | 112 | 106 | 110 | 132 | 146 | 152 | 185 | 178 |
| Rent (²)............................... | *19* | 1,477 | 1,592 | 1,747 | 1,939 | 2,143 | 2,363 | 2,616 | 2,936 | 3,315 | 3,667 | 4,182 |
| Total domestic income before providing for depreciation and stock appreciation ............... | | 25,355 | 27,029 | 29,360 | 31,590 | 33,366 | 34,817 | 37,817 | 40,007 | 43,982 | 48,570 | 54,458 |
| *less* Stock appreciation .... | *20* | −152 | −182 | −292 | −321 | −347 | −187 | −564 | −733 | −1,137 | −1,058 | −1,319 |
| Residual error .................... | *21* | 76 | 31 | 119 | −113 | 38 | 205 | 10 | −106 | −57 | 647 | 345 |
| **Gross domestic product at factor cost**........................... | *22* | 25,279 | 26,878 | 29,187 | 31,156 | 33,057 | 34,835 | 37,263 | 39,168 | 42,788 | 48,159 | 53,484 |
| Net property income from abroad .......................... | *23* | 334 | 398 | 393 | 435 | 387 | 379 | 335 | 499 | 515 | 516 | 456 |
| **Gross national product** ........ | *12* | 25,613 | 27,276 | 29,580 | 31,591 | 33,444 | 35,214 | 37,598 | 39,667 | 43,303 | 48,675 | 53,940 |
| *less* Capital consumption | *24* | −2,354 | −2,503 | −2,699 | −2,912 | −3,149 | −3,353 | −3,658 | −3,965 | −4,447 | −5,082 | −5,824 |
| **National income** .................. | *25* | 23,259 | 24,773 | 26,881 | 28,679 | 30,295 | 31,861 | 33,940 | 35,702 | 38,856 | 43,593 | 48,116 |

(¹)Before providing for depreciation and stock appreciation.
(²)Before providing for depreciation.

# Table 18B (from *Monthly Digest of Statistics*)

## Value of United Kingdom exports (f.o.b.)(¹)

Monthly averages or calendar months £ thousand

| | 1972 | 1973 | 1973 3rd quarter | 1973 4th quarter | 1974 1st quarter | 1974 2nd quarter | 1974 3rd quarter | 1974 Sept. | 1974 October | Jan.–Oct. 1974 compared with Jan.–Oct. 1973 |
|---|---|---|---|---|---|---|---|---|---|---|
| **0. Food and live animals** | 28,802 | 42,673 | 43,519 | 52,051 | 48,029 | 47,532 | 47,439 | 46,217 | 61,102 | + 20 |
| 00. Live animals | 3,363 | 4,903 | 3,748 | 8,691 | 3,285 | 2,963 | 4,344 | 3,903 | 4,689 | − 7 |
| 02. Dairy products and eggs | 1,847 | 3,690 | 3,934 | 3,356 | 4,093 | 3,807 | 2,101 | 1,825 | 2,634 | − 14 |
| 03. Fish and fish preparations | 2,439 | 3,596 | 3,236 | 4,919 | 4,542 | 3,944 | 4,018 | 4,194 | 5,363 | + 28 |
| 04. Cereals and cereal preparations | 2,825 | 4,550 | 5,195 | 5,976 | 5,412 | 5,848 | 6,097 | 7,009 | 8,971 | + 41 |
| 05. Fruit and vegetables | 2,615 | 3,610 | 2,613 | 5,003 | 4,985 | 3,865 | 3,570 | 3,612 | 4,952 | + 29 |
| 06. Sugar, sugar preparations and honey | 3,874 | 5,125 | 5,647 | 4,869 | 4,720 | 8,106 | 9,390 | 7,343 | 9,983 | + 47 |
| 07. Coffee, cocoa preparations, tea and spices | 4,216 | 5,115 | 4,917 | 5,950 | 7,255 | 6,888 | 6,003 | 6,731 | 10,130 | + 40 |
| 01, 08 and 09. Other food and food preparations | 7,624 | 12,083 | 14,230 | 13,287 | 13,737 | 12,110 | 11,913 | 11,599 | 14,380 | + 6 |
| **1. Beverages and tobacco** | 26,194 | 30,293 | 29,902 | 36,222 | 30,435 | 37,988 | 45,788 | 40,077 | 43,151 | + 33 |
| 11. Beverages | 22,195 | 25,449 | 25,337 | 31,110 | 25,572 | 32,362 | 39,932 | 34,457 | 35,487 | + 35 |
| 12. Tobacco | 3,999 | 4,844 | 4,565 | 5,113 | 4,864 | 5,626 | 5,856 | 5,620 | 7,664 | + 18 |
| **2. Crude materials, inedible** | 25,829 | 34,697 | 29,943 | 39,747 | 48,761 | 50,931 | 42,361 | 38,599 | 46,237 | + 38 |
| 23. Crude rubber (including synthetic and reclaimed) | 2,345 | 3,160 | 2,940 | 3,481 | 4,338 | 5,078 | 4,411 | 4,220 | 4,808 | + 49 |
| 26. Textile fibres, not manufactured and their waste | 9,009 | 14,342 | 13,372 | 15,703 | 18,348 | 20,361 | 16,229 | 13,524 | 13,945 | + 26 |
| 27. Crude fertilizers and minerals | 4,115 | 5,014 | 4,821 | 5,553 | 5,651 | 6,699 | 6,823 | 7,030 | 7,922 | + 33 |
| Other crude materials | 10,360 | 12,181 | 8,809 | 15,010 | 20,425 | 18,792 | 14,898 | 13,826 | 19,563 | + 52 |
| **3. Mineral fuels, lubricants, etc.** | 19,883 | 30,834 | 37,169 | 43,566 | 46,817 | 69,537 | 69,810 | 68,864 | 81,302 | +129 |
| 33. Petroleum and petroleum products | 18,272 | 28,376 | 34,775 | 40,625 | 44,928 | 64,392 | 62,347 | 60,612 | 70,669 | +130 |
| Coal, coke, gas and electric energy | 1,611 | 2,458 | 2,393 | 2,941 | 1,890 | 5,145 | 7,463 | 8,252 | 10,633 | +125 |
| **4. Animal and vegetable oils and fats** | 933 | 1,422 | 1,453 | 2,019 | 2,549 | 2,951 | 2,399 | 2,066 | 3,021 | +103 |
| **5. Chemicals** | 80,151 | 106,034 | 103,401 | 118,436 | 144,857 | 184,570 | 190,954 | 178,846 | 214,965 | + 70 |
| 51. Chemical elements and compounds | 21,213 | 30,374 | 30,367 | 35,334 | 46,539 | 64,359 | 66,723 | 63,928 | 76,439 | +106 |
| 53. Dyeing, tanning and colouring materials | 8,832 | 11,708 | 11,532 | 13,372 | 16,642 | 19,221 | 18,477 | 17,000 | 19,274 | + 60 |
| 54. Medicinal and pharmaceutical products | 15,067 | 18,434 | 18,151 | 19,850 | 21,587 | 24,299 | 26,561 | 22,817 | 27,386 | + 34 |
| 55. Essential oils and perfume materials | 6,445 | 8,071 | 8,115 | 8,626 | 9,731 | 12,539 | 12,983 | 12,710 | 15,139 | + 50 |
| 57. Explosive and pyrotechnic products | 884 | 1,003 | 938 | 993 | 1,575 | 1,525 | 1,576 | 1,294 | 1,262 | + 54 |
| 58. Plastic materials and artificial resins | 14,703 | 18,769 | 17,443 | 21,282 | 24,642 | 32,918 | 32,798 | 31,902 | 36,555 | + 67 |
| All other | 13,008 | 17,677 | 16,855 | 18,980 | 24,141 | 29,709 | 31,836 | 29,195 | 38,911 | + 68 |
| **6. Manufactured goods classified chiefly by materials** | 196,218 | 271,543 | 268,234 | 305,307 | 305,212 | 359,570 | 328,965 | 321,237 | 363,838 | + 26 |
| 61. Leather manufactures and dressed furs | 5,583 | 6,985 | 5,905 | 7,560 | 7,661 | 8,740 | 7,151 | 6,208 | 8,505 | + 14 |
| 62. Rubber manufactures, not elsewhere specified | 8,033 | 10,099 | 9,842 | 10,330 | 11,669 | 14,423 | 14,243 | 13,133 | 16,746 | + 36 |
| 64. Paper, paperboard and manufactures thereof | 8,475 | 10,729 | 10,308 | 11,737 | 13,674 | 16,105 | 17,181 | 17,348 | 21,923 | + 55 |
| 65. Textile yarn, fabrics and articles | 37,112 | 49,131 | 47,484 | 54,858 | 59,840 | 68,208 | 59,524 | 56,452 | 67,542 | + 31 |
| 66. Non-metallic mineral manufactures | 51,473 | 84,165 | 93,823 | 91,080 | 74,716 | 111,740 | 88,077 | 90,873 | 85,085 | + 11 |
| 67. Iron and steel | 31,370 | 36,085 | 33,531 | 38,146 | 37,212 | 38,605 | 49,144 | 50,451 | 60,078 | + 22 |
| 68. Non-ferrous metals | 29,024 | 44,816 | 38,529 | 60,102 | 65,885 | 60,288 | 52,114 | 46,693 | 55,066 | + 40 |
| 63 and 69. Other wood and metal manufactures | 25,148 | 29,532 | 28,814 | 31,496 | 34,554 | 41,462 | 41,531 | 40,079 | 48,894 | + 37 |
| **7. Machinery and transport equipment** | 334,520 | 397,924 | 382,191 | 422,229 | 437,912 | 494,426 | 513,656 | 508,232 | 599,989 | + 25 |
| 71. Machinery other than electric | 171,184 | 201,082 | 191,694 | 209,702 | 225,012 | 252,008 | 262,013 | 253,852 | 297,084 | + 25 |
| 72. Electric machinery, apparatus and appliances | 55,159 | 67,274 | 63,803 | 73,726 | 80,606 | 89,894 | 94,324 | 92,470 | 115,972 | + 38 |
| 73. Transport equipment | 108,178 | 129,568 | 126,695 | 138,801 | 132,295 | 152,524 | 157,320 | 161,910 | 186,933 | + 18 |
| **8. Miscellaneous manufactured articles** | 77,208 | 95,821 | 97,501 | 109,802 | 101,878 | 118,543 | 132,277 | 132,136 | 158,087 | + 29 |
| 81. Sanitary, plumbing, heating and lighting fittings | 1,951 | 2,375 | 2,176 | 2,727 | 2,901 | 3,904 | 3,701 | 3,858 | 4,386 | + 54 |
| 82. Furniture | 2,924 | 3,682 | 3,683 | 4,416 | 4,638 | 5,731 | 5,958 | 5,765 | 7,399 | + 60 |
| 84. Clothing | 12,030 | 14,965 | 16,916 | 18,788 | 14,765 | 16,920 | 22,070 | 22,351 | 28,115 | + 30 |
| 85. Footwear | 2,688 | 2,963 | 3,013 | 3,716 | 3,147 | 3,789 | 4,499 | 4,698 | 5,093 | + 37 |
| 86. Professional, scientific and controlling instruments, photographic and optical goods, watches and clocks | 22,804 | 28,649 | 28,479 | 30,368 | 30,906 | 35,544 | 36,464 | 33,616 | 39,979 | + 23 |
| Other | 34,812 | 43,188 | 43,235 | 49,518 | 45,520 | 52,656 | 59,585 | 61,848 | 73,114 | + 28 |
| **5–8. Manufactured goods** | 688,097 | 871,322 | 851,328 | 955,775 | 989,859 | 1,157,109 | 1,165,852 | 1,140,451 | 1,336,879 | + 31 |
| **9. Commodities and transactions not classified according to kind** | 22,411 | 26,685 | 25,391 | 36,124 | 28,026 | 33,767 | 31,587 | 22,478 | 37,458 | + 33 |
| **Total United Kingdom exports** | 812,148 | 1,037,926 | 1,018,704 | 1,165,506 | 1,194,477 | 1,399,815 | 1,405,236 | 1,358,752 | 1,609,151 | + 34 |

(¹) The numbers on the left hand side of the table refer to the Section and Division code numbers of the *Standard International Trade Classification, Revised.*

Source: Department of Trade

# Table 18C (from *Monthly Digest of Statistics*)

## Value of United Kingdom imports (c.i.f.)[1]

Monthly averages or calendar months — £ thousand

| | 1972 | 1973 | 1973 3rd quarter | 1973 4th quarter | 1974 1st quarter | 1974 2nd quarter | 1974 3rd quarter | 1974 Sept. | 1974 October | Jan.–Oct. 1974 compared with Jan.–Oct. 1973 |
|---|---|---|---|---|---|---|---|---|---|---|
| | | | | | | | | | | per cent |
| **0. Food and live animals** | 175,055 | 226,169 | 216,460 | 242,897 | 257,175 | 280,855 | 278,935 | 258,121 | 287,044 | + 23 |
| 00. Live animals | 6,001 | 6,686 | 5,816 | 10,315 | 6,416 | 5,617 | 7,280 | 7,092 | 7,830 | + 9 |
| 01. Meat and meat preparations | 45,009 | 59,661 | 54,288 | 60,917 | 62,298 | 57,813 | 53,704 | 55,950 | 57,612 | − 3 |
| 02. Dairy products and eggs | 21,285 | 18,784 | 12,582 | 16,638 | 24,041 | 21,712 | 30,298 | 30,306 | 31,804 | + 37 |
| 03. Fish and fish preparations | 8,036 | 11,014 | 9,761 | 18,245 | 12,092 | 9,546 | 8,237 | 8,964 | 12,618 | + 4 |
| 04. Cereals and cereal preparations | 21,422 | 30,798 | 33,451 | 32,259 | 48,014 | 54,667 | 50,238 | 38,226 | 41,774 | + 66 |
| 05. Fruit and vegetables | 35,768 | 46,977 | 39,370 | 49,657 | 50,909 | 62,725 | 48,861 | 48,217 | 59,031 | + 19 |
| 06. Sugar, sugar preparations and honey | 12,162 | 14,581 | 17,371 | 13,031 | 14,041 | 23,136 | 34,708 | 31,064 | 35,460 | + 69 |
| 07. Coffee, cocoa and preparations, tea and spices | 15,616 | 20,727 | 22,543 | 22,509 | 22,824 | 29,174 | 29,233 | 25,322 | 21,790 | + 30 |
| Other food and food preparations | 9,755 | 16,941 | 21,276 | 18,526 | 16,540 | 16,465 | 16,375 | 12,979 | 19,125 | − 2 |
| **1. Beverages and tobacco** | 21,267 | 31,969 | 32,476 | 43,385 | 30,192 | 32,241 | 31,705 | 31,971 | 47,149 | + 8 |
| 11. Beverages | 11,141 | 19,152 | 20,879 | 24,607 | 18,323 | 16,453 | 17,735 | 17,628 | 24,994 | − 1 |
| 12 Tobacco | 10,127 | 12,817 | 11,597 | 18,778 | 11,869 | 15,788 | 13,970 | 14,343 | 22,156 | + 23 |
| **2. Crude materials, inedible** | 102,806 | 152,951 | 158,387 | 171,930 | 178,156 | 205,402 | 210,749 | 204,930 | 211,759 | + 32 |
| 21. Hides, skins, and furskins, undressed | 7,093 | 9,379 | 7,956 | 10,102 | 9,766 | 7,894 | 7,192 | 4,808 | 12,595 | − 4 |
| 22. Oil seeds, oil nuts and oil kernels | 4,269 | 8,665 | 9,459 | 9,997 | 11,976 | 13,325 | 11,309 | 8,602 | 9,747 | + 42 |
| 23. Crude rubber (including synthetic and reclaimed) | 3,961 | 6,242 | 6,059 | 7,600 | 8,977 | 8,152 | 8,585 | 8,841 | 8,470 | + 39 |
| 24. Wood, lumber and cork | 21,123 | 38,221 | 46,422 | 50,291 | 46,095 | 51,394 | 58,403 | 54,355 | 50,778 | + 40 |
| 25. Pulp and waste paper | 14,304 | 16,792 | 17,607 | 18,522 | 20,654 | 24,801 | 31,001 | 35,512 | 32,510 | + 57 |
| 26. Textile fibres, not manufactured and their waste | 17,780 | 26,870 | 23,308 | 25,046 | 29,625 | 30,918 | 24,075 | 23,496 | 18,823 | − 1 |
| 27. Crude fertilizers and minerals | 4,990 | 6,737 | 6,863 | 6,977 | 9,100 | 12,145 | 13,013 | 13,110 | 14,402 | + 72 |
| 28. Metalliferous ores and metal scrap | 23,672 | 32,462 | 33,483 | 34,073 | 32,017 | 48,706 | 48,125 | 47,323 | 56,151 | + 36 |
| 29. Crude animal and vegetable materials | 5,616 | 7,584 | 7,228 | 9,322 | 9,945 | 8,067 | 9,047 | 8,884 | 8,284 | + 25 |
| **3. Mineral fuels, lubricants, etc** | 103,465 | 143,938 | 140,673 | 186,363 | 343,741 | 415,706 | 372,502 | 367,753 | 458,836 | +183 |
| 33. Petroleum and petroleum products | 97,168 | 140,147 | 137,735 | 181,428 | 337,507 | 408,574 | 364,000 | 359,178 | 447,262 | +184 |
| **4. Animal and vegetable oils and fats** | 7,448 | 10,793 | 11,199 | 14,261 | 15,302 | 19,913 | 22,054 | 15,962 | 14,290 | + 80 |
| **5. Chemicals** | 54,285 | 74,778 | 77,800 | 85,636 | 115,891 | 132,079 | 148,317 | 146,006 | 160,360 | + 81 |
| 51. Chemical elements and compounds | 22,103 | 30,069 | 31,290 | 35,941 | 48,428 | 62,111 | 67,169 | 68,424 | 67,972 | +109 |
| 55. Essential oils and perfume materials | 2,727 | 4,297 | 4,692 | 4,855 | 6,021 | 6,916 | 7,027 | 6,359 | 6,656 | + 59 |
| 58. Plastic materials and artificial resins | 11,951 | 17,073 | 17,568 | 20,017 | 28,419 | 29,201 | 35,937 | 34,911 | 34,199 | + 89 |
| All other | 17,504 | 23,338 | 24,250 | 24,823 | 33,024 | 34,452 | 38,185 | 36,401 | 41,533 | + 55 |
| **6. Manufactured goods classified chiefly by materials** | 192,654 | 281,943 | 280,628 | 338,457 | 379,336 | 417,468 | 396,550 | 398,406 | 438,538 | + 47 |
| 61. Leather, leather manufactures and dressed furs | 3,933 | 5,696 | 5,364 | 5,145 | 5,815 | 4,606 | 4,974 | 5,376 | 5,445 | − 12 |
| 63. Wood and cork manufactures | 11,826 | 20,352 | 21,330 | 25,934 | 25,802 | 22,239 | 16,391 | 16,310 | 14,191 | + 7 |
| 64. Paper, paperboard and manufactures thereof | 25,947 | 33,523 | 35,456 | 37,455 | 51,367 | 56,317 | 67,799 | 71,024 | 77,176 | + 82 |
| 65. Textile yarn, fabrics and articles | 30,807 | 42,908 | 41,977 | 49,321 | 56,515 | 55,971 | 60,003 | 56,898 | 62,850 | + 38 |
| 66. Non-metallic mineral manufactures | 47,022 | 71,451 | 66,570 | 90,129 | 74,444 | 94,874 | 82,232 | 84,241 | 93,956 | + 23 |
| 67. Iron and steel | 21,009 | 31,151 | 30,412 | 41,268 | 58,655 | 61,034 | 52,555 | 52,588 | 66,259 | +102 |
| 68. Non-ferrous metals | 37,214 | 54,993 | 57,828 | 63,509 | 76,767 | 92,806 | 81,492 | 79,243 | 81,052 | + 56 |
| Other | 14,896 | 21,868 | 21,690 | 25,696 | 29,972 | 29,621 | 31,103 | 32,725 | 37,610 | + 45 |
| **7. Machinery and transport equipment** | 186,527 | 274,436 | 270,838 | 312,088 | 307,561 | 330,770 | 311,071 | 288,369 | 367,894 | + 21 |
| 71. Machinery other than electric | 86,708 | 127,197 | 125,955 | 143,870 | 152,368 | 163,524 | 158,726 | 151,441 | 189,641 | + 30 |
| 72. Electrical machinery, apparatus and appliances | 43,985 | 70,647 | 71,244 | 84,682 | 87,630 | 87,962 | 76,614 | 73,072 | 90,218 | + 26 |
| 73. Transport equipment | 55,833 | 76,592 | 73,639 | 83,536 | 67,563 | 79,283 | 75,731 | 63,856 | 88,036 | + 1 |
| **8. Miscellaneous manufactured articles** | 74,314 | 111,644 | 112,667 | 130,676 | 133,846 | 146,052 | 134,161 | 133,092 | 152,184 | + 29 |
| 84. Clothing | 18,237 | 27,789 | 29,822 | 32,353 | 35,186 | 34,036 | 34,171 | 33,439 | 36,170 | + 29 |
| 85. Footwear | 5,199 | 7,032 | 6,570 | 7,372 | 9,835 | 9,672 | 7,720 | 7,356 | 8,814 | + 29 |
| 86. Professional, scientific and controlling instruments; photographic and optical goods; watches and clocks | 16,643 | 23,519 | 23,874 | 26,300 | 27,604 | 32,404 | 31,158 | 29,993 | 37,336 | + 36 |
| Other | 34,235 | 53,304 | 52,401 | 64,651 | 61,221 | 69,941 | 61,111 | 62,304 | 69,865 | + 26 |
| **5–8. Manufactured goods** | 507,780 | 742,800 | 741,933 | 866,858 | 936,634 | 1,026,968 | 990,099 | 965,963 | 1,108,975 | + 39 |
| **9. Commodities and transactions not classified according to kind** | 10,373 | 12,583 | 12,084 | 15,446 | 16,133 | 17,216 | 14,656 | 17,034 | 19,749 | + 36 |
| **Total United Kingdom imports** | 928,194 | 1,321,204 | 1,313,212 | 1,514,140 | 1,777,334 | 1,998,301 | 1,920,701 | 1,861,734 | 2,147,803 | + 50 |

[1] The numbers on the left hand side of the table refer to the Section and Division code numbers of the *Standard International Trade Classification, Revised.*

Source: Department of Trade

# 19 Personal incomes and wealth

### 19.1 The distribution of personal incomes

'Everyone should receive the same income whether they work or not.' Would this work out in practice?

'Everyone who works should receive the same income whatever job they do.' Would this work out in practice?

Study Document 19A. What do you think decides how much people earn?

One boy decides to train as a civil engineer. Another, equally able, decides to train as an accountant. The training periods are very similar and, at the time when they start to train, civil engineers and accountants receive much the same salaries. Later in life the civil engineer, although good at his job, discovers that he can now earn very much less than his friend who became the accountant. What could have happened to bring this about? What actions do trades and professions take to try to prevent this kind of change occurring?

### 19.2 The redistribution of personal incomes

If for any reason it is thought that the distribution of income among the population which results from the operation of the market economy is in any way 'unfair', then the taxes which are used to finance government expenditure of various kinds can be levied in such a way that they bring about a redistribution of income.

At the time of writing, the system of tax and benefits is in process of change, but the important features are as follows.

#### Taxes

*Income tax.* Each person earning above a certain amount pays this tax directly from his income, hence it is called a 'direct' tax. In most cases, the employer stops it out of the wages and pays it directly to a government department. Each person is allowed to earn up to a certain amount free of tax, the amount depending on personal circumstances (single person, married person, married person with children, etc.). Above that figure, tax is paid at various rates which increase with income, so that, in general, the higher the wages the higher the *proportion* (not just the amount) paid as income tax.

*National Insurance contributions.* These are weekly payments by both employees and employers which go to finance National Insurance benefits (see page 139). As with income tax, the employee's contribution is stopped out of his wages and paid directly to a government department. The National Insurance contribution is dependent on the amount the worker earns.

*Customs and Excise duties* which are paid as part of the purchase price of a limited range of goods – mainly tobacco, alcoholic drinks, and petrol. These are examples of an 'indirect' tax.

*Value Added Tax (VAT).* VAT is a tax paid as part of the shop price of most goods and services except food. It was originally 10% of the final purchase price, but it can be varied according to circumstances (see Section 18), and at the time of writing it is 8%. Again, this is an 'indirect' tax.

## Benefits

*Family Income Supplement* is an amount paid *to* workers with low wages according to their family circumstances.

*Family allowances* are paid to the *mother* according to the number of children.

*National Insurance benefits* – sickness benefit, unemployment benefit, old-age pensions, etc.

1 In some methods of taxation, people pay a higher proportion of their income as their income increases – not just more, but a higher proportion. These are called progressive taxes. In other methods, people pay a lower proportion of their income as their income increases. These are called regressive taxes.

Which of the present direct taxes do you consider to be progressive and which regressive?

2 Do you consider an indirect tax such as VAT to be progressive or regressive?

3 If government expenditure increases, financed by higher taxation, does this necessarily benefit less-well-paid workers at the expense of higher-paid people?

4 Many of the benefits can be considered as 'transfer payments', transferring income from one section of the community to another. For example, family allowances transfer income from those who do not have children (through taxation) to those who do. What transfers are represented by sickness benefit, unemployment benefit, old-age pensions?

5 Suppose the Common Market countries agreed to amalgamate National Insurance benefits. Who might gain and who might lose? Would you agree to the idea?

At the time of writing, the government is discussing a plan to simplify the system of direct taxes and benefits. In principle, each wage-earner would be taxed on the whole of his income at a standard rate (probably about 30%). Each person would have a number of 'credits' according to his personal circumstances – single or married with non-working wife, number of children, etc. If the tax due is less than the 'credits', the employer will add the difference (from government funds); if the tax due is more than the credits, the difference will be sent by the employer to the appropriate government department.

**6** Is this system progressive or regressive? For very high incomes is it more progressive (or regressive) than the present system?

**7** 'Credits' might be paid as part of the father's wages; the present family allowances are paid directly (at the post office) to the mother. What are the advantages and disadvantages?

**8** Can you see any other advantages or disadvantages (from various points of view!) of the system?

## 19.3 The distribution of personal wealth

As well as income from employment, some people have income from wealth which is invested in various ways, such as shares in limited companies. Table 19A shows the distribution of personal incomes and wealth.

**1** Can you explain why the distribution of wealth is more uneven than the distribution of incomes?

**2** Do you think it is 'fair' that some people should inherit wealth? (Think of yourself as a father who has worked very hard to work up a business which he wishes to pass on to his children. Think of yourself as someone who does not have a rich father! Consider whether the keeping-together of inherited wealth benefits the community as a whole.)

**3** In what ways do governments attempt to redistribute accumulated wealth?

TABLE 19A The distribution of personal income and wealth

| *Tenth fractions of the population* | *Approximate % share of income* | *Approximate % share of wealth* |
|---|---|---|
| Top 10% | 30 | 75 |
| Second tenth | 12 | 15·6 |
| Third | 11 | 5·7 |
| Fourth | 11 | 2·4 |
| Fifth | 10 | 1·0 |
| Sixth | 8 | 0·3 |
| Seventh | 6 | 0 |
| Eighth | 5 | 0 |
| Ninth | 4 | 0 |
| Tenth | 3 | 0 |

# Document 19A *Case studies of personal incomes*

(From *The Sunday Times* – note: All wages and conditions of working mentioned are those in force at the time this article was written in 1971.)

**Woolworth's counter girl, Ipswich, 18, £13**
On duty two Saturdays out of three, she works the equivalent of a five-day week for a basic annual salary of £754 (£14·50 a week before tax). This includes a Christmas bonus of £13·89. She gets no discount on Woolworth's goods, but she does get her meals from a subsidised canteen – and is given a day off every year on her birthday.

**Norfolk farmworker, 56, £17**
His certificate as a Craftsman for Machine Operation and Maintenance entitles him to a basic annual wage of £1144·88 (£22 per week before tax) which he supplements with an hour per day overtime. Though he normally works a five-day week, he has been working a 17-hour day seven days a week during the harvest period. He only pays 30p a week for his tied cottage but will have to leave this when he retires at 65 – along with the patch of ground on which he is allowed to grow his own potatoes.

**Barnsley miner, 42, £24**
As a pit-road repairer and salvage worker he is entitled to the post-strike annual basic of £1547 (assuming full attendance), for which he works five days a week underground from 6 a.m. until 1.15 p.m. without a lunchbreak. He benefits from the usual miner's perk of free coal – nine tons a year, worth in his area about £100 – and he won't be sending his son down the pit.

**Metal finisher at Ford of Dagenham, 47, £28**
His basic annual salary of £1768 for a 40-hour week brings him £34 on a Friday before tax and there's no chance to earn overtime at the

A counter assistant in a Woolworth store

moment. He is entitled to an 18 per cent discount on a new Ford but can't afford a car. So he cycles to work every day.

**Bus driver, Huddersfield, 42, £30**
Driving 60 hours, six days a week, he grosses just over £2000 a year from his basic pay, overtime, his bonus for 15 years' service and the productivity bonus he receives for driving a one-man bus and collecting fares as he goes. Having his uniform provided saves him some £20 a year and his bus journey to and from work costs nothing. But that is all the free bus travel he gets.

**Secretary/typist, 22, £30**
She is secretary/typist to an advertising executive in a small London office. She works a 35 hour week, no Saturdays, and in addition to her wages she receives luncheon vouchers.

**South London bingo caller, 31, £32**
He grosses £40 a week which after tax leaves him a net yearly salary of £1650. He works at the Streatham Hill Mecca afternoons and evenings with Sundays off, which adds up to a five-and-a-half-day week, and he reckons he saves 25p a day on the free coffee and rolls he gets while on duty. As other perks, he says, 'I've met Miss Worlds, cabaret performers and other most interesting people. Because we work odd hours we avoid the rush hour. It's an easy-going life.'

**University lecturer in London, 26, £34**
As Lecturer in Greek and Latin at University College, London, he is paid a salary of £2240 which includes his London living allowance. 'Our salaries are worked out on the theory that we do only 200 hours teaching a year but, in fact, preparing a difficult lecture or a five-page article may take me a month or more.'

**London hairdresser, 22, £40**
His basic salary at Crimpers of Hampstead is low, only £1040 a year, and he works a 44-hour week that includes a full Saturday. But he brings his total income up to £3255 a year as follows: £884 commission (he gets 10 per cent of everything he takes); £160 competitive bonus; £156 for teaching juniors (£3 a night); £105 from extra fashion shows (last year he did

Pan's People in concert

A Bingo caller at a Mecca social club

three at £35 each); and, of course, tips, averaging £3·50 a day, £910 a year.

**Pan's People Dancer, 23, £45**
She is self-employed so the gross basic of £2165 paid by the BBC is for just 49 weeks. She rehearses three days a week and spends one day and an evening on the dress rehearsal and recording the show. Her take-home pay is increased by all the expenses she can claim; also, she says, 'All of us do cabarets, promotions and personal appearances at £60 per girl for each event. We do about two of these each week.' There are extra perks: 'We've all been made honorary members of clubs like Penthouse, but we wouldn't dream of going.'

**Insurance Executive, London, 35, £50**
His apparently low take-home pay from his £80-a-week salary of £4275 (£4100 basic plus £175 London allowance) as Sales Manager of Guardian Royal Exchange Assurance (City Branch) is explained by the special help that many insurance companies and banks give their executives with their basic commitments. From his payslip are deducted: the repayment on his mortgage (his company charges only 3½ per cent interest, a saving of at least £500 a year on normal building society interest rates), the monthly repayment of his £72 p.a. Croydon–London season ticket (paid by the company at the beginning of the year interest-free); his BUPA subscription (obtained at a company discount rate); his insurance premiums (all commission-free with the GRE); and then the normal tax, National Insurance and graduated pensions. His car and some of his mileage are also paid for by the company, and the GRE's non-contributory pension scheme will pay him two-thirds of his income at retirement for life, plus death-in-service benefits of four times his annual salary.

**London bank manager, 38, £65**

As manager of the King's Road branch of Lloyds Bank, responsible for over 3000 customers, he earns a salary of £4494 a year with an additional London allowance of £201. His principal perk is a housing loan at the incredibly low rate of 2½ per cent – a saving of at least £400 a year on a £10 000 house purchased with the help of a normal building society mortgage.

**Senior captain flying jumbo jets, 49, £120**

He grosses £9500 a year for working 12 periods of 28 days (80 flying hours) plus an equal time spent preparing for flights and other duties. The salary seems high but, he explains, it is a high-risk occupation and pilots have to retire at 55. Because of the stringent twice-yearly checks many pilots lose their jobs even before then and it has been found that pilots flying repeatedly through different time zones age quickly. He sees his family only eight or nine days a month and the profession has a high divorce rate. However, as a perk, he and his wife and three children get a 90 per cent rebate on air travel.

**Chairman National Coal Board, 53, £192**

One of those who benefited from the rises recently awarded to heads of the nationalised industries, he is now paid at the rate of £22 500 a year gross.

**Chairman British Leyland Motor Company, 58, £304**

As Chairman and Managing Director of the largest British-owned motor company, he is paid a salary of £46 060 a year, on which the annual tax bill, after deducting earned-income and single-person reliefs, is £30 274.

**Chief Executive, Green Shield Trading Stamp Company, 54, £1313**

By far the highest paid executive in Britain, he was paid last year a salary of £260 000 and was entitled to even more. By his service agreement with his company he could have taken a £395 000 pay packet, but made do with £5000 a week before tax, plus £13·50 dividend for each of the 19511 shares he holds in the company he started 14 years ago after a holiday in the USA. Observing the success of trading stamps there he decided to import the idea to this country, so the man who began his working life as a laundry boy now owns two Rolls-Royces, a Belgravia mansion, a Riviera villa and a private jet – and he issues more stamps every year than the Post Office.

# Social consequences of business activities 20

Wildlife conservation in woodland

## 20.1 Ecological disturbance

In a natural environment, e.g. woodland undisturbed by man, it would appear that a balanced community of plants and animals can exist together indefinitely. Why don't they die when they have used up all the foodstuff or when their waste products accumulate? You may be able to answer this from what you have learnt in science; if not, your teacher will organise a class discussion so that your friends who have studied science can explain how this comes about.

In 1967 in Japan, 111 cases of mercury poisoning occurred, resulting in 41 deaths, as a consequence of eating fish or shellfish taken from Minimata Bay. The bay had been contaminated by waste from a factory using mercuric oxide. Lesser outbreaks have occurred in other places.

The mercury compounds discharged as waste are acted upon by bacteria which convert them to methyl mercury. This is soluble, and is taken up by fish. Since the mercury is not a 'natural' constituent of food, there is no process within the fish to excrete it, and it accumulates in the organs and flesh of the fish. Since one human eats many fish, the mercury accumulates at an even higher concentration in the human organs, and eventually causes mercury poisoning and death.

**1** Can you find any other examples of substances which are used, or have been used until recently, which might cause similar damage?

**2** What steps do you think could be taken to stop this kind of 'ecological disturbance?'

## 20.2 Conservation of resources

**1** Looking back to Section 13, do you think there might be a tendency for the amount of goods used up by each person in Britain to increase?

**2** For what kinds of goods do you think production has increased most over the last ten years?

**3** A metal called chromium is used in alloys which form part of many metal products. It is estimated that, at the present rate of consumption, known supplies of chromium will last only for about 30 years. As the supplies run out, which of the following do you think are likely to happen? (It could be all of them):

a) the price of chromium will go up;

b) because the price goes up, it will become economic to mine metal ores which contain very little chromium;

c) there will be research to find substances which could be used instead of chromium;

d) it will become economic to get back chromium from refuse – called 'recycling'.

**4** Increased consumption is caused by increased consumption per person and by increased population. It is very difficult indeed to forecast population changes very far ahead, because this involves assumptions about the continuation of present trends – e.g. whether parents will continue to have the same number of children per family. Some recent population predictions are:

| | 1980 | 1990 | 2000 | |
|---|---|---|---|---|
| Britain | 59·3 | 63·2 | 68·2 | (million) |
| World | 4269 | 5068 | 5965 | (million) |

What do you think will be the effect of trying to find room for another 9 million people in Britain by the year 2000?

Which do you think causes the greatest increased use of resources, an extra 9 million people in Britain or an extra 9 million people in India?

## 20.3 Waste disposal

There are three ways in which waste leaves your house: (a) up the chimney (if you burn coal, coke, oil or gas); (b) as sewage; (c) as refuse in the dustbin.

The Deepham Sewage Treatment works, with the Edmonton Refuse Incinerator Plant in the background

1 Describe what happens to each of the three kinds of waste when they have left the house and in particular what *permanent* effects they may have on the environment.

2 Why might it be thought that these effects would have increased during recent years?

3 What steps have been taken during recent years to try to diminish these effects?

## 20.4 The wealth gap between developed and underdeveloped countries

In your geography lessons you may have studied India. If so, you will have realised that life for most people in an economically underdeveloped country such as India is very different from life for most people in an economically well developed country such as Britain.

1 In what ways do conditions in Britain differ from conditions in India?

2 Make a list of countries which are similar to Britain, and another list of countries which are similar to India.

3 Between 1950 and 1968, the total value of goods and services produced within the developed countries of the world rose from $7\frac{1}{4}$ units to $15\frac{1}{2}$ units, whereas that within the underdeveloped countries rose from $1\frac{1}{2}$ units to $4\frac{1}{4}$ units. One reason for the increase in undeveloped countries was 'the Green Revolution'. Can you find out what is meant by this?

4 Between 1950 and 1968, the population of developed countries increased from $5\frac{1}{2}$ hundred million to nearly 8 hundred million. Did the average income per head in developed countries increase or decrease?

In underdeveloped countries the population increased from $12\frac{1}{2}$ hundred million to $25\frac{1}{2}$ hundred million. How does the change in income per head compare with that in developed countries?

If the average income in a country increases, does this necessarily mean that everyone in that country enjoys a higher income?

5 In developed countries, both birth rates and death rates are decreasing, but, because birth rates are still somewhat higher than death rates, there is a gradual increase in population. In underdeveloped countries the birth rates are decreasing very slowly. What, then, must be the cause of the rapid increase in population in underdeveloped countries?

6 In an economically developed country such as Britain, each year some of the national income is invested in new factories and machinery which in turn increase the flow of manufactured goods. What is to prevent this happening in economically underdeveloped countries?

7 Referring back to Section 20.2, what might prevent the standard of living in underdeveloped countries ever catching up with that in developed countries?

# Population 21

We discovered that many of the problems discussed in Section 20 are becoming more acute because of rapidly increasing population, to some extent in Britain, but more especially in other parts of the world. In this section we are going to try to discover how this increase is caused, whether it is likely to continue, and what opportunities and problems are associated with it.

1 Table 21A gives the population figures every ten years since 1801. Do you know why the figures can be given accurately for these particular years? Why is the figure for 1941 an estimated figure? How can the Registrar General calculate population figures for the intervening years?

2 Draw a graph of the population figures against a time scale in years. What factors could cause an increase in population?

3 Table 21A also gives the 'crude birth rates' (births per year for each thousand of the population) and the 'crude death rates' (deaths per year for each thousand of the population). From these figures, what would you deduce has been mainly responsible for the increasing population since 1801?

4 What factors do you think have been responsible for the change in death rate?

5 If you had to predict the population of Great Britain in the year 2000, how would you go about it? Tables 21B, C, and D will give you some ideas.

6 Why do you think the Registrar General's estimates vary from year to year, as shown in Table 21E?

7 From what we have found out in previous sections, why might an increasing population tend to cause the British economy to expand?

8 An expanding population requires:
a) space for housing and recreational facilities, and more factories;
b) water (this is really a demand for space for the necessary reservoirs);
c) food (which is also partly a demand for space for growing more food) and raw material for industry;
d) waste disposal.

Explain as fully as you can how problems are likely to arise in Britain if the population expands.

**9** The latest figures show a very steep fall in the birth rate in Britain. If this trend continues then the population of Britain will fall slightly from the present 56 million over the next 20 years, and after that the decline will get much steeper. If this proves to be correct, what will be the opportunities and problems for Britain?

TABLE 21A Population changes in Great Britain

| *Year* | *Population (millions)* | *Crude birth rate* | *Crude death rate* |
|---|---|---|---|
| 1801 | 10·5 | 37 | 27 |
| 1811 | 12·0 | 37 | 24 |
| 1821 | 14·1 | 36 | 21 |
| 1831 | 16·3 | 36 | 22 |
| 1841 | 18·5 | 35 | 23 |
| 1851 | 20·8 | 34 | 23 |
| 1861 | 23·1 | 35 | 22 |
| 1871 | 26·1 | 35 | 21 |
| 1881 | 29·7 | 34 | 20 |
| 1891 | 33·0 | 32 | 19 |
| 1901 | 37·0 | 29 | 17 |
| 1911 | 40·8 | 25 | 14 |
| 1921 | 42·8 | 21 | 13 |
| 1931 | 44·8 | 17 | 12 |
| 1941 | 46·6 | 16 | 12 |
| 1951 | 48·9 | 16 | 12 |
| 1961 | 52·9 | 17 | 11 |
| 1971 | 55·6 | 16 | 12 |

TABLE 21B Marriage statistics, Great Britain

| | *1911* | *1931* | *1951* | *1961* | *1971* |
|---|---|---|---|---|---|
| Average age at first marriage: | | | | | |
| Women | 25·9 | 25·7 | 24·7 | 23·2 | 22·6 |
| Men | 27·5 | 27·5 | 27·0 | 25·7 | 24·6 |
| Percentage of women age 40 to 44 ever married | 81 | 81 | 85 | 90 | 92 |

TABLE 21C Average number of children per family born in marriage

| *Year of marriage* | *Marriage duration (years)* 5 | 10 | 20 | *Completed family* |
|---|---|---|---|---|
| 1931 | 1·14 | 1·66 | 2·11 | 2·14 |
| 1936 | 1·06 | 1·64 | 2·04 | 2·05 |
| 1951 | 1·20 | 1·87 | (2·23) | (2·23) |
| 1961 | 1·48 | (2·12) | — | — |

TABLE 21D Births in the United Kingdom

| *Year* | *Total number of births (thousands)* |
|---|---|
| 1951 | 797 |
| 1956 | 825 |
| 1961 | 944 |
| 1966 | 980 |
| 1967 | 962 |
| 1968 | 948 |
| 1969 | 920 |
| 1970 | 904 |
| 1971 | 902 |

TABLE 21E Estimated future total population of the United Kingdom

| *Year projection made* | *Estimated population (millions) in year* | | | |
|---|---|---|---|---|
| | *1968* | *1980* | *1990* | *2000* |
| 1956 | 53·2 | 54·7 | 55·4 | — |
| 1961 | 55·6 | 60·1 | 63·6 | 67·5 |
| 1966 | 55·4 | 60·0 | 65·1 | 72·1 |
| 1968 | 55·4 (actual) | 59·3 | 63·2 | 68·2 |

When you were discussing Britain's population problems, you probably became aware that Britain's ability to support its population depends on the willingness of other countries to exchange their raw materials and food products for Britain's manufactured goods, and the present situation might be expected to change if the population of other countries increases and/or they become more industrialised.

**10** Table 21F shows predicted population figures for various parts of the world. Identify these areas on a world map, and list the principal countries in each area.

**11** The population of every part of the world is not known with the same accuracy as that of Britain. Why not?

**12** Why is it not possible to predict future populations with great accuracy?

**13** Calculate the percentage increase in population in each area between 1970 and 1980 using the 'A' figures in Table 21F. Which three areas show the greatest percentage increase? From what you know of the history of population changes in Britain, why do you think the predicted increases in these areas are so high?

**14** Under what conditions might the increases in these areas be lower than predicted?

15 What other differences are there between areas with low percentage population increases and those with high? For what reasons is it thought to be unlikely that the standard of living in underdeveloped countries (the 'Third World') will catch up with that of the advanced industrial countries? What might possibly be the consequences of this?

TABLE 21F Predicted increases in world population (based on UN Provisional Report on World Population Prospects, 1963)

A: prediction based on continuation of recent trends.
B: prediction based on probable changes in recent trends.

| | *Population (millions)* | | | | |
|---|---|---|---|---|---|
| *Area* | *1960* | *1970* | *1980* | *1990* | *2000* |
| Latin America | | | | | |
| A | 212 | 284 | 387 | 537 | 756 |
| B | 212 | 282 | 374 | 488 | 624 |
| Africa | | | | | |
| A | 273 | 348 | 458 | 620 | 860 |
| B | 273 | 346 | 449 | 587 | 768 |
| South Asia | | | | | |
| A | 858 | 1092 | 1418 | 1898 | 2598 |
| B | 858 | 1000 | 1366 | 1677 | 2023 |
| East Asia (includes Japan) | | | | | |
| A | 793 | 941 | 1139 | 1419 | 1803 |
| B | 793 | 910 | 1038 | 1163 | 1284 |
| Oceania | | | | | |
| A | 15·7 | 18·4 | 22·0 | 26·7 | 32·5 |
| B | 15·7 | 18·7 | 22·6 | 27·0 | 31·9 |
| North America | | | | | |
| A | 199 | 230 | 272 | 325 | 388 |
| B | 199 | 227 | 262 | 306 | 354 |
| Soviet Union | | | | | |
| A | 214 | 253 | 295 | 345 | 402 |
| B | 214 | 246 | 278 | 316 | 353 |
| Europe | | | | | |
| A | 425 | 460 | 496 | 533 | 571 |
| B | 425 | 454 | 479 | 504 | 527 |
| World Total | | | | | |
| A | 2990 | 3626 | 4487 | 5704 | 7410 |
| B | 2990 | 3574 | 4269 | 5068 | 5965 |

# How decisions are made 22

### 22.1 The decisions to be made

In Parts 1 and 2 of this study we were concerned with setting up, and subsequently enlarging, a business enterprise which would make a profit. We could argue that in doing this we have contributed to the nation's prosperity, that we have been able to provide for the comfort and security of our families, and that we have also given opportunities to our employees to do likewise.

In Part 3, however, we have stood back and viewed our business activities from a wider perspective. In Section 16, for example, we saw how the prices/profit mechanism is the chief means by which resources are allocated in our type of economy. More generally, we have also seen that some of the decisions it seemed necessary and wise to make for the sake of our business could have profound implications for contemporary society, for future generations, and for people living in other parts of the world. With these considerations in mind, we may feel we should give additional weighting to social factors in our gains and losses accounts.

This different perspective on industrial activity highlights the following three problems confronting the world today:

1 natural resources are being consumed at an ever-increasing rate;

2 present methods of disposal are inadequate or unsafe to cope with the types and amounts of waste now being produced;

3 the population is out-growing its means of support with a marked and increasing inequitable distribution of wealth, especially between those nations that have and those that have not.

In turn, attempts to find short-term solutions to these problems interact to such an extent that they are upsetting the ecological balance and thus creating further anxieties.

There is no easy solution to these problems, which different people view with varying degrees of concern. Some feel that the measures already being taken to curtail the worst abuses of the environment are sufficient to prevent disaster until technological developments can provide effective solutions. Others feel intensely that, unless direct action is taken immediately, the end of human existence in the world as we know it is in sight. Obviously, these are world-wide problems that can be solved only through some form of agreement among the wealthy industrialised nations, each of which could be called upon to make a major contribution, which might require considerable sacrifices from its inhabitants. If change is thought to be desirable and necessary, the governments of these countries will be asking to what extent their people are prepared to make sacrifices for the sake of future generations and for people living in other parts of the world. Through the various processes of government of individual countries, decisions would have to be made. Let us consider how, in Britain, such a decision could be arrived at.

There is no reason to suppose that a decision of such magnitude would be made in Britain in any but the most conventional of ways. Can you think of any occasions in the past when the government introduced measures as a direct result of:

a) a national referendum?
b) public demonstrations?
c) a national petition?
d) the influence of the national press?
e) the influence of radio or television?

Perhaps the three most memorable decisions made by British governments in the last decade have been:

1 the abolition of the death penalty,

2 the introduction of decimal currency,

3 joining the EEC.

How were these decisions arrived at? Did they have the support of the majority of the electors in Britain?

It is not our purpose here to go into the complexities of the British system of government or the various channels through which decisions have to pass before they become law. We wish to know at what point these decisions are made and something of the pressures that can be brought to bear on the processes of decision-making. Nevertheless, it may clarify our thinking if we consider a much simplified model of the British system.

### 22.2 The decision-makers

First, we must understand that Britain, unlike many other countries, has no single document legally and specifically defining the nature of its government and the relationships between the various institutions that make up the government. The British system of government has been fashioned by tradition over the centuries to meet the particular interests of the nation. On the one side it reflects the independence, stability, and unity that the country has enjoyed and, on the other, many of those characteristics that have become regarded as typically British, e.g. the desire for strong government yet a certain distrust of 'the expert', the loyal support given to one or the other of the two main political parties by the vast majority of the electorate, and the lack of noisy and ostentatious displays at election times.

At least every five years the country has the opportunity to choose a new government. Traditionally, the Queen will ask the parliamentary leader of that political party which has by election secured most seats in the House of Commons to form a government. Thus the new Prime Minister (he may be the old one if his party has been successful again) chooses his Cabinet ministers, who collectively accept the responsibility for the government of the country. The decisions this team takes and the measures it proposes have to be justified first in the House of Commons, then in the House of Lords, and finally receive the Queen's assent. As the government can count on the votes of its backbench party members, who form the majority of MP's in the House of Commons, its propositions are not likely to be defeated there, although amendments are often made in the light of adverse criticism. Nor can the House of Lords (since the Act of 1949) delay the passing of a Bill for longer than twelve months. The Queen's assent has become more or less a formality. Hence, as a general rule at least, the Cabinet is responsible for governing the country, and Parliament is simply the place where decisions have to be justified, but not often made.

It seems, then, that in Britain the Prime Minister and his Cabinet are given a relatively free hand to make and implement major decisions. There are of course some constraints, the greatest of which is the knowledge that to a certain extent their performance in office will be judged at the next general election. Similarly, most ministers are sensitive to criticism in Parliament and, although they can rely on the votes of their backbenchers in the House of Commons, they know that at their own political party conferences their actions may meet more outspoken condemnation. But the British people like their governments to have strong leadership, which is neither afraid to govern nor impeded from doing so. This is the prime reason why national referenda have never been popular in this country, nor noisy, violent public demonstrations very effective. (Can you think of exceptions?)

### 22.3 How the decision-makers are influenced

So we have identified our top decision-makers: the forty or so government ministers, especially those some twenty who are members of the Cabinet. However, two questions still need to be answered:

1 how do they arrive at their decisions?

2 do they in practice make all the decisions of government?

The volume of work of each ministerial department has grown so enormously in the twentieth century that ministers can no longer be acquainted with every important issue. Consequently, there are now over 400 000 officials in Whitehall whose job it is to advise ministers. By far the greater proportion of decisions that have to be made are routine and non-controversial, arising out of the ordinary business of administration. It has become established practice for these decisions to be made by senior civil servants, albeit in the name of the minister, who may be called upon to justify them in Parliament. On those questions that are likely to cause political controversy, a Permanent Secretary has to decide whether to put them before the minister, who, in turn, has to decide whether to take them to the Cabinet. Similarly, when a minister wishes to introduce one of his own ideas, he will first discuss it with senior officials, and then put detailed proposals before his colleagues in the Cabinet for their criticisms and the criticisms they anticipate they will receive in Parliament. If the proposed measures stand up to this onslaught, they will eventually be implemented. If they do not, the minister may resign from the Cabinet, but this is a rare occasion.

It is clear, therefore, that the Civil Service plays a fundamental role in the processes of decision-making. But senior civil servants, like ministers, are not expert, in a technical sense, in many of the issues that are the direct concern of their departments. They, too, must spend much of their time listening. The spokesmen to whom they listen hold the key to the machinery of decision-making.

These spokesmen who have the ear of Whitehall are the representatives of interested groups: the various trade unions, the Farmers' Union, the Confederation of British Industries, the Howard League for Penal Reform, the RSPCA, the AA and the RAC, the Central Council for Physical Recreation, and the Association of British Chambers of Commerce – to name but a few. Each department has its own collection of groups whom it traditionally consults about particular interests. This process of consultation is valued alike by the government and by the groups concerned. On the one hand it provides the government with information, and on the other it provides the groups with prestige in the eyes of their members.

This model of the British system of government may have suggested to you a course of action that could be followed if you wished to bring about legislation concerning the problems we raised at the beginning of this section. Now make out a plan of campaign which you would use to give your proposals the greatest chance of acceptance by the government, clearly indicating the four or five steps that it would be necessary to take. In addition, make a list of those influences and activities which appear to have little effect on government legislation.

# Part 3* Allocating our resources—the choice before us

# How does the customer get what he wants? 16*

How is it that, whatever the customers want, there is usually just about enough in the shops – neither too much nor too little? How do the manufacturers know how much to produce?

## 16.1* Prices

Suppose that we are manufacturing a new product. By effective advertising we have stimulated a strong demand, and orders are coming in much faster than we can produce the goods.

We decide that if customers like our product so much, they will probably pay more for it, and we find some excuse for putting up the price. Also, we do not need to advertise so much, at least for the present. The higher price gives us more profit, and, since we are not spending so much on advertising, this increases our profits as well. We use some of these profits to buy more factory space, machinery, etc. to increase production.

Unfortunately for us, another firm notices our higher prices. This firm has factories producing goods which are going out of fashion. As the firm is making very small profits, it is decided to close these factories and use the capital to enter into competition with us. It makes its product slightly different and at a slightly lower price, and it runs a big advertising campaign to try to persuade customers that its product is better and cheaper. We are forced to respond by cutting our price a little and stepping up our advertising to keep our customers 'loyal' to us – both of these actions mean less profit.

Can you think of any examples of this kind of thing happening? We can now see how resources of raw materials, capital, and labour have been changed from producing one type of goods for which the demand was falling to producing another type of goods for which there was a high demand. The way in which individuals spend their money 'signals' to firms through higher profits, and, at the same time, these higher profits are used to make available the means of producing more goods.

1 Although as the owner or manager of a firm you may not like this kind of competition developing, how do you feel about it as a customer?

2 In order to start up production in competition with us, a firm needs more capital. What means exist for public companies to obtain more capital?

3 What factors might prevent the supply adjusting itself to the demand quickly in the way we have described?

4 Are there any countries which do not have a 'free-enterprise' system in which private firms make profits? How do you think the resources are allocated in these countries?

5 Which of these decisions are made on the basis of how individuals spend their money:
a) that more sweets or more cigarettes will be produced?
b) to produce a car with shock absorbers which last 30 000 miles or to produce a car with shock absorbers which last 100 000 miles?
c) to produce more beer and cigarettes or more roads?
d) which postal service to use?
e) to produce more cigarettes or build more hospitals?

### 16.2* The changing pattern of demand

In Section 16.1* we referred in the third paragraph to a company which had factories producing goods for which the demand was now falling. This often happens because of new inventions. For example, the demand for many articles previously made in metal fell because of the invention of new plastics. Can you think of any other examples?

How do firms try to resist a falling demand for their products? (Refer back to Section 13.)

In the long run, firms producing obsolete products must change to producing new products or close down so that the capital and labour can be moved to other industries. This is obviously a situation which is resisted by all concerned – the shareholders because they will lose money, and the workers because they will lose their jobs.

The workers may be unable to find other jobs in the same trade in the same part of the country. There may be jobs in the same trade in other parts of the country, but it will be difficult to get a council house in the new area, or sell a house in an area of high unemployment.

The other possibility is to change the type of job, and, because of the rate of technological change, many of you can expect to change your type of job at least once during your working life. Do you know any ways in which governments have tried to help people who have to change their jobs?

# Should more firms be nationalised? 17*

So far we have been looking at those goods and services which are produced by private individuals or companies. They are usually offered for sale in shops, and we can choose whether or not to buy and, if we decide to buy, we can choose between different makes. I can choose whether to spend my money on a jacket or a pair of shoes, and if I decide on the shoes, I can choose between different makes.

But there are two other ways in which goods and services are supplied. One way is through public corporations and nationalised industries, e.g. the British Broadcasting Corporation (BBC), the Post Office, the gas boards. In most cases where there is a public corporation or nationalised industry, we can choose whether or not to buy, but, if we do decide to buy, we have no choice about where we buy from – if you decide to post a letter, you must use the Post Office; if you want to use gas, you must get it through the gas board.

At various times it has been proposed that certain industries which are now run by private enterprise should be nationalised, e.g. shipbuilding and insurance.

The following arguments have been put forward in favour of nationalising insurance:

a) It would be more secure than private firms. (In recent years some car-insurance companies have gone bankrupt.)
b) Profits from insurance should benefit the country as a whole, not just the shareholders in insurance companies.
c) Insurance should be available to everyone on a non-profit making basis.

Arguments put forward against the nationalisation of insurance are:

a) customers would have no freedom of choice.
b) because there was no competition, the industry would become inefficient and the cost of insurance would become higher.

1 Using the above arguments, and any others you can think of, write a short speech which a minister might use to introduce a Bill to Parliament to nationalise insurance.

2 In a similar way, write a speech which the Opposition spokesman might give.

3 Because some public corporations have a monopoly, e.g. the Post Office, you might think they could charge as much as they liked. If it were left to you, how would you control them?

4 Are there any ways in which you think it would be to the consumer's benefit to allow private enterprise to compete with nationalised industries or public corporations? For example, ITV already competes with BBC TV.

Another way in which goods and services are provided is by the government or the local government (the county council or the district council). For example, medical services are provided through the National Health Service organised by the national government in London. On the other hand, refuse collection is organised by the district council.

Using a local rate-demand form, a recent copy of *Britain: an Official Handbook*, and any other sources of information you can discover, find out how the following goods and services are provided:

Milk
Water
Sewage disposal
Protection of property (from thieves)
Electricity
Roads
Newspapers

5 How does the national government get the money to pay for the services it provides?

6 How does the district council get the money to pay for the services it provides?

7 How is it decided how much money shall be raised, and how it shall be allocated to the various services?

8 What are the arguments for and against including a lending service for pop records as part of the public-library service?

# Is it the government's fault? 18*

Pound falls again as prices go higher

Sharp upward trend in unemployment

You will often have seen headlines such as these. What do they mean? What can the government try to do about it?

### 18.1* Unemployment

We talked to some people who were queueing up for unemployment benefit. Here is what they said:

A: The place I was working for went bust five weeks ago. I'm living off the unemployment benefit until the labour exchange find me another job. I think they'll find me one this week.

B: People call me a hippy. I live on a barge on the canal. Most of the time I live off the unemployment benefit. I just get a job when I need some more money.

C: I work on the fun fair at Blackpool during the summer. I make very good money during the season, and during the winter I don't do anything – I live off what I saved in the summer and the unemployment benefit.

D: I'd like to get another job, but I'm 55 and I had this accident to my back last year, so nobody will have me.

E: There's nothing wrong with me, but these . . . can't find me a . . . job. I've been on the dole over a . . . year now. There's a lot like me now. When's the . . . government going to do something about it?

1 Can you think of any other type of person who may be unemployed? Write a paragraph about what they might say.

2 These people mentioned unemployment benefit. What is this, and what other help is available to people who have to change their jobs?

3 People like Mr E who have been looking for a job for a long time are part of what is called 'hard-core' unemployment.
In which parts of Britain is there most 'hard-core' unemployment? Why is it mostly in these parts of Britain? What have governments tried to do about it? (Refer back to Section 10.)

How can governments get rid of unemployment?

They could let people have more money to spend, then firms would want to produce more goods, so they would take on more workers to make them.

One way of letting people have more money to spend would be to reduce income tax.

Another way would be to lower the Value Added Tax (VAT) – the tax added to most goods we buy – so that the goods we buy would be a lot cheaper.

4 Can you think of any other ways in which the government could get us to buy more goods?

### 18.2* Economic growth

Most people would like more radios, cars, washing machines, and so on. People would like to go to watch more football, to go to the hairdresser more often, to go to Majorca for their holidays – in other words, they would like more services as well as more goods.

The value of all the goods and services produced within a nation during the year, plus any income from abroad, is called the gross national product (GNP). By and large, the higher the GNP, the more there is for all of us – provided it is shared out, which is what we shall be looking at in the next section.

The GNP is likely to increase if

a) there are more people working;
b) people work longer;
c) workers use more and/or more efficient machinery;
d) people work more effectively, e.g. they are working to produce what is most needed and they produce goods which can be sold for a high price at home or abroad, rather than goods which can be imported more cheaply from other countries.

Which of these do you think the government should try to bring about?

### 18.3* Inflation

A sudden or sustained rise in prices is called *inflation*. One way of measuring price changes is by the retail price index. Market-research techniques (see Section 2) are used to find out what goods and services are bought by a 'typical' household, and at what prices. The total for the period chosen as a starting point is scaled up to 100, and the totals for other periods are scaled up correspondingly. For example, suppose we choose as a starting point the period January 1955 and the total for a typical household for that period was £20. The total for March 1962 is, say, £25. Then if the index for January 1955 is 100, the index for March 1962 is 125.

Figure 18A on page 131 plots the average index for each year since 1955. The graph also shows how earnings have increased, both for those who are paid weekly and for those who are paid monthly (salaries).

**1** Why are average weekly earnings higher than weekly rates of wages?

**2** In terms of what money will buy, what was the approximate percentage increase in real wages between 1955 and 1968?

**3** What are the bad effects of inflation?

**4** Which sections of the community will suffer most?

There are a variety of possible causes of inflation. The difficulty is to know which causes are the most important at any one time.

a) Suppose the average household feels able to spend up to £10 a week on food, and the cost of the average family bill is £9. The shopkeepers would be able to push up their prices to £10 before people would start buying less. This is sometimes called 'too much money chasing too few goods', or 'demand-pull' inflation. It can happen in general when purchasing power of consumers or money supply rises faster than the output of producers.

b) Producers' costs may rise. There may be an increase in the price of imported raw materials, or powerful trade unions may obtain wage increases which are not accompanied by more goods being produced, or a fall in demand may result in a higher cost per article (See Section 3). This is often called 'cost-push' inflation.

**5** How might the steps which a government takes to cure unemployment cause inflation?

**6** In what ways may governments try to control inflation?

### 18.4* The trade figures

Britain is a manufacturing country. We import from abroad the raw materials which we manufacture into goods such as cars and textiles. Some of these we use ourselves and some we export abroad to pay for the raw materials and also for much of our food which comes from other countries.

The difference between the value of imported goods and the value of exported goods is called the *balance of trade*.

As well as importing and exporting goods, Britain also earns money abroad by providing services such as shipping and insurance, and we also get money from investments abroad. These are often called 'invisible items'.

The balance of trade plus the balance on invisible items is called the *balance of payments*.

In some recent years the statistics for the UK have been as follows (figures in £ million):

| | *Year A* | *Year B* | *Year C* |
|---|---|---|---|
| Imports | 5024 | 1212 | 1420 |
| Exports | 4471 | 1112 | 918 |
| Income from 'invisible items' (insurance etc.) | 650 | 220 | 310 |

In year A the balance of trade was $4471-5024$, which is $-553$, i.e. a deficit (loss) of £553 million.

The balance of payments was $-553+650 = +97$, i.e. a gain of £97 million.

This has been the pattern in a number of years recently – a loss on the balance of trade made up for by a gain on invisible items.

Calculate (a) the balance of trade and (b) the balance of payments in years B and C.

In recent years, Britain has had great difficulty in avoiding a balance-of-payments deficit. Having a balance-of-payments deficit is like owing money to other countries, and obviously they won't put up with it forever. In the next section we shall see why the deficit arises, and what the government tries to do about it.

## 18.5* What the government is trying to do

Since the last war, all British governments have tried to (a) get rid of unemployment, (b) get faster economic growth – more goods for all of us, (c) get rid of inflation, and (d) stop getting a balance-of-payments deficit. To do all of them at the same time seems to be practically impossible.

When the number of unemployed rises, the government tries to release more money for people to spend, so that firms will want to produce more goods for people to buy and they will therefore employ more workers. Because people have more money to spend, firms tend to put up their prices, causing inflation.

At the same time, all of us are always wanting higher wages, which puts up our firms' costs, which is another reason why they put up their prices.

Inflation tends to cause a balance-of-payments deficit. For example, a particular product which is manufactured in both Britain and Germany cost, at a certain time, £1 in Britain and 8 deutschmarks (DM) in Germany. At the prevailing exchange rate, £1 could be changed for 8 DM. As a result of inflation in Britain, the product some time later costs

£2 in Britain but still only 8 DM in Germany: the exchange rate remains the same. British exporters will therefore not wish to export because they can get £2 in Britain but only the equivalent of £1 in Germany. On the other hand, German exporters will step up their efforts to sell in Britain because they can get twice as much in Britain as in their own country. The effect of inflation is therefore to increase imports and decrease exports, thus causing a balance-of-payments deficit. One way of trying to overcome this is by devaluation. That is, we alter the exchange rate (in the above example) so that instead of changing £1 for 8 DM, we must change £2 (or more) for 8 DM. The trouble with this is that it makes all our exports cheaper (i.e. we earn less money from them) and all our imports cost more, so that we have to export more to pay our way.

So what usually happens is that after a period of 'boom' to get rid of unemployment, inflation gets worse and the balance of payments gets worse, so the government has to 'deflate'. That is, in order to try to stop inflation and remedy the balance of payments, they put up income tax, VAT, and so on so that there is less money to spend. This usually puts up the unemployment figures again.

Thus, since the last war, the unemployment figures have gone up and down in a cyclic manner – but unemployment, inflation, and the balance of payments have got worse each time.

Now the jackpot question: if you were in the government, what would *you* do about it?

# 19* Why does he earn more than I do?

What do *you* think each of the workers shown here should earn? If you think they should all earn different amounts, why do you think this?

Look back in the book to Document 19A to see what some people earned in 1971.

If there are differences between what you think they should earn (relative to each other) and what they did earn, how can you explain the differences?

If it is thought that some people get too little and some people get too much, the government can do something about this through the system of taxes and benefits. The main taxes and benefits are as follows.

## Taxes

a) *Income tax*. As we saw in the previous section, the government gets the money to pay for services such as the armed forces by means of income tax.

A miner

A farmworker

Paint sprayers in a car factory

Each person earning above a certain amount pays this tax directly from his income, hence it is called a 'direct' tax. In most cases the employer stops it out of the wages and pays it directly to a government department. Each person is allowed to earn up to a certain amount free of tax, the amount depending on personal circumstances, e.g. a married man is allowed to earn more free of tax than a single man. Above that figure, tax is paid at various rates which increase with income. For example it might be

| | |
|---|---|
| up to £5000 | 33% |
| £5000 to £7000 | 40% |

(governments alter the rates of taxation from time to time).

Thus a man with a tax allowance of £1000 earning £4000 per year would pay 33% of (£4000 – £1000), which is roughly £1000 or 25% of his income.

A man earning £8000, with the same tax allowance, would pay

| | |
|---|---|
| 33% of £5000, which is roughly | £1666 |
| 40% of £2000, which is | £800 |
| | £2466 |

This is roughly 30% of his total income.

So the man who earns most not only pays more tax, but a greater *proportion* of his income goes in tax.

b) *National Insurance contributions.* These are weekly payments by both employees and employers which go to finance National Insurance benefits (see below). As with income tax, the employee's contribution is stopped out of his wages and paid directly to a government department. The National Insurance contribution is dependent on the amount the worker earns.

c) *Value Added Tax (VAT).* This is a tax paid as part of the shop price of most goods and services except food. It was originally 10% of the final purchase price, but it was later altered to 8%. The government is able to alter the percentage according to the circumstances. Since this tax is not paid directly to the government, but indirectly through the shopkeeper, this is called an 'indirect' tax.

d) *Customs and Excise duties* are paid as part of the purchase price of a limited range of goods – mainly tobacco, alcoholic drinks and petrol. These duties are very high and form a large percentage of the final price of these commodities.

## Benefits

a) *Family Income Supplement (FIS)* – an amount paid *to* workers with low wages according to their family circumstances.

b) *Family allowances* – paid to the *mother* according to the number of dependant children.

c) *National Insurance benefits* – sickness benefit, unemployment benefit, old-age pensions, etc.

1 Suppose the government needs to raise more money. If you were a low-paid worker, which would you prefer them to do: increase income tax or increase VAT? Would you give the same answer if you were a highly paid worker?

2 Many of the benefits transfer income from one section of the community to another – for example, money is taken (through taxes) from those who do not have children and paid in family allowances to those who do. What transfers are brought about by Family Income Supplement, sickness benefit, old-age pensions?

3 Are there any other benefits which you think ought to be paid?

# 20* Can we stop these things happening?

### 20.1* Ecological blunders

In a natural environment, e.g. woodland undisturbed by man, it would appear that a balanced community of plants and animals can exist together indefinitely. Why is it that they don't die because they use up all the foodstuff, or because of the accumulation of their waste products? You may be able to answer this from what you have learnt in science; if not, your teacher will organise a class discussion so that your friends who have studied science can explain how this comes about.

In 1967 in Japan, 111 cases of mercury poisoning occurred, resulting in 41 deaths, as a consequence of eating fish or shell fish taken from Minimata Bay. The bay had been contaminated by waste from a factory using mercuric oxide. Lesser outbreaks have occurred in other places.

The mercury compounds discharged as waste are acted upon by bacteria which convert them to methyl mercury. This is soluble, and is taken up by fish. Since the mercury is not a 'natural' constituent of food, there is no process within the fish to excrete it, and it accumulates in the organs

Discharged wastes – in this case detergents – pollute waterways

and flesh of the fish. Since one human eats many fish, the mercury accumulates at an even higher concentration in the human organs, and eventually causes mercury poisoning and death.

1 Can you find any other examples of substances which are used, or have been used until recently, which might cause similar damage?

2 What steps do you think could be taken to stop these kinds of 'ecological blunders'?

## 20.2* Dwindling resources

1 Looking back to Sections 11 and 16*, do you think there might be a tendency for the amount of goods used up by each person in Britain to increase?

2 For what kinds of goods do you think production has increased most over the last ten years?

3 A metal called chromium is used in alloys which form part of many metal products. It is estimated that, at the present rate of consumption, known supplies of chromium will last for only about 30 years. As the supplies run out, which of the following do you think are likely to happen? (it could be all of them):
   a) the price of chromium will go up;
   b) because the price goes up, it will become economical to mine metal ores which contain very little chromium;
   c) there will be research to find substances which could be used instead of chromium;
   d) it will become economic to get back chromium from refuse – called 'recycling'.

4 Increased consumption is caused by increased consumption per person and by increased population. It is very difficult indeed to forecast population changes very far ahead, because this involves assumptions about the continuation of present trends, e.g. whether parents will continue to have the same number of children per family. Some recent population predictions are:

| | *1980* | *1990* | *2000* | |
|---|---|---|---|---|
| Britain | 59·3 | 63·2 | 68·2 | (million) |
| World | 4269 | 5068 | 5965 | (million) |

What do you think will be the effect of trying to find room for another 9 million people in Britain by the year 2000?

Which do you think causes the greatest increased use of resources, an extra 9 million people in Britain or an extra 9 million people in India?

## 20.3* Waste

There are three ways in which waste leaves your house: (a) up the chimney (if you burn coal, coke, oil, or gas); (b) as sewage; (c) as refuse in the dustbin.

Rubbish may be dumped on a convenient site near the edge of a town

1 Describe what happens to each of the three kinds of waste when they have left the house and, in particular, what *permanent* effects they may have on the environment.

2 Why might it be thought that these effects would have increased during recent years?

Or burnt in an incineration plant such as the GLC's at Edmonton

3 What steps have been taken during recent years to try to diminish these effects?

### 20.4* The wealth gap between developed and underdeveloped countries

In your geography lessons you may have studied India. If so, you will have realised that life for most people in an economically underdeveloped country such as India is very different from life for most people in an economically well developed country such as Britain.

1 In what ways do conditions in Britain differ from conditions in India?

2 Make a list of countries which are similar to Britain, and another list of countries which are similar to India.

3 Between 1950 and 1968, the total value of goods and services produced within the developed countries of the world rose from $7\frac{1}{4}$ units to $15\frac{1}{2}$ units, whereas that within the underdeveloped countries rose from $1\frac{1}{2}$ units to $5\frac{1}{4}$ units. One reason for the increase in underdeveloped countries was 'the Green Revolution'. Can you find out what is meant by this?

4 Between 1950 and 1968, the population of developed countries increased from $5\frac{1}{2}$ hundred million to nearly 8 hundred million. Did the average income per head in developed countries increase or decrease? In underdeveloped countries the population increased from $12\frac{1}{2}$ hundred million to $25\frac{1}{2}$ hundred million. How does the change in income per head compare with that in developed countries?

If the average income in a country increases, does this necessarily mean that everyone in that country enjoys a higher income?

5 In developed countries, both birth rates and death rates are decreasing but, because birth rates are still somewhat higher than death rates, there is a gradual increase in population. In underdeveloped countries the birth rates are decreasing very slowly. What then must be the cause of the rapid increase in population in underdeveloped countries?

6 In an economically developed country such as Britain, each year some of the national income is invested in new factories and machinery, which in turn increase the flow of manufactured goods. What is to prevent this happening in economically underdeveloped countries?

7 Referring back to Section 20.2*, what might prevent the standard of living in underdeveloped countries ever catching up with that in developed countries?

# 21* Are there too many people?

Every ten years since 1801 there has been a census of the population of Britain. In that time, the population has increased from 10·5 million in 1801 to 52·9 million in 1961. The population is now about 56 million.

During most of this period the birth rate has gone down, particularly in recent years. Why, then, do you think the population of Britain has increased?

An increasing population requires:

1 space for housing and recreational facilities, and for more factories;

2 water (this is really a demand for space for the necessary reservoirs);

3 food (which is also partly a demand for space for growing more food) and raw material for industry;

4 waste disposal.

What problems have been caused as the population of Britain has expanded?

The latest figures show a very steep fall in the birth rate in Britain. If this trend continues, then the population of Britain will fall slightly over the next 20 years, and then fall quite rapidly. If this proves to be correct, what will be the problems and opportunities for Britain?

The table below shows the predicted increases in population in various parts of the world (figures in millions).

| | *Europe* | *North America* | *South America* | *Africa* | *East Asia* | *South Asia* | *Soviet Union* |
|---|---|---|---|---|---|---|---|
| 1970 | 454 | 227 | 282 | 346 | 910 | 1000 | 246 |
| 2000 | 527 | 354 | 624 | 768 | 1284 | 2023 | 353 |

Find these areas on a map, and make a list of the biggest countries in each area.

In many parts of the world it is difficult to find out the exact population. Why is this?

Why is it not possible to predict future populations with great accuracy?

Why do you think the predicted increases in some areas are very high?

Is it true that the predicted increases in population in underdeveloped countries are greater than those in developed areas such as Europe? If so, what are likely to be the consequences of this?

# Making a choice *22

**22.1* Our choices for the future**

In Parts 1 and 2 of this study we were concerned with setting up, and subsequently enlarging, a business enterprise which would make a profit. We could argue that in doing this we have contributed to the nation's prosperity, that we have been able to provide for the comfort and security of our families, and that we have also given opportunities to our employees to do likewise.

In Part 3, however, we have stood back and considered our business activity from a rather different point of view. We have seen that some of the decisions it seemed necessary and wise to make for the sake of the prosperity of our business could also make problems for our friends and neighbours, for future generations, and for people living in other parts of the world. With these considerations in mind, we may feel that some of the decisions we took in order to make our business prosper did not sufficiently allow for the cost to society as a whole.

This was some-one elses choice for the future

In particular, our business activities will have brought us right up against the following three problems confronting the world today:

1 natural resources are being consumed at an ever-increasing rate;

2 present methods of disposal are inadequate or unsafe to cope with the types and amounts of waste now being produced;

3 the population is out-growing its means of support, with a marked and increasing inequitable distribution of wealth, especially between those nations that have and those that have not.

We have also seen that attempts to find immediate solutions to these problems have very often upset the natural ecological balance and have thus created further anxieties.

There is no easy solution to these problems, which different people view with varying degrees of concern. Some feel that the measures already being taken to curtail the worst abuses of the environment are sufficient to prevent disaster until technological developments can provide effective solutions. Others feel intensely that, unless direct action is taken immediately, the end of human existence in the world as we know it is in sight. Obviously, these are world-wide problems that can be solved only through some form of agreement among the wealthy industrialised nations, each of which could be called upon to make a major contribution, which might require considerable sacrifices from its inhabitants. If change is thought to be desirable and necessary, the governments of these countries will be asking to what extent their people are prepared to make sacrifices for the sake of future generations and for people living in other parts of the world. Through the various processes of government of individual countries, decisions would have to be made.

### 22.2* How we choose in Britain

In a democratic country like Britain, we may assume that the government will ultimately arrive at a decision after considering the interests and wishes of the majority of the people. It is, however, worthwhile to discuss among yourselves whether this was entirely true of three of perhaps the most memorable decisions made by British governments in the last ten years:

1 the abolition of the death penalty,

2 the introduction of decimal currency,

3 joining the EEC (the 'Common Market').

You may conclude that these decisions were made by British governments irrespective of the wishes of a large number of people. It may seem that on such matters we are prepared to surrender our own individual choice and interests to the government of the day for what it may consider to be the good of the nation. Again, you might discuss what safeguards we have for ensuring that our governments act for the public good and not for their own ends.

Clearly, then, although a substantial body of people may hold an opinion and even suggest a course of action through publicity in the national press, on television, or by a demonstration in Trafalgar Square, there is no guarantee that the government will act in accordance with this sort of demand. The government is much more likely to be influenced by the advice it receives from the civil servants attached to the various ministerial departments. But civil servants, like the Cabinet ministers they serve, are not expert, in a technical sense, in many of the issues that are the direct concern of their departments. They, too, must spend much of their time listening to the spokesmen of various interested groups: the trade unions, the Farmers' Union, the Confederation of British Industries, the Howard League for Penal Reform, the RSPCA, the AA and the RAC, the Central Council for Physical Recreation, the Association of British Chambers of Commerce, etc. Each ministerial department has its own collection of groups whom it traditionally consults about particular interests. It is on the expert advice of these groups that major decisions of government are frequently made.

You will already have discussed the three problems mentioned at the beginning of this section. You may have thought of some possible steps that might be taken towards the solution of these problems. How would you try to ensure that the choices and decisions you have made stood the best chance of being implemented by the government? In note form, draw up a plan of campaign, estimating the time it might take to accomplish the various stages in your plan.

# Index